Fantasies of Gender and the Witch in Feminist Theory and Literature

Comparative Cultural Studies,
Steven Tötösy de Zepetnek, Series Editor

The Purdue University Press monograph series of Books in Comparative Cultural Studies publishes single-authored and thematic collected volumes of new scholarship. Manuscripts are invited for publication in the series in fields of the study of culture, literature, the arts, media studies, communication studies, the history of ideas, etc., and related disciplines of the humanities and social sciences to the series editor via email at <clcweb@purdue.edu>. Comparative cultural studies is a contextual approach in the study of culture in a global and intercultural context and work with a plurality of methods and approaches; the theoretical and methodological framework of comparative cultural studies is built on tenets borrowed from the disciplines of cultural studies and comparative literature and from a range of thought including literary and culture theory, (radical) constructivism, communication theories, and systems theories; in comparative cultural studies focus is on theory and method as well as application. For a detailed description of the aims and scope of the series including the style guide of the series link to <http://docs.lib.purdue.edu/clcweblibrary/seriespurdueccs>. Manuscripts submitted to the series are peer reviewed followed by the usual standards of editing, copy editing, marketing, and distribution. The series is affiliated with *CLCWeb: Comparative Literature and Culture* (ISSN 1481-4374), the peer-reviewed, full-text, and open-access quarterly published by Purdue University Press at <http://docs.lib.purdue.edu/clcweb>.

Volumes in the Purdue series of Books in Comparative Cultural Studies

Justyna Sempruch, *Fantasies of Gender and the Witch in Feminist Theory and Literature*
Kimberly Chabot Davis, *Postmodern Texts and Emotional Audiences*
Philippe Codde, *The Jewish American Novel*
Deborah Streifford Reisinger, *Crime and Media in Contemporary France*
Imre Kertész and Holocaust Literature, Ed. Louise O. Vasvári and Steven Tötösy de Zepetnek
Camilla Fojas, *Cosmopolitanism in the Americas*
Comparative Cultural Studies and Michael Ondaatje's Writing, Ed. Steven Tötösy de Zepetnek
Jin Feng, *The New Woman in Early Twentieth-Century Chinese Fiction*
Comparative Cultural Studies and Latin America, Ed. Sophia A. McClennen and Earl E. Fitz
Sophia A. McClennen, *The Dialectics of Exile*
Comparative Literature and Comparative Cultural Studies, Ed. Steven Tötösy de Zepetnek
Comparative Central European Culture, Ed. Steven Tötösy de Zepetnek

Justyna Sempruch

Fantasies of Gender and the Witch in Feminist Theory and Literature

Purdue University Press
West Lafayette, Indiana

Purdue University Press
West Lafayette, Indiana
Copyright 2008 by Purdue University. All Rights Reserved.

Printed in the United States of America.

Library of Congress Cataloging-in-Publication Data

Sempruch, Justyna.
 Fantasies of gender and the witch in feminist theory and literature / by Justyna Sempruch.
    p. cm. -- (Comparative cultural studies)
  Includes index.
  ISBN 978-1-55753-491-0
  1. Feminist criticism. 2. Women in literature. 3. Witches in literature. I. Title.
  PN98.W64S46 2007
  305.4201--dc22
                                    2008004050

Contents

Acknowledgments	vii
Introduction	1
Chapter One Functions and Risks of Radical Feminist "Witches"	12
Chapter Two Splitting the Feminist Subject	59
Chapter Three The Embarrassed "etc." at the End of the List	119
Conclusion	172
Works Cited	174
Index	183

Acknowledgements

I thank foremost Valerie Raoul, for her unrelenting support and complex dialogue on feminist writing and literature throughout the various stages of the project, as well as her accessibility that has helped me to transcend the many difficult moments in putting the manuscript together. I owe a special debt of appreciation to Sneja Gunew for her inspiring work on diaspora and cultural representation, thoughtful guidance, and deeply resonant responses to my writing. Nasrin Rahimieh first introduced me to women's world in comparative literature and has provided thoughtful comments on the initial theoretical dimensions of my study. Nancy Frelick and Elisabeth Bronfen have inspired me with psychoanalytical insights, which became central to my readings of feminist literature. Daphna Arbel provided an abundance of classical references and has been a crucial interlocutor in my thinking about intersections of femininity and sacredness in Western mythology. Bożena Karwowska has provided valuable insights into Polish literary and cultural contexts and made significant comments on my first readings of the narratives analyzed in my book. I am especially thankful to my life companion, Sebastian Szachowicz, whose ongoing numerous comments and unfailing encouragement were and continue to be indispensable; to my parents and my sister Aleksandra, my friends Catherine Rab and Milja Gluhovic, for their faith. A very particular appreciation goes to Carmen Quennville for inspiring me with her enthusiasm in the most difficult moment of my writing and her critical rereading of the entire study that unfolded subsequently into the first draft of the manuscript. I would like to express my gratitude to the University of British Columbia for the fellowships that made this work possible and for the courtesy that I enjoyed from both faculty and staff. I am especially thankful to Gabriele Griffin, Tamara Trojanowska, and the anonymous evaluators of my manuscript, their enthusiastic comments, and valuable guidance in the final stages of this manuscript. Last but not least, I would like to thank the editor of the Purdue series of Books in Comparative Cultural Studies, Steven Tötösy de Zepetnek, for his interest in my work and the publication of my book in the series.

Earlier versions of sections of this book have previously been published in the following journals as follows: "The Sacred May Not Be the Same as the Religious. Angela Carter's 'Impressions: The Wrightsman Magdalene' and 'Black Venus'" in *Women: A Cultural Review* 16.1 (2005), "The Sacred Mothers, the Evil Witches and the Politics of Household in Toni Morrison's *Paradise*" in the *Journal of the Association for Research on Mothering: Mothering, Religion and Spirituality* 7.1 (2005), and "Feminist Constructions of the 'Witch' as a Fantasmatic Other" in *Body and Society* 10.4 (2004).

Introduction

Theoretical Points of Departure

Focusing on the contemporary representations of the "witch" as a locus for the cultural negotiation of genders, in this book I revisit some of the most prominent traits in past and current feminist perceptions of exclusion and difference. I examine a selection of twentieth-century North American (U.S. and Canadian) and European narratives to reveal the continued political relevance of metaphors sustained in the fantasy of the "witch," widely thought to belong to pop-cultural or folkloristic formulations of the past. Through a critical rereading of the feminist texts engaging with these metaphors, I develop a new concept of the witch, one that challenges stigmatized forms of sexuality, race, and ethnicity as linked to the margins of culture and monstrous feminine desire. I turn instead to the causes for radical feminist critique of "feminine" sexuality as a fabrication of logocentric thinking, and show that the problematic conversion of the "hag" into a "superwoman" can be interpreted today as a therapeutic performance translating fixed identity into a site of continuous negotiation of the subject in process. Tracing the development of feminist constructs of the witch from 1970s radical texts to the present, I explore the psychoanalytical writings of Hélène Cixous, Julia Kristeva, and Luce Irigaray, as well as Judith Butler's and Rosi Braidotti's feminist reformulations of identity complemented with narrative analyses of different cultural contexts.

While early feminist representations of the "witch" fit into the paradigm of US-American feminists helping their "sisters on the periphery," current feminist theory suggests that sociocultural transformations affected by the recognition of difference cannot simply include only those who are usually excluded. They must equally dislocate the centrality of the dominant subject that is not strictly defined by gender. Radical feminist configurations of the "witch" as a *herstorical* fantasy and as an archaic mother mark a turning point in feminist philosophy by indicating new processes of responding to the nullification of "woman" in the social structure. They allow us to move forward today in contesting metaphorical representations of the female subject by undermining the very structure of female subjectivity, as well as the social relations and collective imagery that preserve these representation. Each of the selected texts in my study attests to a particular relationship between the witch and representation (identity), and enables us to read the self-fashioning of the witch literally as a language of cultural negotiation, consisting of constant reformulations of negativity and difference. Bringing in this relational dimension, my study demonstrates that despite distinctive cultural, linguistic, and political contexts, common philosophical threads of difference intertwine the various representations of feminist witches. Their cultural and national heterogeneity is thus set to confirm and to unsettle the function of the witch figure as a token for otherness and incompatibility. In fact, as analyzed here, representations of the witch appear to be somewhat confusing, because two apparently contradictory versions are conveyed simultaneously. The first is that the "witch" as a phallogocentric archetypal construct remains intact across time and geographical space. Like the generally shared conception of "woman," this construct is difficult to displace. The second configuration, introduced strategically by specific writers in particular contexts and with different aims and effects, needs to be differentiated from the archetype. I formulate these particular (differentiated) threads as traces of "cultural un/belonging," a term that denotes a cultural topography of the stigmatized body, and engages the political significance of identity with reference to contemporary feminism that challenges the antagonisms between sameness and difference. This political challenge has as much to do with mainstream North American and European capitalist and (post)communist histories as with the specificities of feminist cultures within these histories, to which the concept of "difference" is fundamental.

My objective is to suggest a theoretical framework for explicating the culturally transgressive locations of the witch as representing feminist configurations of identity. The main argument is that the "witch," deployed in the 1970s to convey the diasporic status of a female sexuality as incompatible with the dominant discourse, has undergone significant theoretical transformations over the last three decades. These transformations reflect on central traits in the reformulation of second-wave Continental and Anglo-American feminist thought into current postulates of transnational difference and the heterogeneity of women's agendas. The book gives a detailed and careful mapping of various positions, while focusing on paradigmatic representations of the "witch," her culturally specific identifications, and how they are influenced by the Anglo-American and Continental discourses of gender and difference. The archetypal "witch," simultaneously a particular and peculiar representation of "woman" in Western history and culture, offers one of the most spectacular and complex metaphors for identification with difference. Always already a fantasized sign, her appearance exemplifies Butler's definition of the body as never free of an imaginary construction. Constituted as hysterical and disordered in relation to logocentric structures, the "witch" is suspended at the point of crossing into the unspoken and forbidden. Her speech perverts the language of philosophers; laughter, spells, and evil incantations flow from her grotesque and filthy mouth. Emerging in asymmetric relation to logocentric thought, the "witch" articulates a force for subversion that exceeds her own representation within the philosophical logos. This recognition offers a point of departure for a politically feminist theorizing that challenges epistemological dichotomies of subject and object, I and the other, or masculine and feminine as central categories of identification.

In reading various narratives emerging from feminist philosophies, I have observed that a distinction between a literary text (a narrative, a fantasy) and a critical or theoretical text is difficult to maintain and persistently displaces itself in auto/biographical, historical, and documentary references. I refer to this tendency as a narrative suspension between fantasy and memory, between auto/biography and fiction, and in the end, between the authenticity and fraud of both the remembering and remembered subject. The second, a question more than a remark, is that despite deconstruction of the category of "woman," there nevertheless remain some universal issues at stake. The question is: for whom? These "issues," along with the treatment of every text (literary or not) as a cultural text, are broached in my analysis of the "witch" as a network of identities, in which somehow, paradoxically, forms of local appropriation, opposition, and resistance contribute to the conceptual dissemination of the archetype. I therefore turn to feminist narrative as a type of theory, as a way to define other theoretical spaces that theory alone does not encompass. The line of argument developed in approaching the fantasy of "witch" parallels both Butler's formulation of "gender as trouble" and Braidotti's definition of "embodied subject." As an ongoing discursive practice the argument is open to interventions within specific cultural and national agendas. For example, the postfeminist proposal to abolish gender as a cultural equivalent to biological sex, a position reminiscent of the anti-sexuality wing of early US-American feminism, does not recognize the transformative power of the feminine in subverting the representational economy of the social order. In opposition to this reduction, Continental philosophers of difference, such as Irigaray and Braidotti, propose to involve a psychoanalytic insight. Sexuality, the materiality of human reproduction, and consequently the kinship system are central to their conception of difference that rests on the combined impact of morphological and social power relations upon the positioning of the subject. The "trouble" with the witch figure (re)created in the 1970s relates to complex feminist beliefs of the alleged mystery of "woman" on the margins of culture. This witch appears as a sudden intrusion of a female subject, who reverses the phallic gaze, contesting the authority of the masculine position. My study creates spaces for discussing both: the tremendous desire to deal with the witch as a troubling gendered category, a woman (but not quite), and the need to dispose of this category. Through the entire book, the argument is developed to elucidate the heterogeneity of feminist thought, as well as to allow representations of the "witch" to have a strong presence in the text itself, to have a voice (voices perhaps) in the text that the reader can clearly discern.

The starting point for my work is a question that I would also place at the center of my theoretical quest: the trace of the "witch"-woman. Corresponding to the "other" as dissociation and incommensurability, the "witch" as a her(m)etic figure offers a philosophical encounter with alterity that extends the boundaries of system towards anarchy. The concept of the trace leads back to the poststructuralist persistence in formulating otherness as negativity (Levinas, Derrida, Lacan), but it also looks into the (feminist) future. Echoing Levinas's philosophical project of "sensibility" elevating otherness and difference above self-identity and presence, Derrida has argued that before any finality can enter a linguistic process (a literary work or a cultural situation) the textual "split" will mark the folly of a/the sign, granting nothing but a *trace*, a hinge, or an *edge* position. Derrida relates this trace to what is at center of Levinas's critique of ontology, that is, a relationship between the knowing subject and the illeity (alterity) of the past that "can never be lived in the originary or modified form of presence" (*Of Grammatology* 42). As a trace of this alienated other, the witch (in the feminist project) becomes a trace of alterity, suggesting an ethical possibility that "begins" in the articulation of that trace. To locate this trace as a feminist strategy, I am specifically turning to Irigaray, Kristeva, Butler, and Braidotti, whose concepts provide central navigating tools from the start. The lack of agreement between these theoreticians on the issue of "sexual difference" is significant and constitutes an important element of my discussion. However, the employed method of thinking is that of convergence of feminist thought, which, in disabling fixed references, shifts our attention towards the interrelations and intersectionality of various feminist positions on the subject of difference.

My theoretical approach focuses on the feminist practice of overthrowing the notion of "difference" as a negative sign of presence permanently inscribed within the dialectics of Self and Other. Irigaray's and Braidotti's poststructuralist philosophies of sexual difference represent these deeply anti-Hegelian positions translated philosophically into the critique of phallogocentric normativity of humanism. Kristeva's "different legality" associated with a provisional, dialogical, but strategically political project also belongs to this line of thought, which, in the context of Anglo-American feminism, culminates in Butler's and Haraway's postulates of the subversion of gender and its (Western) cultural foundations. I enlarge this debate by introducing a postcommunist perspective that builds on the feminist rejection of the illusionary hegemonic Western identity and its opposition to a "substandard" East European identity. What this particular convergence implies is that transnational exchanges of feminist theories/narratives produce "boundary work"—works "on the edge"—that posits the witch as a set of constructs that are both contested and difficult to displace in contemporary representations of women. In order to elucidate this convergence, the witch, in my analysis, goes through the stages that feminism went through: from positing feminist practice as a process developing along with liberal feminist demands of equal access to the symbolic order, towards a radical feminist rejection of phallogocentric sameness, and culminating more recently in a critique of the metaphysical dichotomy between masculine and feminine constructs. Advocating a deconstructive approach to sexual difference, the third (transgender) wave necessarily challenges the very concept of identity; however, its political significance remains in reference to the earlier feminist positions. In this sense, as Butler concludes, there is "no story to be told about how one moves from feminist to queer to trans. The reason there is no story to be told is that none of these stories are the past: these stories are continuing to happen in simultaneous and overlapping ways as we tell them" (*Undoing Gender* 4). In setting up this relational perspective, the book traces the interactions between feminist theories and narrative (cultural) reformulations of the "witch" into a multiple fantasy of gender, transgression, and un/belonging. These reformulations converge with a number of theoretical concepts, such as resistance, parody, and subversion, and finally lead to the emergence of a subculture as a political form of expression. Although configurations of the contemporary witch have been distilled from various feminist standpoints, three theoretical positions prevail and have their precise chronology, which I subsequently analyze in chapters: 1) as a radical feminist (political) figure representing the culturally subjugated and victimized woman (Daly, Dworkin), and her subsequent *herstorical* reconfiguration into a sovereign, mythic, and powerful "superwoman" (Cixous, Wittig, Gearhart, Walker); 2) as a problematic dialogical figure collapsing into the archaic forms of the presymbolic mother and the phallic monstrous feminine (Kristeva, Creed); and 3) as a borderline phenomenon suspending logocentric discourse and opening thus heterogeneous spaces beyond the accumulation of stigmas, but also beyond the mythic origin, maternal *jouissance*, or femininity (Irigaray, Butler, Braidotti).

Relevant to my comparative cultural studies analysis of these positions is the conceptual confusion of femininity and femaleness. The theoretical use of "feminine," understood as a sociocultural construction of woman's biological body, is differentiated from both "female" and "feminist" (Moi, "Feminist" 120-27). "Femininity" as a cultural construct imposes "naturalized" standards on the biological body ("one is not born a woman, but becomes one" perspective). Seen through this constructionist lens, it is in the logocentric interest that "femininity" and "femaleness" stay thoroughly confused, labeling a nonconforming "woman" *unfeminine* and *unnatural* (Moi, "Feminist" 123). Patriarchy, although increasingly difficult to define, operates in this perspective as a paradigm of institutionalized authority. It is best understood as a sociopolitical structure interwoven with complex cultural framework of kinship that rewards the conforming and stigmatizes undesired forms of sexuality. While patriarchy is a shared target of various forms of feminism, it exhibits different characteristics, which I address along the late capitalist and post/communist axis of difference. The blurred categories of the "feminine"/"female" designation have significant consequences for all feminist interrogations of difference as negativity. Irigaray's position, central to my readings of the "feminine," undercuts the use of feminine persistently defined as the masculine other, the "other of the same" ("Questions" 178). Although sympathetic to Levinas's ethical position, Irigaray reads Levinasian "feminine" "as the underside or reverse side of man's aspiration," as its negative counterbalance. The apprehension of the "feminine" is "not in relation to itself" but "through a purely erotic strategy dictated by masculine pleasure" that underscores this ethical gesture. Consequently, what Irigaray suspects "the philosopher" is seeking is "neither the qualities of the other's flesh nor of his own," but the very same phallogocentric play with cartographies of "elusiveness": "with something other, always inaccessible, always in the future" (178). In this aesthetic play,

Irigaray asserts, "the only function of the feminine other is to satisfy the hungers of the philosopher," to "nourish the intentionality of his pleasure" (179). To satisfy this pleasure, the "feminine" needs to remain marginal, available, at service of the philosophical inquiry. More recent feminist interpretations of Levinas allude extensively to Irigaray's standpoint. The Levinasian "feminine," to follow Tina Chanter, is "a condition of 'slipping away from the light' that interrupts the economy of being, whereby a subject who seeks to know the world ends up negating the otherness of objects and reducing the world to itself." Even with most sensible metaphysics of difference, this economy remains intact (16).

In an addendum to Irigaray's readings, my standpoint with respect to femininity adopts Kristeva's, Butler's, and Braidotti's perspectives, which equally question the philosophical marginality of the feminine subject. The symbolic repression of "femininity," according to these thinkers, is to be viewed in terms of positionality and relationship rather than of essence. Like any other cultural construct, femininity and masculinity are shifting *positions* (see Kristeva), fantasies, parodies (Butler) or metamorphoses (Braidotti). If there is anything right in Beauvoir's claim that one is not born, but rather *becomes* a woman, it is that *woman* itself is a term in process, a becoming, ongoing construction. This positional perspective offers an escape from biology (on this, see Moi; Fraser), but it does not resolve the complexity of "sexual difference." Activating a deconstructive approach to sexual difference, recent feminist positions necessarily challenge the very notion of gender identity (Butler), however, their political usefulness is maintained in reference to the feminist past. In this sense, feminist positions, past or contemporary, must be simultaneous. Advocating the "postfeminist" (or third-wave) position as "exclusive of the first two is to lose touch with the political reality of feminism," but more importantly perhaps it is to realize that "labels," such as "femininity," "masculinity," "feminism," or "sexuality," are categories operated for specific political reasons (Moi, "Feminist" 132). The employment of a positional simultaneity is thus a necessary intellectual strategy for any of the feminist futures. What it offers is a perception of sexuality as a physiosocial fantasy combining nature and culture into a form of (repressed) supplementation. As defined by Irmtraud Morgner (one of the authors selected for this study), "sexuality is a precious state of unrest that makes erotic relations possible, not only towards people, but also toward landscapes, sounds, colors, smells—phenomena of this world in general. Without sexuality, there would be no enthusiasm, no intellectual passion, no *esprit*" ("Making Use" 277). Definitions proposed here are thus intended for debate, although they also delineate the ground on which the debate might effectively be staged: identity, marginality, and cultural transgression are the issues of this exploration.

Narratives through the Lens of Trans/feminist Debates

Within the theoretical and methodological framework of comparative cultural studies, I focus on the contextual comparison of literary and theoretical texts across languages and cultures, in particular of less-known literatures (on the framework of comparative cultural studies, see Tötösy de Zepetnek). The choice of narratives is based on my personal experience with Central and East European and North American (U.S. and Canada) theoretical and literary contexts, and my ongoing nomadic interest in cross-cultural encounters. The narratives, written in the English, German, and Polish, have been selected from numerous contemporary stories about witchlike characters that I have come across or that were suggested to me at different stages of my project. This rather transitory research pattern has allowed me to introduce several less-known Continental women authors into the widely discussed North American feminist context. Their narratives, mostly untranslated, and therefore inaccessible to English-language readers, provide a striking literary parallel to the contemporary Continental and North American feminist voices. They demonstrate clearly that feminist representations of witches are not exclusive to Anglo-American or French-language literatures; however, their relation to second-wave feminism is different because of their culturally distinct contexts. My selection creates space for discussion on what these heterogeneous narratives have in common, what their references to witches convey, and whether they are attributable to different cultural traditions, political systems, and feminist ideologies. While writers' biographies are not central to my analysis, the particular contexts in which they write is relevant, and thus their culturally specific agenda as well as their relationship to Western European and North American feminist frameworks will be addressed. Within this relational context, I examine the ways in which the selected authors (as it happens, all having academic backgrounds) interact with feminist knowledge. The literary works serve as equilibrium in a field of theoretical (representational) writing. As "boundary work," this interaction points to some important convergences of French/European and North American influences, although these "national" divisions are inadequate, and should not limit the diversity of feminist approaches, whether US-American, French-Bulgarian, or Polish-German. Neither is this "coming together" to be confused with globalized methods of sisterhood that invokes internationality at best ambiguously, but it is set to draw our attention to boundaries delineating similarities among the various embodied subjectivities precisely through their claims of difference. In all these senses, my work follows one of the main principles of comparative cultural studies, namely the nonessentialist, that is, nonnational approach to literature and culture.

The earliest narratives I analyze, Andrea Dworkin's *Woman-Hating* (1974), Mary Daly's *Gyn/ecology* (1978), and Sally Gearhart's *Wanderground* (1984), are US-American publications representing a radical multigeneric criticism of patriarchal culture. In these formulations, the witch (or woman's alterity) becomes a central strategic signifier, a crucial metaphor for *herstorically* transmitted "female" values. The body contours, metaphors, and parodies providing reference for these formulations are the Middle Ages and Renaissance projections of the witch either as an evil crone who impersonates the mother, kidnaps and devours children, or as a powerful and dangerous seductress, the mythical *vagina dentata*. The identity principle, in a fierce opposition to the dominant discourse, is crucial to this early political practice. Brought into a dialogue with Alice Walker's African American fantasies of gender and Irmtraud Morgner's East German publication from the same period, they are conveyed as narratives of cultural healing and therapies in process. These therapies intermingle in the second chapter with the methods used by "correcting" figures (doctors, hypnotists, psychoanalysts) and "unconscious" returns (see Freud, *Introductory Lectures on Psycho-Analysis*) to the presymbolic maternal space that have also contributed to women's exclusion from culture. In this identification with the loss of the mother, rather than the loss of the phallus, the "witch" is redesignated as an "archaic" mother, the fantasy of the semiotic *chora,* and the feminist revision of the Freudian *unconscious* (hereafter, this psychoanalytical reference appears in italics). The archaic maternal body is no longer marked by "symbolic castration" but by "the real incision" evoked by the cutting of the umbilical cord, deferred and perpetuated by the presence of the scar, the navel. This psychoanalytical context allows me to compare contemporary Polish texts with such narratives as *Alias Grace* (1996) by Margaret Atwood, or short stories by Sara Maitland and Angela Carter, who likewise emphasize the crucial importance of sexuality in the formation of subjectivity. The Polish novels represent a so-called "postcommunist" feminism, formulated as a decisive counterreaction to "socialist emancipation" (as represented by Morgner's text, produced in the secular atmosphere of East German culture). There are few such literary examples from Poland, since this type of socialist fiction was believed to fall into the category of communist propaganda. Although Krystyna Kofta, one of the Polish authors discussed, began her literary career at the height of communism in Poland, she published without a feminist label. Her novel, *Złodziejka pamięci* ("Thief of Memories";1998), belongs to the postfeminist stance of a younger generation of women writers, represented also by Olga Tokarczuk, the acclaimed author of *Dom dzienny, dom nocny* ("The Day House, the Night House"; 1998), and a less known but promising author of *Siostra ("Sister"*; 1996), Małgorzata Saramonowicz.

In the "postcommunist" discourse, two distinct sociocultural developments are present. On the one hand, an increasing masculinization of the political and scientific arenas impacts the management of the social and the most private aspects of women's lives: abortion is illegal, and contraception and divorce are discouraged by Catholic dogmas. There is a return to social policies based on marriage and the family as primary to women's identities. On the other hand, the growing popularity of "intellectual" feminism, borrowed from US-American and French second-wave feminist positions, encourages a local "digging into" a collective "feminist" past. The texts selected for discussion belong to a category that visibly draws on Irigaray's theories, and displays preoccupations with the failure of the sexual revolution and with theorizing women's difference as a source of cultural possibility rather than a source of oppression. Equally these texts reflect on the Western feminist formulations of Freudian and Lacanian psychoanalysis as a discourse normalizing patriarchy, as well as on reevaluations of hysteria as the unheard voice of the woman whose language is reduced to psychosomatic symptoms (as in Tokarczuk's novels). What hinders my analysis is the relatively limited theory related to Polish feminist history, or its resistance to Western feminism perceived as a monolithic antimale stance. In this respect, I follow Barbara Einhorn (1993) and attribute Central and East European antipathy to feminism to previous experiences with socialist slogans and the neoliberal association of feminists with "physically unattractive" and frustrated women unnecessarily politicizing every aspect of life. Indeed, the few politically active women wear the stigma of being elected on the basis of quotas and are viewed by the majority as political tokens. Also, a tradition of refusal, "refusal of propaganda, ideology, political messianism, big liberatory ideas" (Busheikin 14), as part of the Central and East European psyche is certainly felt in Polish feminist context, and more generally in Central Europe. Discussions often become frustrated by the theoretical imperialism of Western discourse (on this, see Nash; Busheikin; Einhorn), and the exclusion of untranslated opinions and voices. In this sense, it is more accurate to describe "postcommunist" women's contribution (or attitudes) to gender debates as "different" rather than noncollaborative with those in the West.

An interesting parallel can be made to African American feminist attempts to define their own culturally specific place within the debates, preoccupied by two closely related questions: What is the relationship between Black feminist criticism and rather Eurocentric forms of poststructuralism, and how should this criticism proceed with a cultural translation of African fantasies and myths? Both questions refer to issues of essentialism and difference, demonstrating an attempt to widen the discipline for the actual voice of the differentiated. However, the problem of elucidating "different" gender sensitivity and perhaps even consciousness is itself problematic, because it is measured in relation to the "same," more established or familiar, Western scenarios that in themselves are far from monolithic. In fact, Western feminism has split into "a large collection of single-issue organizations that press for feminist aims in many different accents" (Walter 44). British feminism, for example, for which the postcolonial question is of central importance, and is relevant in the context of Carter's and Maitland's texts, "grew rapidly as a mass movement [from the late 1960s], peaking in the mid-1970s before dissolving as a coherent organization by the end of that decade" (Segal 9). According to prevailing European convictions, "explanations of cultural difference do not produce a greater understanding or make differences any less real" (Strathern 29), while many women seem to return to and value their roles as mothers and wives, and do not want to be involved in political decision-making (see Nash; Sempruch). Precisely in this light of "dissolving" feminist tradition, I discuss the most recent (Western) German narratives (Korte's and Finckenstein's) that contribute to recognition of the "inadequacies" of the US-American sexual revolution, raising acute questions to present-day third-wave feminists.

Bringing out the effects of these two preceding contexts, namely the valorised *herstorical* rewritings of the "witch" as a fantasy of a "superwoman" and the "witch" as an archaic mother, the texts analyzed in the final chapter propose an encounter with "cultural un/belonging" and suspensions of identity in the process of "becoming." Like gender, the terms ethnicity and race refer to culturally sanctioned but arbitrarily defined categories within the social rather than universal biological conditions. Ethnicity, clearly intersecting with nationality and race, refers to a cultural orientation shaped by specific traditions and historical experiences: "Just as the usage of 'gender' has, until recently, implied a focus on women while masculinity remained the invisible norm, the usage of 'race' and 'ethnicity' has connoted a focus on people of color, as if persons in the white mainstream had no race" (Warhol and Herndl 741). To take any of these constructs for granted implies a retreat to the principle of self-sameness, into futile attempts to return to an origin: "Where and how does it begin...? But a meditation upon the trace should undoubtedly teach us that there is no origin, that is to say simple origin; that the questions of origin carry with them a metaphysics of presence" (Derrida, *Of Grammatology* 46). In this metaphysical framework, feminism involves the constitution and organization of collective memories and desires as well as resistance and consciousness of becoming-a-subject. The trace of the "witch," as discussed in the final chapter, becomes a complex interplay of social and symbolic forces: the "witch" is no longer an essence, let alone a biological substance, but a play of constructs within a complex web of social obligations. Emerging thus as a necessarily dialogical figure, the "witch" represents the split identity of the "embodied subject" that negotiates between subconscious and conscious drives, between repressed and released desires, between the condensation of maternal physiology and social dis/placement. Finally, texts written out of (or representing) particular cultures, such as issues of race and oppression in relation to gender in Morrison's *Paradise* (1998) or nationalist and sexist agendas in Polish texts, intertwine spaces of gender fantasy with age, ethnicity, and religion. Postcolonial and psychoanalytic theories of "othering" are relevant in both cases. A comparative perspective, juxtaposing Morrison's novel with Carter's "Impressions: The Wrightsman Magdalene" (1996) and "Black Venus" (1985), emphasizes the ambiguity or interchangeability of racial roles. Interestingly, these roles go beyond cultural stereotyping of the gendered body to posit women's collective crossing of boundaries and territorial borders as modes of delineating identities that are not exclusively national, gendered, or racial. Rather, their differential positions need to be acknowledged in terms of ideologies of locations, i.e., locally defined social divisions, collective memories, spirituality, or ambivalent family relations.

Consequently, the feminist theory discussed in the final chapter of the book occupies a noncompliant but vulnerable position of negotiating between patriarchy and resistance to it, between the social order and the "unspoken" semiotic territories of the maternal and the sacred. The identity transgressions, or borderline status, as emerging from these negotiating spaces offer the most convincing elements of the discussion, and build theoretical meeting points between Kristeva's, Irigaray's, Butler's, and Braidotti's stances that all seek to destabilize specific codes of logocentric culture. In the end, the question that reoccurs throughout the book is that of how to maintain the complexity of the models proposed while approaching them comparatively. What emerges as central to each of the considered views is that feminist actions do not need to be instituted from some stable, unified gender identity, since every category has in itself a definitional incompleteness. The very form of feminist coalitional politics emerges thus as a multiplicity of positions from which one no longer speaks as a/the Woman. Indeed, the positions represented here are upheld by a split (divided) subject, even a pluralized subject that occupies politically mobile places. The "witch" figure represents such a divided subject, a fantasy deployed to convey the transgressive status of the category of "woman" and gender in general. This position reinvests the concept of fantasy as un/belonging with the strategic purpose of transgressing the confining territories of culture and therefore contesting its restrictions. It undermines the very negativity of un/belonging while bringing it into a dialogue with belonging, and can therefore be seen as a theory of cultural negotiation. I close this introduction with positively transgressive readings of difference, addressed most prominently by Irigaray and Braidotti. In these feminist readings, the subject of feminism is no longer "a/the woman" as a specular other of the universal masculinity, but "rather a complex and multi-layered embodied subject who has taken her distance from the institution of femininity" (Braidotti, *Metamorphoses* 11). Most certainly, there is an imprint of history on that "embodied subject": her traveling through centuries of subordination, silence, and negativity. This historical dimension of difference has left a permanent scar on the present feminist posture. Although a/the woman "may no longer be a she but a subject of quite another story," a "subject-in-process, a mutant, the other of the Other" (12), whoever "she" may come to be today, she wears this scar all along: the repressed past of her patriarchal duties. The ultimate inquiry thus, pertaining to the political meaning of the scar, is how to read it today, without losing its complex relationship with history and its multiple potentials for the "embodied subject." The theoretical approach and concepts presented in these introductory remarks will frame the discussion of selected texts in the three chapters to follow.

Chapter One

Functions and Risks of Radical Feminist "Witches"

Desire as a Place of Herstorical Inconsistencies

While rereading the radical feminist versions of the "witch" figure in 1970s scholarship, it is possible to conclude that no matter who she is, or whom she supposedly represents, the "witch" remains a benevolent "wise-woman," a victim of phallogocentric hegemonies. This particular identity construction derives from mythic stories of the "Burning Times" and beliefs in the "Craft of the Wise," both drawing on the historically documented medieval and postmedieval European witch-craze. Following Diane Purkiss, most of these "mythic" sources were invented (and invention is one of the key words here) at the point when the second wave feminist movement "began to turn away from rights-centred public-sphere issues towards crime-centred, private-sphere issues": "Sexuality was to be identified as the site of women's oppression in the sense that property was for Marx the site of class oppression. Rape, sexual violence, pornography, wife-battering and (eventually) child sexual abuse became the central signifiers of patriarchy, replacing signifiers such as legal asymmetries and pay differentials" (15). This formulation of sexuality, traced back to the so-called sexual revolution of the late 1960s and forming an important aspect of second-wave feminist identity politics in the 1970s, carried in itself the somehow troublesome "freedom of sexual expression." Reflecting the influence of Wilhelm Reich and Herbert Marcuse, whose theories were grounded both in Marxism and Freudian psychoanalysis, the early 1970s feminist voices postulated the "release of sexual energy" as a means of liberation from repressive social forces and, on a more radical note, the right to "sexual pleasure." Sexuality was defined as male centered and organized around phallic pleasure, with women's sexuality defined in terms of meeting male sexual fantasies and reproductive duties. Through this simplified binary lens of sexual relations, radical feminism (see Millett, Rowbotham, Oakley) encouraged women to reclaim their sexuality that has been suppressed and denied to them.

The feminist narratives from this period, such as Daly's *Gyn/ecology* (1978) or Dworkin's *Women-Hating* (1974) shift their critical interest to the witch figure as a signifier for physically abused and culturally neglected "woman," the one Cixous, in the French feminist context, refers to in "The Laugh of the Medusa" (1975): the woman "in her inevitable struggle against conventional man," the "universal woman subject who must bring women to their senses and to their meaning in history" (347). To begin with, this universal subject performs "a sort of tetralogy, tackling the problem of the four elements: water, air, fire, earth, applied to philosophers nearer our time," and simultaneously, it interrogates the philosophical tradition (Irigaray, "Bodily Encounter" 35). Irigaray's focus on the "double syntax" in philosophical debates on desire, that is to say, on a possible articulation of the in-between processes of the conscious and subconscious, masculine and feminine significations of desire, is of crucial importance in this context. It somewhat futuristically delineates what is still out of sight in 1970s: the strategy of a self-conscious mimesis that will highlight the mechanisms that maintain sexual indifference (rather than difference) in place. The very concept of "desire," dense with intertextual connotations, is understood here as used by Lacan in correlation with the exteriority of linguistic experience, that is as the "split" that occurred when we entered language, and a "hole" in the "self" that the subject attempts to "close" through an endless metonymic chain of supplements. This definition of "desire" becomes a point of contention for French and Anglophone second-wave feminists because of the phallogocentric model of "woman," who is said "to be desirable to man" owing to a belief that she will be able to complete him, that she is his Other (all that he is not)" (Warhol and Herndl 485). Within the newly emerging feminist psychoanalysis, this concept of "desire" clearly limits women's possibilities in the world of lived experience, that is, an experience ruled by the symbolic discourse that relegates female types of desire to the dyadic "imaginary." The "symbolic," imposed by Lacanian psychoanalysis "as a universal, innocent of any empirical or historical contingency," is in fact, as Irigaray argues, a "'monosexual' (or 'hom(m)osexual') imaginary, transformed into an order, into the social" (*Speculum* 98). Or, in Butler's understanding, the symbolic constitutes "the sphere that regulates the assumption of sex, where sex is understood as a differential set of positions, masculine and feminine" (*Undoing Gender* 47).

In this fantasmatic system of "topological order" of phallus as a signifier of fullness of being, "woman" (and as a result, women) has been made into a "fantasy" of the "speculum" providing a material support of male narcissism. Projected as "being the phallus," "woman" does neither exist nor belong; she is "in exile" (Irigaray, "Women's Exile" 76), in cultural diaspora. The exilic narratives, especially the Anglo-American radical feminist texts, revalorize the unbelonging roles of midwives, healers, herbalists, and crones, reflecting Cixous's "women" who return from the Dark Continent of desire "from always: from 'without,' from the heath where the witches are kept alive; from below, from beyond 'culture'" ("Laugh" 348). These texts need to be viewed as attempts to remove witches' history (problematically identified with women's history) from the entrapment of their physiological bodies stigmatized by "symbolical castration": the "little girls and their 'ill-mannered' bodies immured, well-preserved, intact unto themselves, in the mirror. Frigidified" (348). They are mostly so-called *herstorical* (in contrast to historical) narratives, and their objective is to escape the stereotypical link between fascination and revulsion as inscribed onto the castrated and melancholic female body. More recently, this and similar radical objectives have come under challenge (see Butler; Purkiss; Pusch), while the subject of a feminist identity, assumed to be shared, obvious, and crucial to the understanding of the radical feminist texts, has since been recognized as far from monolithic. Indeed, the arguments developed by Diane Purkiss, Luise Pusch, and Butler that will frame my discussion emphasize the fragmentation of feminist identity and "the paradoxical opposition to feminism from 'women' whom feminism claims to represent" (Butler, *Gender Trouble* 4). This opposition, as a type of adversative reaction, suggests in itself "the necessary limits of identity politics" (4). In Purkiss's view of this inadequacy, the radical narratives of the witch-craze are particularly troublesome, because the myth of the "Burning Times" has become "such a key part of many feminists' identities that to point to its limitations is bound to be painful and divisive" (26). As a radical feminist identity, the "witch" strategically represents both the historical abject figure subjected to torture and death, and a radical fantasy of renewal in the form of a female figure who desires (and articulates) a cultural transformation "that has not happened yet," and also the one who already marks that transformation. Although the feminist witch succeeds in subverting her abject identity by converting it into a political fantasy of gender, the "category of women for merely 'strategic' purposes" (Butler, *Gender Trouble* 4) remains problematic. The herbalist-witch represents clearly such a fantasy of a superwoman, the feminist heroine of the 1980s and 1990s, a professional woman who has a beautiful country garden, bakes her own bread, makes her own quilts, and demonstrates unconventional sexuality (Purkiss 21). Through all this, the fantasy is strategically set to undermine the inferiority of the feminine sex and to erase paternity (the father and the son) from the symbolically accorded priority. This "feminine," designating a restorative theory/fantasy beyond the signifiers of paternity and fecundity, is clearly meant to refer beyond the biological entrapment of the "female" subject; however, the question remains of what transformative significance this radical term acquires in the end. In an attempt to answer this question, I trace several theoretical routes as taken by Continental and Anglo-American authors.

I begin by focusing on Irigaray's, Cixous's, and subsequently, Daly's and Wittig's philosophical conceptualizations of a/the "universal" woman, all constituting very different intellectual standpoints. In contextualizing their positions (especially Irigaray's and Cixous's), it seems necessary to refer to a mobile discursive locus of the/a "universal" woman: a dialogical impossibility, or incongruence between history and *herstory*, strategically ending up in women's imaginary which "is inexhaustible, like music, painting, writing: their stream of phantasms is incredible" (Cixious, "Laugh" 347). This "stream of phantasms" needs to be retrospectively seen as a therapeutic attempt both to break through the silence and invisibility of female history, and to elevate the notion of "feminine alterity" over the complementarity and symmetricity of the phallogocentric system. Such clearly Levinasian reference to the "exteriority of the Other" (see his *Time and the Other*) has been carefully pursued by Irigaray in her philosophical debate of "alterity" as a "nonreciprocal relationship" that characterizes social life. Posited at the very heart of the relationship with the other, Irigaray's interruption of Levinasian "alterity" is most significant in the context of the "feminine." Elevated by Levinas as "absolute alterity," this formulation plays a crucial part in both unsettling and maintaining the philosophical heritage of the masculine sameness. Although for Irigaray, the Levinasian "feminine alterity" does not constitute the limits of masculinity, but, above all, the site of a masculine self-elaboration, it is the unsettling aspect of the Levinasian Other that becomes attractive for French feminist purpose.

Given that Levinas, against the Western philosophical tradition, claims a priority for alterity over the sameness, the idea that alterity is accomplished in the feminine amounts to a radical claim: the "feminine" is thus inconspicuously rendered a privileged term, since in it alterity is accomplished (Chanter 5). In a similar mode, the "witch" (or the "alterity" of the woman) becomes a privileged term for *herstorical* narratives. To follow Morgner, the witch "is not only possible, but actually she is needed, desired" (*Amanda* 635). The perspective offered is that of an *other woman*, defined by Irigaray as one that is exterior to phallocentric metaphorizations, "a woman who does not yet exist, but whose advent could shake the foundations of patriarchy" (Whitford 29). Indeed, in *The Newly Born Woman* (1975), Cixous's and Clément's witch figures replicate the traces of alterity (illeity, anarchy) in a range of subversive feminine symbols. Evoking both medical and sexual implications, the sorceress and the hysteric are posited as tropes for the feminine condition of the "universal" woman , that is, for cultural incompatibility and deviance which, if excessive, will be vomited "into protected spaces—hospitals, asylums, prisons" (*Newly Born* 6). There the witch-woman is veiled, hidden, and kept under restraint. This feminine condition, according to Cixous, has to be rewritten against the heterosexual ideology of two physiologically different but supposedly complementary halves; an ideology, which Butler would reformulate as "literalizing fantasy": the conflation of desire with the real—that is the belief that it is parts of the body, the "literal" penis, the "literal" vagina, which cause pleasure and desire. This fantasy and its perennial enactments, characteristic of the syndrome of melancholic heterosexuality (Butler, *Gender Trouble* 71), have silenced figurations of alternative subjectivities, and precisely the "alterity" accomplished in the "feminine."

The "dark" origin (alterity) of the feminine condition has been revisited by Cixous in her formulation of a/the woman as Dark Continent, associated symbolically with what Reason leaves behind: "the dark powers of the earth goddesses, immersion in unknown forces associated with mysterious female powers" (Lloyd 2; see also Anderson). This continent is "*neither dark nor unexplorable*" (Cixous, "Laugh" 354), but due to phallogocentric perpetuation of this fantastic belief, "what interests us is the white continent, with its monuments to Lack" (354). Dating back to the Aristotelian philosophy of reasoning in ancient Greece (see Anderson), the/a "universal" woman represents the embodiment of nonreason and antirational procedures, emerging as an icon (or a symptom) of cultural un/belonging. As a contemporary protagonist, Cixous's Medusa (and her subversive laughter) becomes a deconstructive designation for the *difference* that challenges her historical displacement, indicating a permanent breakdown of authority, an anarchic gap between the signifier and signified and the manifestation of an ontological inconsistency. As such she/it relates to the Derridean "past that has never been present," adapted carefully in Cixous's theoretical aspiration to reverse the course of Western history in which the concept of the transcendental "woman" develops in tandem with philosophical and religious denials of the female authority: "And we believed. They riveted us between two horrifying myths: between the Medusa and the abyss. That would be enough to set half the world laughing, except that it's still going on" ("Laugh" 354). This reversal theoretically converges with Butler's "laughter in the face of serious categories" as an indispensable feminist tool, a way to trouble the "historical configurations of a nameless female indisposition" (*Gender Trouble* viii). Cixous's clearly Derridean recognition of the "unexamined" potentials of the dominant culture contributes thus to an important aspect of Butler's parody of gender, i.e., a parody of "natural" identity "vested with an agency that remains intact regardless of its cultural embeddedness" (*Gender Trouble* 142-43).

Cixous's representations of the "universal" woman enter into dialogue with some of the most peculiar phallocentric assumptions that "enabled male culture sometimes to vilify women as representing darkness and chaos, to view them as Lilith or the Whore of Babylon, and sometimes to elevate them as the representatives of a higher and purer nature, to venerate them as Virgins and Mothers of God" (Moi, "Feminist" 127). In discussing these extreme versions, or "limits" of a/the "woman," I view them, following Clément and Kristeva, as "porous" models, models that both interconnect and deconstruct women's cultural bodies. The very contours of these bodies, as Butler suggests in reference to Douglas, "are established through markings that seek to establish specific codes of cultural coherence" (*Gender Trouble* 131). The objective to follow is thus to reformulate the "witch" as a trace of cultural un/belonging, of bodily margins "invested with power and danger" (as referred to by Douglas); a trace that is constantly present and absent in such Western figures as the Judeo-Christian Lilith, Eve, and Jezebel, and the Virgin Mary, or Mary Magdalene, as well as in the classical Greek figures of the Sirens, Circe, or Cassandra, all of whom are evoked in the discussed literary texts. Above all, "the sorceress—the witch, the wisewoman, destroyer and preserver of culture—is she not the midwife, the intermediary between life and death, the go-between whose occult yet necessary labors deliver souls and bodies across frightening boundaries" (Cixous and Clément xiii)? Similarly, in a striking reliance on the "original craft" of words, Daly and Barbara Walker draw on the hag's metamorphosis from the wise-woman into the witch that transforms her medieval cauldron "from a sacred symbol of regeneration into a vessel of poisons" (Walker, *The Crone* 122). According to Daly, the hag is a female *eccentric*, in reference to the Greek *ek* (out of) and *kentrum* (center of a circle; 186), who deviates from established patterns and delineates new cultural topography of the universal woman. This hag, to follow Walker, stands in a direct opposition to the malevolent stereotypical hag that "still haunts elder women today. If a man is old, ugly, and wise, he is a sage. If a woman is old, ugly, and wise, she is a *saga*—that is, a witch" (122). This revival of the crone, the image, and the motif of the "witch" allows for highly emotional "digging" through several layers of history, and lead radical feminism to the inevitable rediscovery of the witch pogroms of the late Middle Ages as an incontestable archaeological proof of female oppression (Bovenschen 230). And although the tension between past established patterns and present feminine condition is experienced in all subsequent second-wave feminist histories, only radical feminism resolves it by presenting its narrative "not as a reconstruction of the past, but an account of the way things *always* are" (Purkiss 10). This *herstorical* tendency to invoke the mythical past, and its insistence on erasing the traces of its own historicity (10), is undoubtedly intertwined with the desire to manifest one's own sovereign presence, even if that presence appears to be hysterical. Alice Walker's references to witches, in the context of her African heritage, also seem to fall into this category of emotional "digging." As explained by Lissie, one of the protagonists in *The Temple of My Familiar* (1989), "the first witches to die at the stake were the daughters of the Moors....It was they (or, rather, we) who thought the Christian religion that flourished in Spain would let the Goddess of Africa 'pass' into the modern world as 'the Black Madonna.' After all, this was how the gods and goddesses moved from era to era before, though Islam, our official religion for quite a long time by now, would have nothing to do with this notion; instead, whole families in Africa who worshipped the goddess were routinely killed, sold into slavery, or converted to Islam at the point of the sword. Yes...I was one of those 'pagan' heretics they burned at the stake" (*Temple* 222). Such emotional "proofs" explain perhaps why "the radical feminist history of witches often appears to offer a static, finished vision of the witch" (Purkiss 10), one that reflects the feminist *desire* for an irrefutable reference that could be considered ultimate and eternal. This form of historicizing, dogmatic and often historically inadequate, can be understood as a resistance to the phallocentric attribution of "deficiency" to the/a "woman" (Felman 9).

In the view of the above, the radical feminist witches "can only represent all oppressed women if we know very little about them. The more witch-history the myth of the Burning Times attempts, the more damage it does to its own mythic status" (Purkiss 13). This *herstorical* blindness to difference in historical and present situatedness of women is characteristic of many radical feminist texts. Their witch figure remains entrapped within the dilemma of a cultural transgressor and negotiator that in history became a convenient scapegoat (the stereotypical frightening witch-woman to be eliminated), and in *herstory* becomes a utopian projection of female power. I therefore propose to consider radical feminist texts as theoretical and narrative forms of spontaneous hysteria, that is, as examples of a revolutionary discourse that carries in itself an inherent division between the methodical, logical, and reasonable on one hand, and the hysterical, that is *eccentric* and out of control, on the other. There is a revolutionary potential in this type of hysterical discourse: "Even in her paralysis, the hysteric exhibits a potential for gestures and desires....A movement of revolt and refusal, a desire for/of the living mother who would be more than a reproductive body in the pay of the polis: a living woman" (Irigaray, "Women-Mothers" 47-48). I illustrate this division between methodology and hysteria while focusing specifically on Daly's, Dworkin's, and Wittig's positions on women's sexuality.

Constructing the Body as a Locus of Fear

To begin with Moi's observation, valid particularly in reference to Daly's writing, the radical Anglo-American phantasms represent the "undeconstructed" form of feminism that, still "unaware of the metaphysical nature of gender identities...runs the risk of becoming an inverted form of sexism" (*Sexual/Textual* 129). One of the risks to be negotiated by the radical feminist projects is that of merging, intentionally or not, with the patriarchal definitions of women that Simone de Beauvoir struggled to contest, confining women to the mysterious and not quite human other, as a muse incapable of taking responsible actions in the symbolic. Thus, although significant as radically positive and empowering rewritings of the historical "witch" into a therapeutic narrative figure, the narratives analyzed here demonstrate how difficult and sometimes risky it is to work against the phallocentric structure, especially once we start to diversify feminist *herstories* across race, class, and political systems. Precisely, because it operates on a basis of assumed identity politics, *herstory* emerges as a form of feminist mythology, and constitutes a challenging alternative to the established (Western) male-centered master-story. One could refer here to a range of narrative fantasies: Elana Nachman's *Riverfinger Women*, Bertha Harris's *Lover*, Wittig's *Les Guérillères*, or Gearhart's *Wanderground*, to name but a few, present communities of strong, witchlike women, drawing on myths of Amazons and prehistorical matriarchies. This phase of "intellectual rebellion, gynocentrism, and critical separatism" belongs to "a crucial period in the experience of women who had always played subordinate roles as dutiful academic daughters, research assistants, second readers, and faculty wives" (Showalter 224).

As an alternative discourse, *herstory*, or rather herstories, taking into account their conceptual plurality, initiates important processes in the cultural interrogation of existing historical and mythical representations of gender. In the 1970s, as Clément and Kristeva remind us, "we heard slogans about the return of witches, the moon, the tides, matriarchy, the primal. There was blood in the air and slaughter on the horizon" (71). In these rebellious circumstances, the alterity accomplished in the "feminine" amounts indeed to a radical claim, and must alter the traditional association of the feminine with negative otherness. The feminist witch (or the alterity of the woman) consequently becomes a central strategic signifier, a crucial metaphor or rather a metonymy for radically transmitted female values. Daly's and Dworkin's texts in particular can be categorized as hysterical and fanatical means to resist an equally hysterical and fanatical misogyny. Their strategies consistently draw on the historical victimization of women accused of witchcraft, and particularly on the exhibition and torture of the female body. Considering that postmedieval accusations of witchcraft were "aimed at particular categories of persons," the majority of which were elderly, and often poor widowed women of low status (Sanders 118), recreating their victimization as a symbol of sisterhood-based on twentieth-century middle class women's solidarity is particularly troublesome. However, in the process of constructing a "universal" feminist story, personal fears, hatred and solidarity are evoked on purpose, and their complexities, such as the conflation of fiction with academic research, are often difficult to examine, leaving little space for analytical perspective. Questioning Daly's self-absorption with historical "discoveries," Pusch addresses her plea directly: "Mary, please don't punish us any more" (106). Cleary disapproving of her "new, true, deep structures," apparently referring to the etymological "original word/craft," Pusch suggests rightfully that Daly's word puns contribute to her theoretical weakness, tangible especially if read in a translation today, at the dawn of transfeminist culture. No doubt, Daly's sharp-witted linguistic deconstructions that have since drawn our attention to the pathologies of patriarchal language end up in a feminist storage: in the "section: patriarchal curiosities" (Pusch 110). Interestingly, to follow up on some possible reasons, Daly's troublesome, deliberately ambiguous wording would still be digestible, if used within reasonable limits. But clearly, such limits are not Daly's venture. In fact, her linguistic intricacies increase from one work to the next, undeniably revealing Daly's engagement in a "truly pleasurable pursuit of new meanings," resulting in such flourishing creations as stag-nation, the-rapist, bore-ocracy, Hexicon or Mister-ek-tomy (Pusch 107). At this point, I propose to open the storage once more and dust off some of the reasons for the *herstorical* rage and its dogmatic practices.

Daly's and Dworkin's radical theses posit the "witch" simultaneously as a female source of authority and as a patriarchal scapegoat, equating patriarchy with the relentless persecution of women by physical torture. In *Woman-Hating*, Dworkin informs us that "the magic of witches was an imposing catalogue of medical skills concerning reproductive and psychological processes, a sophisticated knowledge of telepathy, auto- and hetero-suggestion" (148). Accused, in history, of stealing male fertility, or even dismembering the male body, the all-devouring, death-dealing hag returns in Daly's *Gyn/ecology* to represent the protective maternal instincts of an archaic character. The witch-crone, Daly's most prominent "archetype" of female powers, becomes a guardian of birth-giving as well as of virginity and homosexuality unstained by patriarchal semen. Daly's rewriting of *hagiography* as *Hag-ography* morphs the *hag* into an embodiment of feminist fantasy of sisterhood, i.e., of "hidden history" deeply intertwined with our own processes of identification. Thus, we learn that "our foresisters were the Great Hags whom the institutionally powerful but privately impotent patriarchs found too threatening for coexistence." As "we write/ live in our own story," we are thus inevitably "uncovering their history" (Daly 14). Their story is *our* story, while *we* become crones (the survivors of the witchcraze), "as a result of having discovered depths of courage, strength and wisdom" (16) in *ourselves*. Obviously, this mode of speaking in the name of all of *us* raises questions as to "who has the right to speak about what on behalf of whom," or else "who can possibly be fit to listen" (Purkiss 17). I would argue that it also explains how these reconstructions and/or postmemories of sorts contribute to a constitution of "feminist subjectivity." To follow Butler, the feminist "we" is a fantasmatic construction of a common gender (*Gender Trouble* 142), attempting the impossible: to bring women living under highly disparate circumstances into the same feminist family. This construction has its clear political and therefore strategic purpose, since "at this point, it becomes clear that [Daly's] narrative account of the Burning Times is less a presentation of external events than the story of an internal voyage, a metaphorical journey into the heart of patriarchal darkness" (Purkiss 13). This darkness clearly converges with Cixous's metaphor of the Dark Continent, both representing modes of resistance to women's "cultural castration" and serving as a new territory from which to identify oneself with the "witch."

If Daly's *herstory* of witchcraft is a religious (spiritual) experience, a form of self-actualizing narrative of suffering, Dworkin's is an experience of bodily victimization, a type of masochism, through which she replies to the "gynocide," "a term which at once covers over and gestures at what it replaces" (Purkiss 17). Dworkin "uses both the image of the demonized witch-stepmother of fairy tales and the figure of the persecuted witch-victim of the Burning Times as figures for the suffering woman-victim of pornography and rape" (Purkiss 15). Unlike Cixous's, her narratives are manifestos of female subjection and simultaneously, somehow disruptively, they celebrate the survivor-figure who lives to tell the tale. Particularly valid, in this double context, is Purkiss's observation that radical feminists (such as Daly and Dworkin) equate themselves with witches in order to ensure "that anyone who disagrees with [them] can be cast as an inquisitor" (16). Daly's "notorious intolerance of women not classed as Hags—often stigmatized by her as 'fembots' (female robots)—ironically reduplicates a rigid structure of 'acceptable' behaviour for women" (16). Daly's firm conviction that what happened to Hags once is happening to them again, perpetuates the vicious circle of gynophobia and is no longer effectual in the light of more recent feminist rereadings of history. Similarly, Dworkin's conscious preoccupation with the very linguistic structure, as she writes "with a broken tool, a language which is sexist and discriminatory to its core" (Dworkin 26), reflects on her own failure to invent vocabulary and articulate her pain. Instead, Dworkin appropriates a sometimes coarse and angry style, as if trying to break through the symbolic, through the theory, into something that constitutes the "actual" subversive discourse, into "life" (24), as she says. In this refusal of emotional detachment as a necessity of critical evaluation, radical feminism maintains a highly personal character. To follow Daly, defending a witch equates with declaring oneself a witch, a symbolic Holocaust survivor from the past and the cult figure of the present. As Purkiss suggests, pogroms, lynchings, and the Holocaust make it difficult "to deny the very existence of racism and ethnocentrism. The Burning Times myth offers to play the same role in women's history, to authorise the need for struggle and authenticate the forms that struggle takes" (15). Daly's model of genocide, unreflectively drawing on the paradigm of Holocaust, clearly serves the purpose of a symbolic shock-value, and has been critically addressed by Purkiss as a strategic attempt "to inflate the number of women who died in witch-persecutions into the millions" (15). This form of re-traumatization of historical memory and its identificatory consequences for radical feminism are giving rise to a discourse of the "surrogate victimage" (LaCapra 221).

Despite a detailed analysis of the torture inflicted on witches, Daly and Dworkin are reluctant to mention (historical) names of witches or to describe particular cases of witch trials. To follow up on this reluctance, Purkiss notes that "male historians never tire of observing that radical feminist histories of witchcraft use almost no early modern texts as a source for views about witchcraft except the *Malleus Maleficarum*" (11). Both Daly's and Dworkin's major historical reference is indeed the infamous *Malleus Maleficarum*, published in 1486, in the early period of the witch craze, and known in English as *The Witch's Hammer*. One of the most famous passages in the *Malleus Maleficarum* reads as follows:

As for the first question, why a greater number of witches is found in the fragile feminine sex than among men...the first reason is, that they are more credulous, and since the chief aim of the devil is to corrupt faith, therefore he rather attacks them... the second reason is, that women are naturally more impressionable, and...the third reason is that they have slippery tongues, and are unable to conceal from their fellow-women those things which by evil arts they know...But the natural reason is that [a woman] is more carnal than a man, as is clear from her many carnal abominations. And it should be noted that there was a defect in the formation of the first woman, since she was formed from the bent rib, that is, a rib of the breast, which is bent as it were in a contrary direction to a man. And since through this defect she is an imperfect animal, she always deceives....And this is indicated by the etymology of the word; for Femina comes from Fe and Minus, since she is ever weaker to hold and preserve the faith....All witchcraft comes from carnal lust, which is in women insatiable." (47)

This comprehensive handbook for witch hunters, compiled by Dominican inquisitors Heinrich Kramer and James Sprenger, presents "by far the most important treatise on persecuting witches to come out of the witch hysteria of the Middle Ages and Renaissance" (Guiley 221-22). In the *Encyclopedia of Witches and Witchcraft*, Rosemary E. Guiley informs us further that the *Malleus Maleficarum* "had a profound impact on witch trials on the Continent for about 200 years. Montag Summers, an English author who wrote extensively on witchcraft and demonology at the beginning of the twentieth century, called it "among the most important, wisest, and weightiest books in the world....It was second only to the Bible in sales until John Bunyan's *Pilgrim's Progress* published in 1678" (221-22; interestingly, whether Guiley's encyclopaedia represents an unbiased and reliable academic source is subject to debate; published in 1989, her work certainly follows the herstorical representations of the witches' history). The Latin genitive *Maleficarum* translates literally as "of female evil doers," and, as cited by Dworkin, the questions analyzed in it are such quandaries as "'whether Witches may work some Prestidigitatory Illusion so that the Male Organ appears to be entirely removed and separate from the Body (Answer: Yes),' [or] 'That

Witches who are Midwives in Various Ways Kill the Child Conceived in the Womb, and Procure Abortion; or if they do not do this, offer New-born Children to the Devils (Answer: Yes)'" (128). Elaborating on the interrogational procedures described, both Daly and Dworkin portray the witch hunters as obsessed (religious) maniacs who see themselves as purifying the female mystical body of indigestible elements, to paraphrase Daly's text. It is precisely these elements, in the radical feminist interpretation, that constitute female independence, a spiritual, physical, and economic sovereignty that threatens the phallocentric monopoly of power. According to Daly, references to torture and the death sentence, performed *ad infinitum* on witches in a medieval form of spectacle, do not concern the women actually accused, but their bodies or body fragments that are rendered seductive, fascinating, and repulsive at once. Passages are quoted from the *Malleus* "not for their centrality to witch-beliefs, but for their striking qualities, hence the more or less constant reiteration of the passage about the stolen *phalloi*, a belief rarely recorded elsewhere but striking as an illustration of rabid misogyny" (Purkiss 11). From the fantasy thus emerges a new feminist ideology of female suffrage. And although radical feminist historians are not deluded into thinking that the *Malleus* is central (although they do write as if it is), their criteria are those of the storyteller, in search of the most striking illustration or anecdote.

Furthermore, radical feminists seem to agree with the Foucauldian understanding of torture as forming part of a ritual. The radical symbolism of the inadvertently sexualized female body is extended and designed to illustrate the spectacular martyrdom of the raped pagan goddess. The same symbolism turns the persecutor into a hysteric who applies repetitive procedures of detecting warts and moles on the stripped female body, or verifies its ability to float when it is tied up and thrown into the water. As Foucault writes in *Discipline and Punish* (1975), "from the point of view of the law that imposes it, public torture and execution must be spectacular, it must be seen by all almost as its triumph" (34). Particularly valid, in the radical feminist context, is the observation that "torture does not reconcile (even if its function is to 'purge' the crime)," it rather "traces around...the very body of the condemned" woman, leaving on the reader/spectator visible, and recognizable scars of fear, which "must not be effaced" (34). Ironical as it seems, Daly's and Dworkin's narratives express a similar desire for ongoing torture, even after death, in elaborate descriptions of the burnt corpses, or bodies dragged on hurdles and exhibited at the roadside. If medieval justice had pursued human body beyond all possible endurance, the radical feminist narratives seem to be absorbed with the same abject ceremonial element: with a sanctification of the victimized body that torture invokes. This element, called by Foucault "the liturgy of punishment," marks the victim "either by the scar it leaves on the body, or by the spectacle that accompanies it, to brand the victim with infamy" (*Discipline and Punish* 34). Because of their focus on torture and execution, Daly's and Dworkin's narratives are both problematic and rhetorically significant: "Since we all have a body, and since we all fear pain and death, torture and execution create an illusion of common identity with a witch-suspect which might be shattered if Daly were to enlarge upon her life or quote her words" (Purkiss 14).

Certainly, in the light of such observations, the myth of the "Burning Times" has lost its political usefulness, but it is important to remember that it was logically unavoidable at one stage in the feminist past. This is particularly true in the context of the eventually rejected victimization of the female body as a site of torture evoked famously by Wittig in *Les Guérillères* (1969) or Gearhart in *Wanderground* (1978). Their radical ecofeminist and lesbian manifestos about witch-Amazons, the rebel-warriors riding bare-breasted under a brilliant helm of crescent horns, appear at the point in history when "there was one rape too many" and the self-conscious earth "finally said 'no': There was no storm, no earthquake, no tidal wave or vulcanic eruption, no specific moment to mark its happening" but the refusal was radical and 'apparent,' and 'it happened everywhere'" (Gearhart 171). Although the identifications with the Amazon as a figure of female autonomy and creativity was both too fundamental and too narrow for a critical movement (Showalter 225), in fact, it were these and similar types of acute and legitimate refusal to cooperate with phallocentrism that enabled a turning point in feminist theory. Today, not unlike the *Malleus* itself, the radical narratives appear as abandoned, archetypal monuments, significant because of the reenacted silence of the victimized female bodies.

In a similarly monumental mode of building on the classic sex/gender distinction, Monique Wittig turns into a radical critique of heterosexism and emphasizes the need to free female sexuality from its subjection to the phallogocentric signifier of a/the "woman." In both restating Hegelian dialectics and radicalizing de Beauvoir's constructed nature of femininity, she proposes that we dismiss the signifier "woman" as epistemologically and politically inadequate. Thus, in a "queer" parallel to Daly's proposal of a "hag" approach, Wittig replaces the signifier "woman" with the category of "lesbian." The "lesbian," who is not a woman, has subtracted herself from the Phallus identity, a position being both attractive and problematically universalizing woman into a new model of normativity (see Braidotti). This radicalism leaves no room for more fluid and dynamic definitions of lesbianism that would reflect on the transformative force of the alternative proposed, and through this, empower different groups of women, such as Rich's concept of the lesbian "continuum" (*Blood, Bread and Poetry* 52) or Irigaray's notion of a female homosexual "libidinal economy" ("Women's Exile" 62-67). Moreover, Wittig's position excludes a priori the possibility of optional hetero- or bisexuality. In a parallel to Daly's heterosexual "female robots," these options are seen as coextensive with domination, and consequently result in a "voluntary servitude"; a position reminiscent of the most extreme antisexuality wing of US-American feminism (Braidotti, *Metamorphoses* 35).

Certainly, in their quest to locate new empowering paradigms for women, radical theoreticians have taken stereotype and archetype as synonymous and therefore ignored the "projective" and "futuristic" capacities of the archetype (Pratt 135). The rhetorical danger of this approach lies however in the evocative, metaphorical power of the archetype itself, resulting, in this case, in perpetuation of phallogocentric desire and victimization of "woman" who has to take rescue in new signifiers. Pratt herself offers vivid examples of *herstorical* tendencies to elaborate on "insanity and womanhating for which there can be no reparation," on the "female martyrdom in death" which "took the forms of burning at the stake, strangulation, crushing with stones, whipping, hanging, drowning, and unspeakable and vile tortures" (175). Without doubt, her archetypes have not become more fluid or dynamic, and remained equally excluding. This indomitable persistence in articulating fear of rape and women's victimization "helps to explain the very dangerous preoccupation with torture and execution in radical feminist narratives of witchcraft," which has turned the historical figure of the witch "into a spectacle of violation and dismemberment" (Purkiss 15). Often difficult to control, fears evoked by radical feminist texts have universalizing tendencies that, not unlike the fear of death itself, are irreversible and impossible to cure. In the fear of rape, as Angela Carter notes in *The Sadeian Woman* (1979), there is "more than merely physical terror of hurt and humiliation—a fear of psychic disintegration, of an essential dismemberment, a fear of a loss or disruption of the self which is not confined to the victim alone" (6). The *herstorical* fantasies, strategically called feminist, are therefore both escapist and political, taking a withdrawal into the *fantasmatic* as a "spontaneous" tool for cultural transformation. In positing the "witch" as a powerful "other" of the victimized woman, these radical fantasies impose otherness as a political strategy, based on the identity principle that is crucial to early radical feminist work. I now proceed to expand the quality of this *fantasmatic* while drawing on the poststructural French feminist stances, such as those of Cixous and Clément, Irigaray and Kristeva, whose distinct proposals take a new position on women's sexuality.

The Orgasmic Freedom of the Newly Born Woman

In French *herstorical* deconstructions of "masculine" sameness, "femininity" becomes a state of permanent conceptual reconfiguration (a permanent lack of authority), since, as Felman has put it, the "possibility of a thought which would neither spring from nor return to this masculine Sameness is simply unthinkable" (8-9). At the same time, paradoxically, *herstory* attempts to challenge the unthinkable, and this is perhaps the most (politically) hysterical part of it, since the challenge comes very close to trying to normalize the unthinkable: "More present than ever," the feminist witch becomes (or transgresses into) *the newly born woman*, "the ancient/innocent/fluent/powerful/impossible woman," as Cixous and Clément have described her. And everything about her is "intense, indeed hyperbolic" (x). They write:

To dance: at the heart of *The Newly Born Woman* is the story of a southern Italian ritual, the tarantella. Early in the book, as she discusses the rebellious celebrations with which repressed (female) subjects have responded to their subjugation by patriarchal hierarchies, Clément tells a tale of women in the Mezzogiorno who can be cured of imaginary spider bites only by doing a ceremonial dance, which sometimes lasts for twenty-four hours. A village orchestra plays; a woman/patient dances—dances in a ferocious "festival of metamorphosis"...which subversively...expresses her passionate rage....At the end of the episode, she transcends the divine bite and "leave[s] risk behind...to settle down again under a roof, in a house, in the family circle of kinship and marriage...the men's world"...But she has had her interlude of orgasmic freedom. (xii)

It is in her "orgasmic freedom" that Cixous's witch personifies the assimilated abjection of the witch's body, her ambiguity of form, and her reenactment of the absence of patriarchal culture that cannot be conceptualized in the historical language of the symbolic. As a linguistically abstracted, imaginary position assigned to the witch, Cixous's and Clément's cultural absence defies symbolic "cultural castration" by a strategic reenacting of inconsistency, transgression, and trance.

Embedded in these hyperbolic allusions, the conceptual categories of the virgin, mother, wife, whore, or postmenopausal crone constantly overlap, disturbing a range of "taboos regarding the appropriate limits, postures, and models of exchange that define what it is that constitutes bodies" (Butler, *Gender Trouble* 131). It is within these overlapping categories that un/belonging appears as a parody and pollution within the system. As Douglas observed, the main function of purifying, demarcating, or punishing transgressions is "to impose system on an inherently untidy experience....It is only by exaggerating the difference between within and without, above and below, male and female, with and against, that a semblance of order is created" (4). According to Butler, Douglas's analysis, although clearly subscribing to a "structuralist distinction between inherently unruly nature and an order imposed by cultural means," provides "a possible point of departure for understanding the relationship by which social taboos institute and maintain the boundaries of the body as such" (*Gender Trouble* 131). Within their specific theoretical frameworks, Cixous, Irigaray, and certainly Butler (following Douglas), seem thus to suggest that what constitutes the limit of the body is not only biological material, but that the "surface," the "skin," is systematically signified by taboos and anticipated transgressions. The contingency of these transgressions translates the boundaries of the body into the limits of the socially sanctioned, the hegemonic, the phallocentric. The term "phallocentric" refers in this context to a (post)-Lacanian concept that claims to distinguish the "phallus" from the "penis" and therefore represents divergent sexual positions, yet remains unable to erase the immediacy of this association, and fails to represent an abstract (gender-neutral) cultural condition. Gallop, for example, questions the Lacanian project of abstracting the phallus (le/la phallus) from its association with the male organ: "By denying the 'phallus' as a fantasy, Lacan denies it as an object, and even as an organ (penis or clitoris, which it symbolized) and renders it dangerously abstract and detached from a cultural context: Is the phallic signifier intrinsically neutral, transgressing the linguistic rules of gender? The Lacanian subject is castrated, that is to say, deprived of the phallus, and therefore can never satisfy desire....Most of Lacan's explanations of the phallus's privilege are 'vague,' that is to say, veiled" (*Daughter's Seduction* 134-54). "Being" the Phallus and "having" the Phallus denote, on Butler's suggestion, "divergent sexual positions, or nonpositions (impossible positions, really), within language" (*Gender Trouble* 44). Caught in the mode of Hegelian dialectics, to "be" the Phallus is to be (and *appear*) as the "signifier" of the privileged desire. To be desired, on the other hand, is to reflect that desire, to be the object, the Other of a "masculine" desire.

Following precisely this line of reasoning, Cixous and Clément's analysis of the hysteric figure leads us back to the Greek *hyster* (womb), to the witch-woman as a creature with a "wandering womb" that manifests a "distinctively female bonding" (*Newly Born* xiii). This radical alterity of the newly born woman is thus anchored in the "forgotten" history of a/the woman: her "inescapable female connection between creation and procreation," (xiii) the destiny, inexorably determined by anatomy. In this sense, Cixous and Clément pursue the radical feminist path but reverse the argument of the second (marked) sex in focusing precisely on the eluded representation of a/the woman, on her symbolically suppressed female transgressions: desires, fears, and rage. These transgressions integrate the new (radically reinvented) qualities of the witch as a metonymic extension of the female limits in the symbolic, an extension that should in fact eradicate these limits. Consequently, Cixous and Clément both associate with and disassociate themselves from the conflictual and self-perpetuating desire to celebrate an exclusively female (*herstorical*) type of suffering. The momentary disintegrity of the dancing, carnivalesque body, as posited by Cixous, revives the experience of inquisitorial interrogation, and links this experience with the possession of the/a woman who "by her opening up is open to being 'possessed,' which is to say, disposed of herself" ("Book" 42). But the witches' sabbath is also evoked as a recurring spectacle of *trans-*, a *trance*, and a *trace* associated with permanence through strategic repetition of dislocating experience. To follow Cixous, "those" who did not experience the "festival of metamorphosis" can neither articulate nor negotiate it. But "she" (the female pronoun, the one designated She, the orgasmic witch-woman), who has participated in this experience has to return in order to speak of it, and so she no longer speaks from, but only about the/a position of otherness. The "she," once placed in the symbolic structure, can no longer speak from the place of the Other since this place resists symbolic articulation. Cixous's otherness of the "witch," deriving precisely from the negotiating status between speaking and speechless (impossible to be articulated) positions, refuses to complement the Law of the Father. In this refusal Cixous's position distinguishes itself most prominently from the radical U.S. formulations of female sexuality. Her witch figure, embodying in fact this refusal of otherness, carries a transgressing value that has already been symbolically castrated, but cannot (yet) be culturally mapped. The concept of "place" (*lieu*), clearly elevated in this cartography over more mathematical *locus* (*lieu géometrique*), does not convey any precise cultural localization. In particular reference to Kristevan psychoanalysis (of which more in my second chapter), *lieu* remains "a hypothetical place, even though constrained by actual forces or presences" (Kristeva, *Desire* 17). In "speaking" thus "hypothetically," the "witch... laughs at the solemnities of sacrifice that constitute culture" (Cixous and Clément xiii), and refuses the historical construction of the abject hag as a zone of exclusion from the symbolic. The phallocentric construct of the hag represents therefore, as with Daly, a salient challenge to *herstory*, which sets another equally imaginary zone against it, the zone of fantasy of the positive other.

The philosophy of the positive other has been most effectively explored in Irigaray's proposal of the "fantasmatic" woman who "will not yet have taken (a) place" ("Volume" 53). The "not yet" points to a "hysterical fantasmatic" that acknowledges its own historical condition: "experienced as all-powerful where 'she' is most radically powerless in her indifferentiation" (53). Distinct from Cixous's, especially in its pertinence to the question of anatomy, Irigaray's feminine sex, which is a "plenum," has a similarly radical point of departure. It is placed in a linguistic absence, which, as Butler would argue, "is not marked as such within the masculine signifying economy" but "eludes the very requirements of representation, for she is neither 'Other' nor the 'lack'" (*Gender Trouble* 10). Irigaray's alterity pertains above all to the question of identity as assumed in the symbolic language, but strategically coincides with, and in her later work, exceeds, the radical feminist claims that the only possible subject position is that of a phallocentric order. For the sake of my present analytical focus, I therefore employ the term of "*herstorical fantasmatic*" (deriving it from Irigaray's *hysterical fantasmatic*), emphasizing the theoretically shifting ground of "sexual difference." Whether written in opposition to Lacanian phallogocentrism (Irigaray) or as a critical reelaboration of Lacan (Kristeva), this appropriation attempts necessarily to transgress the "feminine" while employing contradictory positions. First, it attempts to view the "feminine" "as the unrepresentable absence effected by (masculine) denial that grounds the signifying economy through exclusion" (*Gender Trouble* 28). Second, it subverts its own exclusion in its radical claim of the positive difference (see Braidotti) that will prove necessary to overcome the split between the incompatible sensibilities of the maternal and the paternal versions of desire. Although Irigaray's philosophical texts, like Cixous's, "are dazzling, allusive, deliberately polysemic, difficult to unravel, and for the most part still untranslated" (Whitford 9), they are significant for reminding us that it was Freud, and not Lacan, "who brought to light something that had been operative all along though it remained implicit, hidden, unknown: *the sexual indifference that underlies the truth of any science, the logic of every discourse*. This is readily apparent in the way Freud defines female sexuality. In fact, this sexuality is never defined with respect to any sex but the masculine....The feminine is always described in terms of deficiency or atrophy, as the other side of the sex that alone holds a monopoly on value" (Irigaray, "Power" 119).

The *herstorical fantasmatic* draws our attention to the inconsistency of the *herstorical* locations that meet at the crossroads of the "transatlantic divide" (Braidotti, *Metamorphoses* 29). Standing at this crossroads, the witch as a "fantasmatic other" emerges thus as a project for the feminist future. In its futuristic form, she/he will no longer embody any antithetical or previously missing addendum to subjects of feminist research. Instead, formulated as running counter to the subjects of Hegelian dialectics, the "witch" will represent "cross-thinking, counter-questioning, counter-seeing, contradiction, protest" (Thürmer-Rohr 164). And as long as s/he does not reduce herself to the universal essence of female specificity, she will uncover the phallacy of standardized systems, understandings, and contradictions of the androcentric worldview (see Braidotti). Notwithstanding this metamorphic vision, I now return to the *herstorical* meeting at the crossroads of theory. This meeting, as a conflation of distinct feminist standpoints, builds a theoretical core of my analysis that attempts to bring or even piece together the inconsistence of the *herstorical* witch. Of all the metamorphoses of her "alterity," I choose one that clearly prevails and therefore interconnects the various theories of difference: the alterity as a range of metaphors of flying. I go through some of the images briefly now and return to this alterity in my readings of the narratives to follow. According to Dworkin, witches most certainly could and often flied on broomsticks: "Before going to the sabbat, they anointed their bodies with a mixture of belladonna and aconite, which caused delirium, hallucination, and gave the sensation of flying" (148). The trans-formed broomstick, "an almost archetypal symbol of womanhood, as the pitchfork was of manhood" (148), serves here as an excellent example of Cixous's "orgasmic freedom," the *herstorical* trance beyond the symbolic, in which the flying broomstick also denotes escape from housework, domestic ties, and oppressive confinement to the sphere of home. In flying on her broomstick, the radical witch of the seventies personifies an alarming "indifference to the boundaries between memory and invention, fact and fancy, truth and fiction" (Purkiss 53). These fantasies do not address the phenomenon of flying itself, but undoubtedly its metaphorical potential. As Cixous explains, "Flying is woman's gesture—flying in language and making it fly. We have all learned the art of flying and its numerous techniques; for centuries we've been able to possess anything only by flying; we've lived in flight, stealing away, finding when desired, narrow passageways, hidden crossovers. It's no accident that *voler* has a double meaning, that it plays on each of them and thus throws off the agents of sense. It's no accident: women take after birds and robbers just as robbers take after women and birds" ("Laugh" 356-57). In turn, for Irigaray, the emancipation of the female body is inseparable from a female self-knowledge (self-touching and opening up physical and metaphysical borders), and related to her plural and "perverse" images of anatomy: her self-touching is that of the/a woman, who is both unable and unwilling to close up, a form that is in(de)finitely transformed ("Volume" 59). Embodying reinscriptions of the archaic mother, the self-touching witch "lives with her body in the past," referred to by Cixous as the past of "forgotten roles: the ambiguous, the subversive and the conservative" (Cixous and Clément 12). She is subversive, "because the symptoms—the attacks—revolt and shake up the public," (the phallic gaze of the inquisitor) and conservative, "because every sorceress ends up being destroyed, and nothing is registered of her but mythical traces." Finally, her ambiguity is "expressed in an escape that marks the histories of sorceress and hysteric with the suspense of ellipses" (5). The flying as an embodiment of her herstorical Sabbath is thus a rite of the past, an apotheosis of the emancipated body and it is also a repressed desire for the imaginary space prior to gender, the forbidden maternal zone, and a fantasy of fragmentation as well as of union. During her performance, the witch-woman "is open to being 'possessed,' which is to say, dispossessed of herself" (42). Perhaps it is a question of a particular phase which, later, one could call "transitivism," some sort of phase of excessive identification with the other being: always on both sides, double. In the end the Sabbath, like a hysterical attack, "provides a return to regular rhythm" (19), reiterating as well as subverting the standard form, the cultural pattern. This Bakhtinian carnivalesque structure is composed of distances, analogies and nonexclusive oppositions that need to remain essentially dialogical (Kristeva, "Stabat Mater" 48). Out of a dialogue then, established between her possession and her dispossession, the "dyads of carnival" appear: "high and low, birth and agony, food and excrement, praise and curses, laughter and tears" (48).

In a similarly dialogical suspension between fantasy and memory, between autobiography, theory, and fiction, feminist narratives employ "fantastic qualities of imagination" that "go far beyond what theoretical discourse, hostile towards images as it is, can transmit" (Bovenschen 232). In a similar vein to Purkiss's argument, Bovenschen notes that elevating the historical witch *post festum* to an archetypal image of female freedom "would be cynical, considering the magnitude of her unimaginable suffering" (232). But there is more than a carnivalesque optimism to this dialogical structure of trespassing. It is rather the witch's hysterical placement on the border between suffering and freedom that evokes the desire to perform, to take part in the enactment of deliverance, the emancipation of body, form, and structure. This borderline position does not simply add to the answers of existing research but fills the historical gaps and omissions in the answers with *herstory*, which in itself might no longer be relevant, but needs to be acknowledged as a necessary and extremely empowering stage of development in feminist research. This borderline location remains central to the contemporary feminist politics of resistance. In the end, the fantasmatic witches, in particular as sustained in the metaphor of flying, represent a much cleaner break with standardized academic reasoning "than anything feminist historians have produced or have wished to produce" (Purkiss 53). The phenomenon of *herstory* demonstrates perhaps "what feminist history might be like if it *really* abandoned empiricism altogether instead of simply calling it into question—from time to time" (53). Beyond doubt, the *herstorical* assumption that patriarchy has operated in similar ways across national borders neglects historical and material differences in women's situations and political struggles. Beyond doubt, it allowed many of Western feminists to avoid confronting painful differences among women in their own cultures, while obscuring the dominance of middle-class women around the globe (on this, see Kaplan and Grewal). Undeniably, however, the *herstorical* stream of phantasms enabled to the next generation new formulations of protest and rebellion against the cultural imprisonment in gender. They have provided the necessary, albeit contentious, points of departure for criticism currently exercised by Braidotti, Butler, or Haraway, namely, the criticism of the prevailing representation of "the metaphysics of substance" (Butler, *Gender Trouble* 24) that shakes the constitution of the very notion of subject.

When the Symbolic Order Collapses

To open a discussion of the "symbolic" collapse, I start with Kristeva's observation that "a woman has nothing to laugh about when the symbolic order collapses. She can take pleasure in it, if by identifying with the mother, the vaginal body, she imagines she is the sublime, repressed forces which return through the fissures of the order. But she can just as easily die from this upheaval...if she has been deprived of a successful maternal identification and has found in the symbolic paternal order her one superficial, belated and easily severed link with life" ("Stabat" 150). The relevance of Kristeva's thought becomes clear in reference to the identification with the mother/nature as a persistently reoccurring theme in radical feminist fiction. As I argue, Gearhart's *The Wanderground* and Walker's *The Temple of My Familiar* contribute equally to the Kristevian "taking pleasure" in the collapse of the symbolic. Although deriving from different cultural backgrounds (Anglo-German and African American, respectively), both stories represent the *herstorical fantasmatic* that is similarly inspired by "rediscoveries" of the repressed, "forgotten" origin, with leading metaphors of the sovereign queen/witch and the healing mother/earth. In blending the myth with history, and fantasy with 1980s ecofeminist standpoints, they speak in the name of the "feminine alterity" as contained in and conflated with nature. Reflecting on Ynestra King's and Rosemary Ruether's ecofeminist postulates, nature represents a somewhat utopian flux of everything that is organic, symbiotic, and untouched by human technology. This *herstorical* archeology of writing has several characteristic features: it is synthesizing (working against analysis), speaking the body/nature rather than self-consciously writing literature, and finally articulating rather than evaluating desire. The witch, as she appears in these narratives, belongs to the newly valorized sphere of the feminine: she speaks about herself, about her presence, and about her origin. Her voice, persuasive, seductive, and above all charismatic, resonates with the voice of a fortune teller whose predictions turn into an intrinsic model of her narrative, a metaphoric/metonymic picture of her own therapeutic methodology.

Both the post/memories of origin and the prophesies of return involved in this *herstorical* archeology translate the "universal" female oppression into an equally universalizing fantasy of the symbolic collapse. This fantasy restores the appealing/appalling powers of the archaic womb, celebrating women's difference or their "natural" uniqueness that is at odds with culture. It draws in fact on the troublesome division of sexuality into heterosexual and lesbian issues that in the 1970s produced a fundamental rift between US-American feminists and shattered the potential unity of feminist claims to "forgotten origin." In particular, the mythic versions of a/the lesbian culture have been read today both as political identifications and as forms of therapeutic consolation. In Butler's commentary, they appear as "a strategic tactic within a narrative that, by telling a single, authoritative account about an irrecoverable past, makes the constitution of the law appear as a historical inevitability" (*Gender Trouble* 36). Indeed, imagining a postpatriarchal future, Gearhart offers an ecofeminist construction of Womanpower, which intentionally deploys the binary of witchcraft (feminine nature) as opposed to reason (masculine technology). *The Wanderground*, a radical separatist lesbian manifesto, addresses specifically female incompatibility with masculinist society and technology. Gearhart's Hill Women live in a somewhat near future: one could imagine an apocalyptic year of the twilight zone, the end of the twentieth century; the end of history of capitalism. Clearly, what is at stake in the 1970s, when Gearhart's, and many similar narrative manifestos were written, was "not so much literature or criticism as such, but the historical, social, and ethical consequences of women's participation in, or exclusion from, either enterprise" (Kolodny 171). Invented as a counterstatement to this exclusion, Gearhart's characters represent harmoniously synchronized, telepathic witches, integrated within the organic world, and further contrasted with an apocalyptic, collapsing (male) civilization. This conditioning reminds us both of Wittig's and Irigaray's challenges to the symbolic order, in which women inevitably stand in an archaic and primal relationship with themselves and, therefore with homosexuality, since the first object of their love and desire is a woman (Irigaray, "Volume" 44). Gearhart's Women act in plural, act *now*, and finally act for themselves, developing magical relationships with nature, reproducing by ovular merging, learning to fly and to live by noncompetitive values and sensibilities unique to female homosexual economy. They are activists of the future (which follows "the collapse of the symbolic"), continuing in fact Gearhart's biography, and projecting her own ecopolitical agenda.

Indisputably, the "Wanderground" (the witches' geographical but also hypothetical location), builds on the "Gaia hypothesis" proposed by such scientists as Margulis, Lovelock, Sahtouris, and further developed in Ruether's work on "the intelligence that guides evolution" and that is not outside nature, but embodied in it as the "wisdom" of the earth (118). However, in Gearhart's story, gender division becomes a prerequisite for the Gaian condition of "evolving," as "masculine values" remain excluded from this "co-evolution": "Love man? The idea did not fit. It was uncomfortable and backward in her mind. She tried it from every angle but it would not adjust" (2). Rather, in a dialectical suspension, Gearhart's proposal resonates with de Beauvoir's and Irigaray's notion of "natural homosexuality." Her lesbian witches demonstrate a "natural" refusal of the male. Their "linking for feminine flesh" is "instinctive," resulting from fear of penetration and "certain repulsion for the male body" (de Beauvoir 428). The dystopian atmosphere of the male-dominated City, reminding us perhaps of the sociopolitical conditions endured by women under Islamic fanatism, the compulsory marriages, polygamy, male escorts, sexual harassment, and institutionalized prostitution from which Gearhart's women have escaped, still haunts the memories of the Hill Women. These postmemories, stored telepathically, serve as historical awareness for the youngest generation, born parthenogenetically in the "Wanderground." Following Wittig's postulates of lesbian departure from the constitution of womanhood, Gearhart draws on a female biological predisposition, a natural difference, affirming the possibility of collective solidarity, and enabling lesbians to effectively rebel against the politics of heterosexuality. Echoing thus Wittig's radicalism in *Les Guérillères*, Gearhart's narrative offers no alternative unless a mutual understanding and acceptance of lesbian autonomy is granted. However, if Wittig has strategically differentiated between women's and lesbians' political agendas, Gearhart offers the most radical split between biological sexes that resists Levinasian elevation of the feminine, the most radical elimination of the negative other, the alterity of the second sex as accomplished in the feminine. In order to preserve its sovereignty, the lesbian, as the "other of the Other," alludes to the semiotic pleasures, and is not bothered to know by whom or what it has been named. *It* neither reads books nor produces culture; *it* refuses to recognize a linear advancement (progress) as transforming the natural into the artificial.

Owing to this fanatical refusal to cooperate with the signifiers of culture, Gearhart's matriarchal fantasy remains suspended between two poles of desire: the lesbian alterity and its incompatibility with phallocentric culture. As Seja, one of the warriors in the story, explains, "it is not in his nature not to rape. It is not in my nature to be raped. We do not co-exist" (26). In this particular sovereign deadlock between contrary forces, Gearhart's account resonates with Walker's African American perspective on matriarchal fantasy of tribal women healers untouched by the symbolic order. Like Gearhart's, Walker's matriarchy celebrates the hypothesis of the mother goddess and radically expands the Western concept of women's participation in the so-called historical time. As analyzed by Carol P. Christ, historical time is usually discussed within the framework of the Babylonian creation epic: "the Enuma Elish, which depicts the slaying of the primordial Mother Tiamat, and the Epic of Gilgamesh, in which the hero curses the Goddess Ishtar and refuses her gifts, may be mentioned as providing evidence about the origins of religion in the Near East" (76). Frequently, these religious sources, attesting to historical denigration of female authority, are presented primarily as backdrop to the "distinctive and superior" contributions of Greek philosophy, Hebrew religion, and subsequently of Christianity. To follow Christ, the naming and chronology attributed to "time" "is not a trivial matter, as Christian rulers recognized when they took control of the calendar" (77). Both Walker's and Gearhart's reinventions of matriarchy draw tangibly on this recognition in their proposals of the positive and powerful alterity that expands the symbolic chronology of the paternal order. In Gearhart's particularly utopian projection of matriarchy, the future of women's time takes place in fact instead of in history. Perceived in this matriarchal dimension, the cult of the Earth has a symbolic, even religious quality that connects with the denigration of the mother in the Babylonian epic and subsequently with the patriarchal fear of the archaic mother. This link becomes most evident in the imbedded story of eleven warriors emerging from the forest to fight against demoralized militant males. In supplying her female warriors with all the unfeminine characteristics that phallocentric oppression attempted to avoid (woman as a maternal warrior, a self-sufficient family provider, an active political body), Gearhart attempts to transform the powerlessness of the mother in culture. The mother, conflated with earth/planet, opposes militant technology associated by Gearhart with numerous evils such as rape, pornography, imperialism, starvation, homelessness, and the poisoning of the environment (126).

Characteristically for U.S. radical feminist positions, the narrative identifies with the culturally victimized women/nature, clearly deriving from Carolyn Merchant's ecofeminist postulates of the technological exploitation of nature understood as a "feminine principle" (99). Certainly, both the "nurturing mother" and "dominating father" metaphors have existed in Western philosophy and religion, but, to follow Merchant, "as the economy became modernized and the Scientific Revolution proceeded," the metaphor of domination "spread beyond the religious sphere and assumed ascendancy in the social and political spheres as well" (100). Further, the depiction of culturally unpredictable nature echoes King's influential essay on feminist ecology discussing "life on earth" as "an interconnected web" of dependencies in which the earth is "like a lover" who has suffered, "yet with great intelligence, has survived" (19). It is precisely in this metaphorical employment that Gearhart effectively links the feminine with mystical maternal powers acting as vital elements in women's favor. In this *herstorical* vein, Gearhart's witch turns from a carnivalesque figure into a figure of ritual. The Hill Women live and survive thanks to a complex ceremonial sharing: they sleep, eat, work, and love in constant communication with nature. Their awareness is no longer that of a self, it has a plural, ritualistic and, to large extent, sacred character, converging with ecofeminist aims to reveal the complexity of interconnectedness. In her allegorical reinscription of the culturally abject menstrual blood into a sacred ritual, Gearhart introduces a monstrous generative womb, "crowded with women, sitting on the upward spiralling path, naked and gleaming bodies moving rhythmically to and fro to the sound of their own humming...never ceasing steady vocal rumbling" (55). This image offers a powerful envisioning of the semiotic chora, and a return to its repressed forces. Consequently, it is this maternal feminine that in Gearhart's narrative makes it into the communal, holistic, and intuitive and that offers a viable choice for survival. In contrast, the masculine powers are projected as fundamentally evil, allowing no cooperation, perhaps with the exception of "gentle" homosexual men who have initiated contact to the witches in order to learn from them but have so far been rejected. This separatist position is particularly relevant to the context of radical feminist rethinking of the feminine in relation to the unquestioned character of cultural normativity and its deep suspicion of even most progressive theory that might emerge from there. In fact, 1970s attentiveness to power relations, with its acutely gendered character, demonstrates what feminist theorizing needs to take into account today in formulating the cultural, social, and economic conditions for divergent "embodied" subjects and their fair participation in the cultural landscape. In the end, however, Gearhart's *herstory* operates with mythically static, disabling rather than empowering versions of women. In its remedial blend of female biology and spirituality, it problematically persists at preserving women's alterity. As a conceptual deconstruction of the symbolic, the very "feminine" cannot be limited to an inherent "femaleness" that "gives women emotional satisfaction...at the price of obscuring the real conditions of life" (Carter, *Sadeian Woman* 5). Either way, Gearhart seems to reject Beauvoir's assertion that one "isn't born a woman, but becomes one" (see *The Second Sex*) and that it "is in the patriarchal interest that these two terms (femininity and femaleness) stay thoroughly confused" (qtd. in Moi, *Kristeva Reader* 123). Her ecofeminist search for a natural female origin works against feminist theories of no return by defeating their premise that biology is not destiny after all. Whether "feminine sexuality is articulated here through a discourse of biology for purely strategic reasons," or whether it indicates a return "to biological essentialism," to formulate "female sexuality as radically distinct from a phallic organization of sexuality remains problematic" (Butler, *Gender Trouble* 30). The witches, and Gearhart herself as a radical feminist, are to some extent aware that their identity politics is too simplistic, but their mistrust and wariness are stronger than reason, especially since reasoning, entangled in a paternal tradition, is based on technology, the logical development of thought, and its empirical dichotomies. In imposing culturally enhanced oppositions, Gearhart's witches ignore the actual, acute differences between women and the distinct ways through which their cultural positions are manifested, repeating precisely what Daly's and Dworkin's texts have accomplished: the radicalization of the "feminine alterity."

Drawing on the commonality of women's culture propagated by such feminist traits, Showalter and many other race- and class-sensitive critics in the 1980s have reexamined the essentialism of the female subject. The *herstorical fantasmatic* has thus been "open to charges of racism, especially since black women's texts were rarely cited as examples" (225). In articulating this feminist dilemma, Showalter has contrasted a color-blind or an "uncolored" woman theoretician as already "in exile" (because "she speaks a paternal language") with a nonwhite female theoretician as "in double exile," "for she speaks a white paternal language" (214-15). In this sense, balancing the heterogeneity of women's exile, Gearhart's and Walker's fantasmatic returns to nature are perhaps good examples of the second-wave political conflation of difference and similarity among women. Developed in Walker's narrative into a specific "Afra"-American fantasy, this exile demonstrates its own linguistic consciousness, distinct from the "white" feminist field. "Afra"-American criticism, unfolding in 1974 with the publication of *Black World*, essays by June Jordan and Mary Helen Washington, and Alice Walker's critical work (see Smith; Humm), is preoccupied with the relationship between Black feminism and poststructuralism, as well as with the position of African myths in the Western cultural order. Both issues refer to essentialism and difference, demonstrating an attempt to open the Eurocentric discipline of literary criticism towards other races and cultures. Myths are thus interpreted in terms of textual opportunities for the actual voice of the differentiated. Walker proposes a mixture of conscious and subconscious uses of language, interweaving her autobiography with mythic history that moves decisively beyond Western tradition. Referring to herself as a "womanist" rather than a "feminist," Walker provokes the emergence of a much wider spectrum of Black womanhood. "Womanist," as she writes, "is to feminist as purple to lavender" (*In Search* xxii) and she calls for a return to a mythical African spirituality that survives in Black women's culture.

In reference to Walker's manifesto, *In the Search of Our Mothers' Gardens* (1983), Showalter posits Walker as a storyteller and a philosopher, describing her position as a mediator between contemporary culture and the suppressed creativity of black women under slavery, poverty, and the denigration of African art. Charting and analyzing culturally distinct mythical pasts in *The Temple of My Familiar*, Walker simply invents her own, as it were, maternal mythology. Also, rather than envisioning the future, she returns to the prepatriarchy, a process that in her writings often conflates with spirituality. Consequently, the responsibility for the revision of the past is attributed to women artists, weavers, and musicians, rather than to academic thinkers. Walker describes spirituality as a move "away from sociology, away from the writing of explanations and statistics and further into mystery, into poetry and into prophecy" (*Temple* 8). Her female characters, depicted as spiritually richer and more powerful than their male counterparts, are not the victim-figures repeatedly found in white feminist criticism of the same period. Pratt, for example, who criticized her radical sisters (Daly and others) for remaining in a dialectic deadlock of binary poles, seems "always to find that women in fiction are cut off from autonomy, from self-actualization and ethical capacity. In her view, women are victim figures either succumbing to madness or marriage or frequently to both" (Humm 69-70). On the contrary, Walker's polyphonic stories, proverbs, and gospel recreate entrances to the pre-ancient pasts, a gesture, as Walker frequently reminds us, that leads away from analysis, criticism, and accusation towards meditation upon cultural difference. Eleonora, one of the characters in *The Temple,* observes in her diary: "There is a little serpent here [she writes in 1922] that is exactly the color of coral. It lives only in certain trees and comes out of its hole, far up the tree, near dusk. It lives on the tree spiders and bugs, and is known to sing. The natives tell me that it sings. They claim they have heard it sing millions of times, and act as if this is entirely ordinary. Furthermore, they ask why I have not heard it and why it should be so strange. Everything sings, they say" (239). In a way, Walker's mythic constructions of a/the woman of color provide the post/colonial perspective to the reinterpreted past of the 1970s feminist agenda. A key role in her agendum is assigned to the "forgotten" crone figure, the third figure in the matriarchal triad. Her crone, Miss Lissie, moves consciously from one life into the next, maintaining the narrative pattern of *her* story retelling the cosmologies of various religions and people. Her story unfolds like the intrigue of gossip: she is the mythmaker, the fortune-teller and the archaic mother of mankind. By transferring her messages from one era and culture to another, Walker's heroine repeatedly emphasizes her need to go beyond (Western) culture, and, apparently, to recover the "pre-ancestral heritage" as a form of women's *unconscious*. Her voice travels in time in order to reach and "open a very important door against memory, against pain" (*Temple* 389) often unacknowledged in academic writing. Miss Lissie is a fully mature female character and a timeless creature, ultimately representing all three aspects of the triad (virgin, mother, and crone), and bringing any one of them into play at any time. She is universal (as Daly's hag), fantasmatic (as Cixous's sorceress), subversive, and extremely knowledgeable all at once: a presymbolic virgin-whore and a wise mother who lets her children go at the right moment, an act that if precipitous or delayed can lead the maternal element to become destructive. In other words, she is a superwoman, and even more so, as she is sensitive to difference as well as sameness between human and nonhuman embodiments of the underrepresented subject positions.

Lissie, like Gearhart's Atheca, one of the highly skilled witches in *The Wanderground*, presents thus a visionary projection of the past, when women were apparently united with nature. This affirmative projection of the bond between women and nature could be directly contrasted with de Beauvoir's twentieth-century woman who abandons her "disquieting plantlike mystery" (de Beauvoir 444) willingly, as well as with Irigaray's extension of that "woman" and her masks and decorations that cover a void of her desire, the absence of her self-love, and the "I" in discourse. Both de Beauvoir and Irigaray refer to the "significance of woman's attire," her "decoration" as a means to be offered in and to culture (de Beauvoir 444). This adornment has a diametrically different implication in Walker's envisioning of a prehistorical woman who is "entirely used to herself, while man [is] still infatuated with his relative newness. Woman [is] already into adornment....She [is] more like playing with herself" (*Temple* 61). In the mirror-image of de Beauvoir's woman, she uses "feathers, shells, stones, flowers," but she does it narcissistically, entirely for her own pleasure: "For days she and her sisters hung over the edge of the reflecting pools in the jungle, trying this or that" (62). This blend of female/feminine specific pleasures has a religiously utopian character; it is *the unconscious*, semiotic pleasure of coexisting with nature. Its strategically dogmatic aspect becomes most evident when confronted with the newly emerging phallocentric order (*Temple* 61-62), most effectively used in Walker's juxtaposition between the "natural" separation of mother and child in childbirth and its "primitive" effects in the symbolic. In one of the scenes, Walker inscribes Lissie's childbirth with the cultural abject precisely to unfold the complexity of the nature/culture flux. After delivering her baby, which she does without professional assistance, Lissie frantically looks for a knife to cut the umbilical cord, unnecessarily extending the bodily connection that was brought to a close. By the time her horror-struck partner is able to find one, "Lissie had bitten through the cord with her teeth" (127). Subsequently, Walker lends voice to Lissie's partner to describe the abominable scene from his culturalized point of view: "'God, it's like rubber,' she said, making a face and spitting into the rag. And I looked at Lissie sitting up now with the naked baby next to her naked body, and I thought to myself how primitive it was. When the afterbirth came—a lump of bloody, liverish-looking stuff that made me feel even woozier that I was—she wrapped it in newspaper and gave it to me to bury at the corner of the house for luck, so that we could have a houseful of babies. When she wasn't looking though, I threw it into the fire. It wouldn't burn. It put the fire out" (127-28). But we can approach Lissie's character from yet a different, a more Deleuzian angle. As an embodiment of metamorphoses, Walker's crone is a living memory; her mind has the capacity to transgress, and "just as the memory exists at a deeper level of consciousness than thinking, so the dream world of the memory is at a deeper level still" (*Temple* 99): "I lied when I told you I have always been a black woman, and that I can only remember as far as a few thousand years....In addition to being a man, and white, which I was many times....I was also, at least once, myself a lion. This is one of those dream memories so frayed around the edges that it is like an old, motheaten shawl" (391-402). As ever changing and ever becoming narrative figure, Lissie offers a fantasmatic prepast as totalizing vision of the relationship between the unacknowledged fragments and the whole. This, revealed by the simultaneous deployment of world history and individualized psychic processes (Braidotti, *Metamorphoses* 185), offers a remedy against the universal exclusion of marginalized forces. And clearly in concert with Gearhart's vision, Walker posits nature on the very top of the marginalized subjects.

If Gearhart has postulated a radical separation from incompatible culture, Walker's narrative proposes an ultimate symbiosis, a feminine striving toward an androgynous ideal, that is, towards "the ultimate lack of mastery over the one" as "related to the lack of mastery over the other" (Weil 36). Bringing together the writings of Schlegel and Barthes, Kari Weil analyzes androgyny as the paradoxical body, a personal and social ideal of "completed humanity" (Schlegel's *vollendete Menschheit*) that clearly links with Walker's concept of androgyny as a "completed, united wo/manhood" (36-39). This politically utopian enterprise is certainly marked by the naïve production of powerful celebrations of womanhood at the cost of ignoring its own illusionary suspension in the "collapse of the symbolic." Completed in crossing all the boundaries of cultural discourse, both Gearhart's and Walker's narratives could be in consequence categorized as compelling fantasies with an astonishing capacity to resist criticism that effectively bring together militant proponents of matriarchy with worshippers of a fecundity goddess. In this therapeutic function, with its inherent tendency to elevate the "unattainable" future or the lost past of the subject (matriarchy, nature), the "feminine" inevitably confronts its own suspended contemporaneous subject position. In this suspension a/the woman (and many women as a consequence) have perhaps "nothing to laugh about when the symbolic order collapses." Their identifications with the loss, indeed their imaginary sublimations, remain deprived of a link to the very order they seek to reestablish. Thus, reviving Goddess worship and spirituality as sustained in the metaphor of "mother nature" is not automatically a simple step forward for feminist practice. For how far can anyone be sure that the modern religious depictions of the Goddess, especially in their association with the absence of civilization and technology, are actually not disguised borrowings of the patriarchal imaginary, perpetuating ever present phallogocentric fantasies of gender? To associate female powers with values of the semiotic remains thus inherently divisive, having an intrinsically valid therapeutic function but at the same time writing women's agenda out of the picture. The radical mythologies succeed, however, as proposals for alternative forms of female mimesis. Miming, which for Irigaray suggests breaking from within, (deconstructing ones own subject position), implies maintaining a very difficult position of internalized oppositions, of being in-between, sentenced to a permanent compromise. Irigaray's mimesis is difficult to achieve since it borders on mimicry (a concept often used by Moi) that fakes power, that manifests possession when there is dispossession, and that denies gender difference in order to deny gender imbalance. Considering both the problematic and therapeutic aspects of Gearhart's and Walker's narrative disassociations from the symbolic, they must be taken into account as powerful feminist *thealogies*. Dancing through the minefield (Kolodny 175) of the social, cultural, and religious, their methodologies strategize "feminine" pleasure, and constitute, so to say, Irigaray's therapeutic location of self-touching and self-exploring. They cleverly demonstrated the 1970s need for a different mythology from which to address the stubborn oppositions between nature and the female/feminine on the one side, and everything that accounts for cultural representation on the other side of the dialectic pendulum. Their innovative techniques, although associated with a certain North American radical current of second-wave feminism, provoked a range of parallel standpoints across Europe. They have taught us how "to negotiate the minefield" across the transatlantic divide, and if not yet "with grace, then with at least a clearer comprehension of its underlying patterns" (Kolodny 175).

Women are Flying When Men are not Looking

My section title here echoes the title of Maitland's collection of short stories *Women Fly When Men Aren't Watching* (1988). In order to enlarge the cultural framework of the *herstorical* tradition of witches, I have selected an East German narrative *Amanda. Ein Hexenroman* (*Amanda: A Witch Novel*; 1983), written with a far more ironical and detached type of feminist engagement by Irmtraud Morgner. My analysis of this narrative is followed by a choice of German short stories published twenty years later in reunited Germany. Both the choice and chronology of the stories, to follow my reading of *Amanda*, reveal an astonishing complicity with the phallocentric thinking (denounced by Morgner), and further complicate *herstory* as related to the concept of a "universal" female writing-as-desire.

Exceptionally for the socialist political climate, Morgner was granted trips to the political West, and celebrated cautiously as a feminist. In 1974, her major work, *Leben und Abenteuer der Trobadora Beatriz* (*The Life and Adventures of Trobadora Beatrice*) was published in East Berlin, although with difficulties, due to its unacceptably elaborate title as well as its strict feminist position, inappropriate irony, and ideologically suspicious fantasies. The latter in particular challenged both the socialistically defined feminism and patriarchal order of socialist Germany. In 1976, after being rejected by a Western publisher, *Trobadora Beatriz* became an East German bestseller and Morgner was acclaimed a major feminist of the German Democratic Republic. Although Morgner is little known outside German-speaking countries, the author of an extensive study of her work, Alison Lewis, claims that her experiments with forms of the fantastic offer one of the most comprehensive examples of a feminist critique of the history of patriarchal institutions to emerge out of second-wave feminist movements (1). In East German culture, as in other countries of the socialist regime, the very term feminism has long been in mistrust. "In contrast to the United States," feminism in (both East and West) Germany was a term "fraught with a fear of aggression, anarchy, misandrism. Hitherto it was almost completely unknown, and in our first women's movement it played only a marginal role" (Moltmann-Wendel 241). With specific reference to the East German dilemma, Lewis has noted that feminist philosophy "is somewhat problematic when applied to Morgner since she herself repeatedly rejected the label in interviews." As a communist, Morgner "did not need to be a feminist since the sweeping social changes brought about by the socialist revolution automatically envisaged the abolition of all forms of exploitation, including those based on gender" (1).

My understanding of Morgner's philosophical position takes yet into account a fundamental influence of Western feminism (e.g., de Beauvoir, Irigaray, Mies, Schwarzer) on Morgner's vision of a socially transformed society, in which women would have equal rights to education, employment, and public life. Clearly sharing Irigaray's political standpoint, Morgner is not opposed to women's struggles for equal rights, but she does not believe that equality can be achieved as long as women are caught within the paradigm of the exchange (see Rubin, Butler) within a masculine sexual imaginary. This standpoint is most clearly addressed by Morgner in *Amanda*, the work selected for analysis here. *Amanda* appeared in 1983 as a continuation of the intricate story of Laura Salman who, inspired by Beatrice, initiates a cultural revolution against the universal masculine subject. Intended as a "training work to recall the forgotten Sirens' voice" (*Amanda* 657), the novel rewrites the concept of "heresy" as a means of preserving "the possible of the day after tomorrow" (246), and as an allusion to the "impossibility" of the present (unless otherwise stated, all translations are mine). Referring to the 1970s and early 1980s in East Berlin, the present embodies a blend of communist reality and *herstorical* fantasy, employing a heterogeneous mixture of female characters, from mythical women and witches to Greek goddesses, Sirens, and legendary medieval characters. "Reality," understood thus as a historically determined system of dominant philosophical assumptions upheld as reality, offers in Morgner's text a homogeneous, one-dimensional, and undeniably oppressive entity. In contrast with Gearhart's story, the female fantasy coexists within the phallocentric dominance, but far from unified, its plurality denotes both fragmentation and an anarchical potential. In thus supplementing socialist veracity with surrealistic motifs, Morgner focuses on the illusionary character of the communist state that remains suspended in a rigid binary opposition between the phallocentric (both realistic and mythic) world and the dispersed subversive and fantasmatic women. When Laura, the main character, is visited as a child by the daughter of Frau Holle, the witch figure emerging from German folklore, her male playmate, Gerhard, appears not to notice anything unusual and remains unaware of the conspiratory exchange taking place between the two women (Lewis 36). Thus, from the very beginning, a female homosexual economy (Irigaray) is clearly established among various women in their attempts to forge alliances with one another. The borders separating the real/historical and the fantastic/grotesque are sometimes abandoned altogether, but the fusion does not necessarily indicate that choices are available or that plurality is favored. Rather, the borderless coexisting of incompatible systems masks the conflictual power relations, political paradoxes, and gender imbalances permeating, according to Morgner, every aspect of women's lives in East Germany. To put these power relations into postsocialist perspective, I quote Frigga Haug's observation in "The End of Socialism in Europe" (1992): the "former socialist model did not eliminate women's oppression, in fact, the situation of women was not even relevant to the dominant theory, which saw feminism as a bourgeois deviation. Nevertheless, it is above all women in movements in the former socialist countries who appear to be ready to think about an improved model of socialism" (167). Morgner herself explicitly draws on the difference between the West and East European representations of gender roles in her 1975 interview with Karin Huffzky: "But you'll find, for instance, differences in the way things are advertised in your country and ours. Advertising that flatters people by saying what they want to hear always states things very directly. Here advertising for laundry detergent shows men doing the laundry, and in store ads, there are men doing the shopping. It's not something we even notice, except in contrast to advertising in your country, where women are expected to have a guilty conscience if their laundry isn't fluffy enough" ("Making Use" 276).

And yet, parallels to Western *herstorical fantasmatic* are indisputable in Morgner's text. At every turn, like Walker's narrative, Morgner reinvents and refeminizes mythology. In her version of the myth of Pandora, she rejects the classical depiction of Pandora as a dashingly beautiful but calamitous woman sent to earth by vengeful Gods who planned to destroy mankind's happiness. According to Hesiod's account, as summarized by Morgner, when Epimetheus, against the will of his brother, offers shelter to Pandora, she opens her box and all the evil elements in it are distributed over the earth. Only hope remains inside the hastily covered container (*Amanda* 99). Morgner, however, introduces a correction to the story by depicting her Pandora as a source of knowledge about "woman," that is, as an "Allgiver" (87), and as a womb that, depending on the speaker, dispenses "all the good or all the evil things" (267). Again, a parallel association with Irigaray's work can be drawn. In *Speculum*, Irigaray refers to the dominant fantasy of the mother, a "receptacle for the (re)production of sameness," and analyzes the phallocentric need "to represent her as a closed volume, a container": "his desire is to immobilize her, keep her under his control, in his possession, even in his house. He needs to believe that the container belongs to him. The fear is of the 'open container, ' the 'incontournable volume,' that is to say, the volume without contours" (Irigaray, *Speculum* 53). Morgner's model, provided by Goethe's *Pandora's Return* (*Pandoras Wiederkunft;* 1808), refers to a container of the "figures of the imagination and goods with wings: images of the future" (*Amanda* 82). To follow Lewis's detailed analysis of this reference, Goethe's unfinished portrayal of Pandora "is significantly at variance with the Greek sources and subsequent versions of the myth. Goethe recasts his Pandora with the classical grace and beauty of her box, which was once the source of 'all the Spites that might plague mankind' but now contains 'figures of the imagination' and 'happiness in love'" (237). Whereas the figure of Pandora is introduced in Hesiod's epics to explain the necessity for humans to work for their livelihoods and the existence of such social evils as hunger and illness, Morgner uses the same mythological figure to explain the loss of human qualities that have traditionally been associated with the feminine (237). In Morgner's narrative, it is Epimetheus who opens the box, and he does so against Pandora's will. All the attributes cultivated by women over the ages, and summarized by Morgner (love of the earth, a sense of harmony and nurturing, the ability to compromise and to make peace) fly out, and only hope remains (*Amanda* 83). Pandora realizes that in order to preserve her only remaining gift to humanity she must abandon the phallocentric space in which she lives; she must flee/fly, and like Cixous's sorceress, perform a *herstorical* act of "repossession" of the "forgotten" roles. One of these roles will be that of Zoharic Lilith (Patai 223), an ambiguous "reflex of the earth goddess" (Milgrom 227) that, in many *herstorical* narratives of the early 1980s, closes the metaphoric gap between historical civilizations and the myth of the archaic mother. Enveloped in such imaginary returns, Morgner's concept of hope "is entirely stripped of the negative connotations it has in Hesiod's account and becomes—instead of a synonym for delusions—the key to the salvation of the human race and to maintaining faith in [the] future" (Lewis 237).

Although phallocentric space is conceptualized in *Amanda* in direct opposition to what we might denote as the "feminine principle" (of 1970s ecofeminism, notably of Ruether's Gaian ecosystem discussed in the context of Gearhart's narrative), Morgner's concept of the feminine is not as straightforward as it might seem: it is neither a phallocentric construct nor a utopian projection. As Lewis suggests, Morgner contrasts Pandora (as well as other witch figures) with the heroes of the "performance principle"—Prometheus, Faust, and Don Juan. Pandora draws here on Marcuse's reiscriptions of Orpheus and Narcissus, and "stands for alternative modes of social interaction and peaceful, non-aggressive forms of knowledge" (Lewis 219). The feminine principle is simultaneously "unreal," "unrealistic," and "irresponsible," forcing women like Laura to continue to be content with private responsibility, the heterosexual matrix, and patriarchal safety blankets, while delegating public responsibility to specialists (the "chosen few"; Morgner 222). In questioning the political effectiveness of such delegation, Morgner proposes her own specialists (Arke, the serpent daughter of Gaja, and Beatriz, the Siren) who stand for the culturally "monstrous" rather than the "feminine" gender, and take over the responsibility for political activism on the behalf of the paralyzed women. Beatriz, for example, as the only siren already awakened, has the difficult task of coordinating the various ecofeminist activities to bring the planet back from the edge of destruction (Lewis 239). Sirens, having the ability to warn of pending danger, have yet to learn how to divert Prometheus from his self-destructive path, so that he recognizes "his work as fragmentary," and "recall Pandora and her one remaining gift to humankind" (Morgner, *Amanda* 40). At present, Beatriz, whose embodiment converges clearly with the various frustrations of feminist writing, represents an alienated creature that lives on the borderline "between suffering and freedom," to borrow from Cixous and Clément (6). Soon upon her awakening, the Siren finds out that although she has claws, she has been reborn as a mute creature. This truly depressing discovery is directly contrasted with her excellent ability to fly, the *herstorical* capacity per se. Moreover, her voiceless status (as explained by Arke) is nothing new, since sirens had already been silent enough during Odysseus' lifetime. "For the first time," Arke continues, "I have seen the Sirens at the navel of the world....In the old days all wise women lived their second lives in the form of Sirens. There were many Sirens then" (Morgner 15). The navel serves here as a metaphor of centrality in the sea-abyss, the "strange lands beset by powerful females"—Cirke, Calypso, the Sirens, Scylla (Brilliant 167), and of a lost connection with the archaic maternal body often associated with the ocean. Arke's own situation is even less encouraging: Her wings are scratched, her corpus missing numerous scales: "A sad sight of a scabrous face, mysteriously smiling as usual" (*Amanda* 35). Arke's major task is to persuade Beatriz to exercise her voice, since it will be needed, and to write in the meantime; that is, like Arachne, to weave her/story on paper.

In an increasingly bizarre development of events, Arke remains consistent in fulfilling her goal to mobilize and unite women. She does not give up, even when Beatriz, imprisoned in a zoo cage and classified as a "strix sirensis" (479), has to put up with frequent visitors admiring her as "a rare type of a bird" (435). Eventually, the Siren, kidnapped by the witches, undergoes a tongue operation, retains her speech, and will be installed as Pandora "in woman-hating cultures" against a particular type of masculine desire ("the desire for the forbidden"; 52). The job itself is a long term investment since, as Morgner explains in an interview with Huffzky, paternalistic habits "that have evolved over thousands of years cannot be changed in decades" (272). Thus, in concert with *herstorical* politics, Morgner's fantasy offers a form of estrangement, enabling women to remove their femininity from entrapment in a masculinized economy of desire. Morgner's argument that women not only live in patriarchy, but patriarchy also lives through them (*Amanda* 94) connects precisely with the "imaginary zone" of culture, as envisioned by Cixous and Clément, and its importance for what it excludes and what "we must try to remember today" (6).

Laura, like many other "real" women, has been split into two women-halves by Kolbuk, the "major devil" who, as we find out later, simply follows the divine example. Laura, the smaller and thicker half, remains as the "real" single working mother in the city, at a time when "the much-propagated double burden was beginning to peak: Hold down a job on the side and at the same time be the perfect housewife, good mother, smooth lover" (Schwarzer 221). The other half, the tall and slim Amanda, has been kidnapped by Kolbuk and imprisoned in the mythical underworld of East Germany's magic mountain, which in recent times (in the novel) doubles as a brothel. Amanda, who to a degree functions in the story as a Lilith figure, provides a symbolic image of the female beyond the maternal, conveying her "dark," uncontrollable, and threatening attributes in culture. Following the Near Eastern and Judeo-Christian figurations of Lilith as a female demon and "polluting other" (see Frymer-Kensky; Koltuv Black; Milgrom), Lilith's body as a grotesque construction fluctuates between femaleness and animality. It accentuates the connection between evil and femaleness as a specific reinforcement of gender difference.

Lilith's violence, unrestrained sexuality, and lack of encumbrances can be seen as early manifestations of the Western witch figure, a mouth-dominated female creature in a double understanding of the female *labia*, the dangerous lips of the speaking female mouth and the uncontrolled lips of the vulva, usually in the form of the *vagina dentata*. Her body has an indefinable status, and hence it is depicted in different, often contradictory, forms that convey her status as a variable, ambiguous container of divergences, deviations, and deferrals. Indeed, drawing on the Zoharic legend of Lilith, Morgner rewrites her with radical feminist values. However, representing the potentially rebellious part of Laura, Amanda-Lilith is paralyzed, suspended, and isolated in the zone of the imaginary, the only proper place for heretics, lesbians, and witches.

Linked with sexual promiscuity, lasciviousness, and rebellion, Amanda falls outside the symbolic and the social order, and can be further associated with Michelet's witch, who "will be arrested when she has finally become beautiful—in insolently good health, too comfortable in her own body, not sickly enough" (Clément and Kristeva 130). Morgner's strategy of reclaiming the power of female homosexuality parallels in many respects the previously discussed feminist theories, but her belief in the transformative power of this sexuality is tempered with skepticism. To "be banished to the margins means that the heretics and dissidents in fact occupy an intermediary position, a space in the interstices between East and West, between antagonistic systems" (Lewis 214). Simultaneously, it is also a severely controlled military space that remains off-limits and out-of-bounds to the average women, such as Laura. In this somewhat pessimistic closure, Morgner's belief in the reunification of women's halves is "linked to the survival of wishful thinking" (*Amanda* 284), because of the growing gap between feminist theory (as represented by Amanda) and feminist practice (Laura). In fact, Laura's bodily deformity and spiritual weakness result in a fear that "could be defeated by Amanda only," but it will not happen "by means of violent speeches and argumentation alone. The words mean little against the devil's prohibition" (153). Although Amanda and Laura alike want to find out what is the "mother of all things" (141), the first is a visionary full of confidence and hope, the other a skeptical single mother under the pressures of the "double burden." As in her 1975 interview, Morgner asserts that, after all, equal rights are of little use to working mothers if they continuously experience physical and emotional exhaustion. These laws do not simply guarantee the right to work; they also stir up dissatisfaction on the part of women and, in fact, encourage their political disengagement ("Making Use" 276). But there is more to the laws and "words alone," as Morgner seems to suggest in her depiction of the socialist version of the witches' Sabbath, taking place in the Berlin City Hall at night.

When Laura, disgusted and tired, attempts to leave the witches' assembly (which she previously discovered by chance), she is held back and effectively forced to stay by one of the participants. Further on, Laura witnesses "sharp sexual and political jokes, cacophonic singing, partly sung with full mouths, since the women not only drank, but ate without restraint. They ate the richest food, high in calories: Hungarian salami, pickled pork knuckles, whipping cream, sweets. Were they not personally responsible for their figure, or socially responsible for keeping their workers' bodies in healthy condition? And what was really amazing: were they never tired at all? Laura was dog-tired. Did this type of women make it through the nights by sleeping all day? Laura suspected there were housewives around her. Naturally, not the real ones who had to serve the household, the husband and children—but women with housekeepers" (323-34). On the contrary, Laura finds out that these "homoerotic" housewives are fully involved in all sorts of private and public activities, and far from being privileged in patriarchy. When the sabbath night is over, they hurry home on their broomsticks "to prepare breakfast, send their kids to school, gently wake up their husbands, and leave for their places. 'What places?,' asked Laura. 'University, conveyor belt...music school, editors' office, marriage fraud office, hospital, poets' society'" (325). These housewives, Morgner's ironic versions of "superwomen," allude to communist achievements in women's mobilization and entry into the labor force. The socialist ideals supporting women's legal and economic independence, providing affordable childcare and increasing participation in education and politics, have clearly remained part of Morgner's own vision of a women-friendly world. In adopting thus a more critical stand toward the West, Morgner connects conceptually with Western feminist hesitation as to whether to refer to the superwoman as a syndrome or as a necessity. To quote Ursula le Guin, writing in a capitalist context, "it's a lot easier to write books while bringing up kids than to bring up kids while working nine to five plus housekeeping....Talk about superwomen, those are the superwomen. Those are the mothers up against the wall. Those are the marginal women, without either privacy or publicity; and it's because of them more than anyone else that the woman artist has a responsibility to try to change the life in which she is also immersed" (235). In addition to flying, most of Morgner's witches, and this connects them with Laura, enjoy their kitchen as a *herstorical* place of inconsistency and subversion. The kitchen in fact is a central metaphor for the fantasmatic place of female alchemists' experiments (*Amanda* 144). Both sovereign and "safe," it is the place of witches' cauldrons, potions, and brews. Laura's former husband, now married to her best friend, Vilma, never enters a kitchen, a place inscribed with secrecy, containing magic potions and forbidden, half-finished formulae against melancholy, the threat of stagnation, and imposed immobility. This fantasmatic kitchen, in fact, encourages "faith in the possibility of social change and therefore in the improvement of existing conditions for women" (Lewis 17).

In subverting the usual representations of the socialist patriarchal realities, Morgner's imaginary marks the return of values repressed by these realities (Lewis 2), but does not offer substitutes as temporary solutions. Rather, engaging in a Bakhtinian dialogical discourse, her fantasy simultaneously reinforces and undermines the matrix of normativity, echoing the medieval laughter that signals suspension of authority, of fear/death, and of the holy and forbidden. It is precisely in this association with the medieval carnivalesque safety valves that the socialist Blocksberg, the site of witches' rites, is demystified as a site of patriarchal control, a measure of the degree of oppression of the feudal/patriarchal order (*Amanda* 510). Its authority tolerates and actually enhances rehearsals of a revolt, because these rehearsals, including the witches' orgasmic laughter (feminist demonstrations), are fake substitutes for conditions that have not been created. After the performance, the witches' leader, along with the devils' leader and his omnipresent raven, reverse the upside-down universe back into the norm. Ultimately, the fantasmatic carnival of bodies has a "critical rather than celebratory" character; meant to trivialize the tyranny of a regime in an exhibitionist display of pluralist thinking (Lewis 204). Reported to replicate patriarchal relations of exploitation, the Blocksberg remains therefore highly ambivalent in its status. It is a "place of double standards" (*Amanda* 548), oscillating between fascination and terror, depending on the participant's gender. Calling to mind Carter's phallocentric constructions of female sacrifice and "annihilation" ("Scarlet House" 421), of female entrapment rather than sovereignty, the Blocksberg is a place where women can experiment with the "mimetic mode of appropriating the world" (*Amanda* 461). Vilma, for instance, explains proudly that she has swallowed her "unruly half," which is now safely stored in a place (the womb) where her "body speeches" are. The invention of body-speak allows her and many other women to satisfy their need to communicate among themselves, especially since she has realized that most of the energy she requires for living had to be spent on conforming to the system. Gender relations are not necessarily divided between the feminine and the masculine codes of behavior, but the division echoes here ironically the communist assumptions of gender and class equality. The subversive gender, primarily represented by the women-witches, is modeled as a "third" (alternative) gender, and works against the traditional heterosexual matrix. Morgner's task, as a reminiscence to Daly's venture, is to normalize this third gender, in other words, to "rationalize the phenomenon of the witch on a broom" (36) as a future representative of the entire female sex/gender. Therefore, Laura's insistence on an alliance with men, who, according to Morgner, suffer another type of enslavement, is not an endorsement of heterosexuality but a necessary political strategy to ensure the emancipation of both sexes (Lewis 185). The witch, as a gender deviation from the existing fe/male binary, has a political character and transforms the monopoly of patriarchal power into a dialogue of genders. Consequently, the responsibility for Laura's split is assigned to women themselves, and in particular to those who are "blind," nourished with patriarchal dogmas, generations of grandmothers and mothers who urgently need to be reeducated. As Schwarzer postulated in 1975, it is not "biological difference, but its ideological consequences" that Morgner posits as a predicament to be eliminated from women's lives. In the end, Morgner's witch becomes a mediator between the women's "forgotten" knowledge and their future im/possibilities, where, to follow Bovenschen, "elements of the past and of myth oscillate, but along with them, elements of a real and present dilemma as well" (231). In rejecting Amanda (her other "half") as an eccentric witch, and the very word "witch" in connection with herself, Laura is convinced that she can do without theory and "lofty ideas," "a cry not unfamiliar to feminists in the West—to solve her immediate practical problems of sleep deficiency" (Lewis 184). On the other hand, Amanda dismisses Laura's intention to combat tiredness with alchemy as a "piecemeal solution" (*Amanda* 284), one "that fails to address the underlying problem of the fragmentation of East German women" (Lewis 177). Out of these two particular positions, Morgner herself favors Laura's form of pragmatic, down-to-earth feminism, "satirizing the type of radical militant feminist opposition represented in the figure of Isebel" (184). Thus, Laura, still reluctant to cooperate with Amanda's strategy, recognizes it finally as a political necessity in the witches' overall project to unite, since their fragmentation serves patriarchal interests. The "break through the wall," as an attempt at reunification, has a clear reference to Germany as a divided country and the envisioned collapse of the Berlin Wall, alluding to German feminisms divided along the same political axis. Realizing "that even practical short-term goals cannot be achieved without Amanda's theoretical guidance" (Morgner 233), Laura overcomes her skepticism towards feminist ideals. This political overcoming attests to Morgner's conscious narrative focus on how to end the fruitless war between sexes, and to shape the political consciousness of gender relations instead. *Amanda* played a relevant role in building the gender awareness of East German women, and in fact, became a well-known feminist manifesto of the 1980s, influencing various German feminisms since then.

As represented by the next generation of German witch stories (written, one might say, by Morgner's and Irigaray's "daughters"), the political *unconscious*, although given shape, demonstrates that the reinscribed woman's identity is still entrapped in a masculine sameness and phallus envy, while the common experience evoked by the feminist "we" prevents women from seeing how certain differences are constructed as relations of subordination. I now turn to Sabine Korte's "Hexenhochzeit" ("Witch's Wedding") and Iris von Finckenstein's "w.i.t.c.h.," two German short stories published in 2000 (unless indicated otherwise, translations of these texts are mine). These literary proposals of "mystic dances, magic convocations, refined trophies, enchanting and poisonous at once, never harmless" (*Walpurgistänze* back cover), grippingly reflect on the reminiscence of the second-wave fantasmatic traces at the turn of the century. Published twenty years later, they reveal an astonishing complicity with the phallocentric thinking previously denounced by such writers as Morgner and Schwarzer. These rather pop-cultural representations of the feminist witch complicate indeed the relation between theoretical spaces of feminist *herstory* and the actual articulations of female desire that continues to represent a hysterical inconsistency, despite the feminist theories/therapies in process. The question forming itself upon the following readings is that of a suspicion of *herstorical* failure in sustaining a politically useful and common ground from which to act upon culture. Has the "newly born woman" returned to the worship of the phallus, to heterosexuality as a type of biological binary that "has crippled us and created a rift which is seemingly impossible to overcome" (Schwarzer 223)? Do we have to agree with Irigaray that so-called "sexual liberation" has done absolutely nothing for women? "Precisely. And they lay traps for us. Not that I think we should hold it against individual men. But all the same, they do lay traps for us. The superegoization of sexual excess: you aren't a liberated woman if" ("Limits" 107). To continue this thought, both Korte and Finckenstein emancipate their "witches" financially and abandon the privacy of traditionally marginalized witches' locations. Like many contemporary women in Germany, the protagonists have their own income that enables them to travel and explore various opportunities. Yet this sovereignty remains enclosed within a persistent phallogocentric discourse that reduces them to miming and "taking pleasure" in the privileges of men and as their accomplices. In analyzing this phenomenon, I link these narratives to a much earlier and far more didactic configuration of an "active witch," found in Colette's 1958 short story, "The Rainy Moon," and pursuing a witch theme deliberately erased in the *herstorical* imaginary. Colette's story, serving hence as a prelude to my discussion of the German narratives, presents a hysterical and "altogether mad" Délia who makes use of witchcraft in order to kill her husband, Eugène. Eugène, although already separated from her, repeatedly comes to see her because she has "cast a spell on him" (121) or "convoked" him: "Convoking, do you know what that is?...Convoking is summoning a person by force" (122), asserts Rosita, Délia's sister, in a dialogue with the surprised narrator who does not believe in things like "doing evil" (123). Colette's text, underscored with irony, introduces magic as a popular and not exclusively female affair, a secret yet conventional means of getting rid of one's spouse and achieving the liberty of widow(er)hood.

Depicting Délia as one of those knowledgeable in the art of black magic, Colette draws on the power of superstitious belief as well as on a linkage of sexual bonds with possession: "Possession gives you the power to summon, to convoke, as they say" (130). Eugène is lost, according to Rosita, since his body once "belonged" to Délia, but he could be saved if he bonded with another. Unfortunately, Rosita continues, "Eugène has never even thought of wanting me....If he had wanted me, even just once, I'd be in a position to fight against her, you understand." But Colette's narrator does not understand, she has everything to learn. "'Do you really attribute so much importance to the fact of having...having belonged to a man (sic!)?' 'And you! Do you really attribute so little to it?' I decided to laugh" (130). Rosita, however, proceeds to elucidate the convoking procedure, while all that the narrator expects now from her detailed informant is the "one final picture" of Délia, "arriving at the crossroads where, amidst the vaporous clouds produced by each one's illusion, the female slaves of the cloven-footed one meet for the Sabbath. 'Yes, indeed. And where does the devil come in, Rosita'" (133)? And here comes Colette's radical feminist reply, in the form of an innocent but persistently political response: "'What devil, Madame?... An honest amazement was depicted on Rosita's face and her eyebrows flew up to the top of her high forehand. 'But Madame, whatever trail are you on now. The devil, that's just for imbeciles. The devil, just imagine....' She shrugged her shoulders, and, behind her glasses, threw a withering glance at discredited Satan" (133). Délia does not need any form of complicity with phallic figures; she is perfectly self-sufficient in her work with "pointed things, scissors, pins," as Colette assures her readers in the final image of Délia strolling along the aisles of a flea-market as a widow. If anything, she must compete with her sister. Two interesting thoughts are thus suggested by Colette's text: first, that witchcraft is a private (secret) but popular affair, and, second, that it is a serious, competitive undertaking. Irony and detachment discarded, these ideas continue to be used in Korte's and Finckenstein's stories, both fascinated with convoking procedures. The central theme of "Witch's Wedding" is inscribed, however, with the female castration complex and her subsequent seduction by the phallus, ironically reflecting the Lacanian theory of the feminine that substitutes phallus for "lack." Korte's witch, madly in love with her (male) lover, focuses obsessively on his masculinity, a troublesome subject from a radical feminist point of view. Like Rosita, Korte's narrator attributes great importance to the fact of having belonged to a man, but assuming her "natural" inborn castration, she desires an adequate tool that will balance her desire. The knife is what she dreams about: "the witch's knife for the blood wedding" (Korte 266), that is, a fetish, a temporary substitute for the erotic catharsis and a narcissistic identification (in a Freudian sense) with the phallus. Traveling through Africa as somewhat of an eccentric but clearly a tourist, she succumbs to a nomadic condition that should surprise and challenge her lover: "You don't know your witch well enough. I have used all my magic to escape the city. Not with husband and child. Not as a married couple. But alone, enchantingly free, perfectly close to myself and as far away as possible" (257). Joining thus various expeditions to remote places, she articulates her desire while writing letters (convocations) to her lover, likewise on a journey to the Philippines with his wife. The colonizing spirit of these parallel adventures attests precisely to the kind of postmodern and nihilist tradition of Western writing that Korte's text seems to uncritically recreate. In this sense, the narrator's "cultural castration" attains a doubly violent significance, simultaneously intermingling with a culturally sanctioned desire to become the conqueror of a "unexplored" continent and with a culturally abject desire to become a castrator figure, to steal the phallus, to penetrate with the witch's knife. Because of her culturally reinforced submissiveness to the dominant culture and the powerful organ that she strives to possess, she is in a struggle against her own sex, and specifically against her lover's wife, a woman in competition with her. Her unruly libido will thus be tolerated as it continues to cultivate the phallic function, while the relationship between her and the lover progresses as a typical love affair between two unhappily married people.

On her journey, the narrator resembles Cixous's sorceress, suspended between her salient suffering in a particular culture (Germany, home, family obligations) and her "orgasmic freedom" (Africa, journey, erotic desire). The ambiguous in/visibility of her own desire, articulated in a hysterical attack, reflects the narrator's alienated, even lacking, sexual identification, and feeds her eccentric perception of the African landscape as an erect phallic construction. She, the conqueror, has given her lover an ultimate choice, but he has asked for time and place to reflect: "And yet, the fight is not decided, not yet, lover. Perhaps, you will burn me, your Satan's woman, at the stake of lost chances." Or, perhaps, "you will take me as your wife. In a black mass, at a white altar, the elbows bound, the arms thrown over the head, the legs so wide open that the thighs chant, united" (Korte 266). The narrator's vision of the witch's wedding initiates her black-and-white, yes-or-no journey that metaphorically converges with her quest for the knife and her fight for her lover. Resonating thus with the phallocentric voyages of the male hero on his way to self-realization, Korte narrates a somewhat unaccomplished version of Irigaray's mimesis. To play with mimesis for a woman, as Irigaray suggests, is "to try to recover the place of her exploitation by discourse, without allowing herself to be simply reduced to it" ("Power" 124-25). The latter contributes precisely to the narrator's dilemma. If mimesis indicates the kind of "resubmission" by an effect of playful (Irigaray) or otherwise strategic (Butler) repetition of unacknowledged possibilities in culture, the narrator's mimesis barely manages to unveil the fact that women are "simply" good mimics, exercising in this function for centuries. Unquestionably, Irigaray's mimesis is difficult to achieve, since it borders precisely on this type of mimicry that fakes power and manifests possession when there is only dispossession. I mention these two types of miming because "Witch's Wedding" demonstrates how easily one falls into the other. The story shows, perhaps inadvertently, how mimesis turns into mimicry, and how it becomes entangled with a discourse in which a woman, the subject of the new century, cannot articulate her difference, her body, or her *jouissance*, and continues to mirror the universal gender. In this state of not knowing what she might otherwise want, she will be "ready for anything, even asking for more, so long as he will 'take' her as his 'object' when he seeks his own pleasure" (Irigaray, *Speculum* 47). Although in speaking, writing, and acting (all the necessary prerequisites in cultural participation), Korte's narrator inadvertently continues to enact a role of "the beautiful object of contemplation" (Irigaray, *Speculum* 47), of a hysterical woman who, more than anything, desires herself without being able to internalize her desire. At once revealing and ignoring her own ethnocentricity, the narrator becomes a cultural transvestite, playfully projecting herself as a white fe/male Other. In this playful "as if" suspension that easily rejects one subject position in exchange for another, she allows herself to wonder, somewhat narcissistically, who might be afraid of the white woman, who might be fascinated, and who will be seduced by her body of an apparently fake color (Korte 258). Her body, so distinct from the blackness of an African woman, (a blackness that is projected as plural, indistinct) naively denies its own subjectivization. Most certainly, "the Africa" she encounters, to follow Alice Walker, "had already been raped of much of its sustenance...made an uninhabited region, except for its population of wild and exotic animals" (*The Temple* 168-69), and other objects of European desire. But Korte's narrator never "deals" with the black woman, does not approach her, but curiously observes her "exotic" body: the breast full of mother's milk, the child carried proudly in a wrap on her hip like a heavy jewel that accentuates her femininity (Korte 258). The black female body, an actual Other of the other in the story, is a silent witness to "all the action"; the Other does not play, and is not aware of its "authenticity." Falling into the Levinasian category of incommensurability, the Other passively constitutes the narrator's private *speculum*, where she enjoys her own displayed body as an object of ridicule and fascination. Like Irigaray's woman, "she exposes, exhibits the possibility of *nothing to see*" (*Speculum*

47), and this *nothing* entertains her, excites her "lacking" sexuality. Moreover, she is proud of "being allowed" to transgress her gender as a white foreign wo/man, as an eccentric freelance witch.

Her pathetically colonizing and privileged perspective remains entangled in a universality of the "white explorer" who can afford occasionally the encounter with poverty, a postmodern model of boundary-crossing. The fact that she "is allowed" to do "certain things," to transgress taboos is never questioned, because in fact her exceptional position (white European, eccentric) liberates her from her particularly female indisposition. Tolerated and even respected as a stranger, she is not an intruder but a credit card holder, and a freak of sorts (Korte 268). For this very reason, she can forge alliances with (black) men, to negotiate with them and to meet the fetish man. She can thus afford the transgression; she can afford to pursue her desire to detach the phallic organ that does not belong to her yet. Unlike Colette's Délia, who is entirely, *eccentrically* on her own in pursuing the goal of disposing of her husband, Korte's witch assumes that she "has to look for the black magic" that will secure for her the man's love/death (260). Contrary to Délia, she "signs a pact with the devil," since she does not know how to be on her own, in a state defined by Irigaray as "within the intimacy" of her female body. The fetish man, taking on the role of devil discredited by Colette's tale, is thus appreciated, believed indispensable, and even longed for. That devil, the archaic father, will have to teach her how to seduce; his eyes are abysmal, his mouth open as if he wants to talk with her, and the tent is flooded with the presence of his goat-body: "The fetish man squatted on his heels closely to my body and gently opened my legs. I could smell him. He smelled of black skin and male sweat, spicy, intense and strange. My legs trembled under the weight of the stone. The mouldy scent of the menstruation blood flowed from my womb...and the fetish bathed in the chicken's blood. It soaked my skirt, wet my slip and mixed with my own blood" (262). And so, in mimicry, she gives herself away, balancing her desire for the man with an obsessive objectification of her own position. Her body, seen through the man's eyes, excites her, because the phallic gaze has eroticized it. Desiring thus herself, she parodies her self-desire, just as the *herstorical* witch, unable to speak, returns to the language of the archaic mother. This schizophrenic status of the woman, as encoded in the Western philosophy of masculine sameness and its social practices, imposes duality on Korte's figure: She is an object in the language, while her body offers the linguistic home-place inviting masculine desire. The narrator's desire is induced and focused on imagining her own eroticized body intermingling with her masochistic fantasies and obsessions with rape (Irigaray, "Poverty" 90-92): "When, after weeks, I looked at myself in the mirror of the hotel's room, I sank deep into my eyes. I am beautiful, lover—you will see. My eyes are as clear as those of a wo/man who has fasted for a long time. My lips are so dried out that you can no longer bite them to blood. My body is so surfeited with swellings, bites and blue marks that you can no longer lie down on me. There is yet a spirit of the desert shining in me like a sparkle" (Korte 271-72). Proud of her accomplishments in cooperation with black men, she opens her bag which is heavy with what it contains—the fetish and the knife. She has deserved it, having been initiated into the men's world. The story ends with a warning directed to her lover, should he disbelieve her mimic potential. And until the end, the narrator remains anonymous; she does not sign her letters, but represents the nameless: one of the many Walpurgisnacht's witches invited by the Devil to dig up and consummate fresh corpses. Colette, in her story, wants monstrosity to belong to Délia (a problematic issue in itself), to be her private affair, and evokes the devil's centrality on Walpurgisnacht only to deny it. Korte's witch prefers to warn her lover: "It is dangerous to leave a woman devoted to magic to her own devices" (259). It is better to take her home, domesticate her desires, and let her worship the phallus. Let her "be" the Phallus, "reflect the power of the Phallus," and "supply the site to which it penetrates" (Butler, *Gender Trouble* 44).

The second story to be analyzed here, Finckenstein's "w.i.t.c.h.," attempts to relate to the True Craft of the Wise, the one launched by Rosita as a serious business. The secrecy and fear resulting from the witches' persecution, as propagated, for example, by Dworkin and Pratt, has been successfully eliminated in Finckenstein's story and exchanged with the notion of strict business relations. Disrupting the secrecy of witchcraft, Finckenstein installs the witch as a businesswoman immersed in the commercial, money-making aspects of life. The "true craft," advertised on an internet site, is accessible to everybody who joins the workshops organized by w.i.t.c.h. In suggesting that the "forgotten wisdom" can now be bought in a variety of personalized packages, Finckenstein's narrative draws on the growing popularity of esoteric studies offering introductions to magic crafts, psychological archetypes à la Jung, and Tarot readings. As a fully commercialized business, The True Craft of the Wise ironically reinscribes Dworkin's figures of the witch-herbalist and midwife, standing "both for agriculture and for untamed nature" with their "unchanging identity...in an unchanging world" (Purkiss 21). The witch in Finckenstein's text is an active, competitive, and public authority. She takes over the role of the wise old woman, the hag of Daly's (re)creation, as Lu, a grown-up Lolita, the witch-psychoanalyst, and simply the boss: "You will receive your own broom and a new name. She made a dutiful break. Emily admired the obviousness with which Lu spoke about such things" (Finckenstein 33). There is no metaphysics in the foundations of Lu's power, no fundamentally magic phenomena in her witchcraft. As she promises in the folder outlining the course content, relations are reciprocal, pointing out "the perpetual gaps between intentions in relation to one another" as if borrowing from Foucault ("Space" 164). This transition, indeed, the metamorphosis of a phallocentric victim into a businesswoman, meets precisely with the lifestyle of a feminist healer in the seventies, the first owing to business etiquette, the latter to notions of a simple life and increasing commercialization of traditional, antique, or natural products. Both figurations are problematic because they substitute an often unattainable fantasy (the business-witch, the herbalist-healer) for a solution to women's problems (Purkiss 21). The fantasy of Lu, the postmodern witch, is problematic precisely because of the surrealistic status she claims to have achieved. As Emily observes, "an outsider would have taken her for a totally crazy person" (Finckenstein 33). Before she joins Lu's workshop, Emily in fact is an "outsider" leading an unexciting life as a secretary. For a long time now she has been looking for something "original," "thoughtful," and "different." She has tried out many other product remedies (reminiscent of the 1970s), such as Ayurvedian massage, ritual Eskimo chanting, or Indian sand painting, "but nothing was right." While surfing on the Internet, she eventually realizes that "the right thing might be nearer than she thought" and might even be "rooted in European culture" (28). Emily calls the institute only to find out that in the coming workshop there is one place left, and that it is "entirely up to her whether she feels worth it," that is, the 7000 Deutsch Marks that she would need to supply immediately: "It was a short but violent emotional struggle. Then Emily made another phone call and registered for the workshop. The night before the workshop she had really bad dreams. Wild dreams about witches with green pointed nails and yellow bloodshot eyes. They wanted her purse where she kept the check for 7000 DM. She managed to escape, but when she opened her purse, she found an ugly slippery toad instead of her money" (29). In fact, the Institute of Witchcraft, with its main location in California, has long since discarded the witches' history, along with their bad reputation and "European character" (32). Portraying thus, inadvertently, another case of mimesis/mimicry, Finckenstein's institute follows the current fashions for a professional enterprise: The entrance of w.i.t.c.h. resembles the lobby of a financial institution rather than a witch's kitchen. "Glass, stainless steel, immaculate white walls, a light leather sofa with matching armchairs, the name of the institute in sleek golden letters above the bright glass-topped reception desk. Behind the desk a woman, an elegant, dark haired middle-aged woman, a friendly smile on a carefully made-up face" (30). The workshop itself, both a type of masquerade and a form of "initiation into a different womanhood" (as suggested arrogantly by Lu in her welcome speech), sells a modern fairy tale to lonely secretaries and bored nobody-loves-me housewives (the reference is to Doris Dörrie's film *Keiner liebt mich* (*Nobody Loves Me*) [1995]): "And yes, [Lu] is as old as she feels she is...and totally free in terms of relationships. This doesn't mean, she added in a silky voice, that she does not treat herself to a man from time to time. It sounded as if she was talking about a tasty but calorie-laden morsel" (35).

As a postmodern parody of the True Craft then, Finckenstein's narrative, like Korte's, remains uncritical of heterosexual patriarchal normativity targeted and challenged by radical feminism. It can be read, most certainly, as an ironic warning against fraudulent institutes and as a proof of witchcraft addressed to skeptical unbelievers. But, above all, it raises questions as to what has remained of the impact of 1970s feminism on the younger generation of women writers. Although the slogans of w.i.t.c.h., such as "join us, the workshop will change your life," might ironically echo U.S. radical feminist "healing methodologies," the narrated images of female professionals represent a spectacular collage of everything that proves problematic from these feminist positions. The workshop does, in effect, change Emily's life; the w.i.t.c.h. stands proudly for "Where I Take CHances." Emily's major goal, like that of Korte's narrator, to find the right man and get rid of her "loneliness," has been achieved. However, everything that happens seems to have also been possible without the workshop. In this sense, Finckenstein does score a feminist point, as she seems to be aware of irony as an important mimetic enterprise. In the rewriting of the witch's historical characteristics, her story shows that the contemporary witch is seen as both a humorous and an arbitrary figure. Her "postmodern nature" is fully adjusted to the phallocentric capitalism of the late twentieth century. Enveloped in the needs, desires, and fantasies of such system, her masquerade, as Irigaray has suggested, offers a protective skin in the absence of a language specific to her body and her own desire. But her triumph is that of the complicitous woman; she acts and speaks in a language that invariably articulates her "lack" of autonomy. Most probably, rather than "escaping from her loneliness," Emily abandons her (wasted) independence, and ends up denying her own hysterical status/body, while accepting the pleasurable aspects of phallocentric rather than eccentric desires. Although showing witches as an "active, public and financially self-sufficient" group of women, both narratives speak from the perspective of phallocentric fantasy and can be interpreted as subconscious returns under the patriarchal security blanket. This position, characterized often as that "of the castrata" (Baym 280) and forced into various forms of tokenism, continues the tradition of a masquerade. "In the masquerade, they submit to the dominant economy of desire in an attempt to remain 'on the market' in spite of everything. But they are there as objects for sexual enjoyment, not as those who enjoy" (Irigaray, "Poverty" 136). The transgressive potential recognized in some herstorical narratives as enabling the mimetic to break out from within might thus appear as a fantasmatic illusion. The/a "woman," no longer confined to the private home, is still entrapped in hysteria, in a phallocentric "vacuum" (Whitford 54) where autonomous herstory has not yet taken place. This entrapment, which confirms the cultural castration of women, draws on Irigaray's "mimetic appropriation" of the hegemonic discourse, which is "still the most terrible thing of all because it is practiced without any feminine ideality or model" (Whitford 110). Korte's and Finckenstein's stories, and to varying degrees all of the texts discussed in this chapter, are thus Irigaray's "reservoir of a yet-to-come" imaginary in which women would be nomads (but no longer in exile), mobile, dancing, taking their own "house with them."

Tracing Cultural Un/belonging

The narratives analyzed in this chapter illustrate the second-wave feminist sense of urgency, and the need to construct a political "we" and create a common identification with the historical oppression of women (Irigaray's bringing together of mothers and daughters). The figure of the "witch" represents here a dimension of radical (feminist) identity that inserts the history of her invisibility into contemporary ideological and political spaces. Conveying the tension between past and present, the witch becomes a central signifier of women's cultural sovereignty in a "curious epoch in which 'cold' hypertechnicity goes hand in hand with rustic magical passions, with a rather worrying irrationality" (Whitford 140). This witch figure becomes a crucial metaphor for *herstory*, that is, a form of feminist mythology constituted in relation to and as an alternative to the established male-centered master narrative. In response to the poststructural dismissal of traditional identities and what in psychoanalytical theories has been diagnosed as "cultural castration," radical feminism employs strategies of appropriating and reenacting the cultural locations of the witch as "the newly born" woman. Cixous and Clément address specifically the "extensions" of the historical witch towards a woman traditionally exiled from the symbolic order: There is thus an intrinsic connection between the philosophical, the literary, and the phallocentric. Philosophy, constructed on the premise of subordination of the feminine, gives the appearance of universal condition that keeps the machinery intact. If this "suddenly came out," to follow Cixous, "all the history, all the stories would be there to retell differently; the future would be incalculable; the historic forces would and will change hands and change body" (Cixous and Clément 116).

I develop the concept of the *herstorical fantasmatic* as an attempt to assess this "incalculable change," positing the feminist "witch" as a radical denunciation of Lacan's *object petit a*, the embodiment of the woman's lack. Evoking images of the culturally abject and "an implacable enemy of the symbolic order" (Kristeva, *Powers* 70), the "witch" interferes with patriarchal discourse, as does Cixous's "newly born woman" in her imaginative journeys across the frontier of prohibition. After all, it is the physical absence of *her* mother (her unacknowledged identity) that contributes to the dream of presence ("a new earth of her own invention"), a dream that in fact should be taken literally, since its fulfillment lies within the "newly established" limits of culture. In defining history as "a fantastical and slippery concept, a making, a construction" (McDowell 234), the narratives employed in this chapter clearly address the feminist need to rehistoricize the "witch," and through that to revitalize the "woman" and show in *herstorical* perspective how knowledge about her was constructed, by whom, and with what consequences. This need, in retrospection, has to be seen as a form of *herstorical* desire to establish an unchanging point of historical reference from which to start autonomous processes of rewriting the past. An emotional and very personal feminist engagement with the witch as a victim of phallocentric metaphors enters here into a dialogue with institutional knowledge and the homogeneity of phallogocentric discourse. What *herstory* comes to realize is that it works, as a consequence of history, with its tongue cut out, but that it has the capacity to weave her/story in reminiscence of Ovid's Arachne. At stake here, to follow Nancy K. Miller, is the premise "of a female signature, the internal delineation of a writer's territory." Likewise, it is the feminist desire "for another logic of plot which by definition cannot be narrated," and "looks elsewhere for expression" (279). Radical feminist writers are thus often located "inside" the discourse they construct; as narrators and protagonists they are incapable of distance, textual disconnection, or self-criticism. In analyzing the narratives selected for this chapter, I read them as literary unveilings of the "witch" in her ability as well as inability to reenter history as a speaking, autonomous, and self-reflective subject. Most importantly, I view the radical feminist archetype of the witch as attempting, and to some extent failing, to be "fluid and dynamic, empowering women's personalities to grow and develop" (Pratt 135). Instead, *herstorical* narratives focus hazardously on constructing an identity and therefore a theory of "woman." And to have a theory of woman "is already to reduce the plurality of woman to the coherent and thus phallocentric representations of theory" (Gallop, *Daughter's Seduction* 134). The false universal of the "white middle class woman" subject and identity ideals, in particular, "had not promoted feminist solidarity—they led on the contrary, to anger and schism, to hurt and mistrust" (Fraser, *Justice* 179). Reconstructing the history of second-wave feminist debates on sexual difference, we can thus close its first chapter—from the late 1960s through about the mid-1980s—with its radical focus on the erasure of gender difference, and shift our attention to the second phase—from the mid 1980s to the early 1990s—embracing a cultural recognition of "differences among women" and the current position on "multiple intersecting differences." Of course, to plot the trajectory of debate in this way is necessarily to simplify and abstract. But it is also to make us remember an inner logic of the past positions, from which new insights emerge, especially those, as postulated by Fraser, integrating social with cultural demands and seeking to change culture and political economy in tandem (*Justice* 177).

Like a feminist theoretician, to conclude this thought with Braidotti, the witch figure "can only be 'in transit,' moving on, passing through, creating connections where things were previously dis-connected or seemed un-related, where there seemed to be 'nothing to see.' In transit, moving, dis-placing—this is the grain of hysteria without which there is no theorization at all" (*Nomadic Subjects* 93). In exploring the witch's cultural incompatibility in the following two chapters, I continue to use "un/belonging" as a term to convey the location of gender fantasy as a cultural topography of the stigmatized body. The ethical value of difference, as in Irigaray's rereadings of the Levinasian Other, is crucial to my use of stigma as a concept both deriving from and defining un/belonging. Un/belonging is a form of Levinasian "resistance" of the other to the same, of the stigmatized (signified) to the stigmatizing (signifying). This resistance as a point of exteriority to the philosophical logos is located in the face of the Other, but still articulated in the language of logos (see Levinas, *Totality* 290). Un/belonging refers thus to the fantasmatic, the semiotic, and the heretic space of gender associated with the Otherness of the witch. It responds to phallocentric constructions of the witch as the ambiguous ("invested with power and danger") limit or "pollution" of the patriarchal order. This ambiguity, explored in Irigaray's analysis of *Oresteia*, points to the foundations of Western culture as both of patricidal (Freud's hypothesis) and of matricidal order. In her rerereading of Clytemnestra story as "an account of the installation of patriarchy built over the sacrifice of the mother and her daughters (one daughter, Iphigenia, literally sacrificed by Agamemnon, the other one, Electra, abandoned to her madness, while Orestes, the matricidal son, is designated to found the new order)" (Whitford 25). Irigaray returns to the major cultural taboo: the relationship with the mother. "The stress on Oedipus, on castration, serves to conceal another severance, the cutting of the umbilical cord to the mother. This relationship with the mother needs to be brought out of silence and into representation" (Whitford 25). The unacknowledged matricide, followed by "the burial of women in madness," institutes the new model of the virgin/goddess, one "born of the father and obedient to his law in forsaking the mother" (38). If we link Irigaray's reevaluation of the maternal with Douglas's anthropological readings of pollution as associated with the feminine, it becomes apparent how Irigaray's notion of the placenta as the "first house to surround us...like some child's security blanket" (40) constitutes itself as nothing but a waste to be disposed of. And how it is constructed, naturalized, and misrepresented in culture as the "openness" ("ouverture de la mere") that is threatening, that unleashes the danger of pollution, contamination, and "engulfment in illness, madness and death" (40). In Douglas's words, "pollution is a type of danger which is not likely to occur except where the lines of structure, cosmic or social, are clearly defined" (113).

The witch as a fantasy of gender, emerging from this structuralist thinking, has thus crossed over some line that should not have been crossed and unleashed danger through this structural displacement. Both as the "trace" of an archetype and as a specific literary character, the witch displays gender resistance to the phallocentric culture in which she is physically and philosophically placed. Her transgressive character relates to her un/belonging that allows for a type of subculture and relates to the ontology of the interval "between the two" which finds echoes in a range of contemporary theories on gender, most notably in Irigaray's more recent work *Entre deux* (1997). But it is also already present in questions posed by Douglas, and later elaborated by Kristeva and Butler, namely, why should bodily margins be thought to be specifically invested with power and danger" (Douglas 121)? Kristeva, in particular, assimilates Douglas's notion of body boundaries to her post-Lacanian reformulations of defilement as "what escapes that social rationality, that logical order on which a social aggregate is based." This social aggregate "becomes differentiated from a temporary agglomeration of individuals and, in short, constitutes a classification system or structure" (*Powers* 65). The very structure, in a more recent feminist perspective, has traveled, so to say, a full circle of signification. Today, margin and body are categories more slippery than ever, tending, on one side, to slide towards essentialism, and on the other, to be caught in positivist reductions or new age naïve celebrations (see Purkiss; Braidotti). Far from attempting to reduce the discussed images into a blending picture of a/the "woman," I thus refer to the witch as a "differential network," a fabric of *herstorical* and historical traces alluding endlessly to something other than the image itself. The witch, posited in this differential network as a dynamic figure, connects and disconnects culturally distinct narratives, all enveloped in various ways in Western imagery of the very figure. The cultural validity (identity) of this witch appears in sequences of differential processes, and, as I argue in the chapters to follow, releases a multiplicity of meanings. Hence, the seemingly contradictory representation of the witch as a universal Western archetype on the one hand, and as a specific literary character on the other, needs to be acknowledged as a necessarily dialogical and paradoxical structure of "being-the-two." This, in a link to a Levinasian understanding of the concept, does not imply a fusion of one and the other, but the interval between the I and the You, the in-between, employed by Irigaray and Braidotti as the site where the feminist work might take place. The strategy, as employed in this interval, is that of a self-conscious mimesis pointing to and questioning the mechanisms that maintain sexual indifference (rather than difference) in place. In Butler's understanding, specifically, this kind of mimesis does not result "in a slave morality, accepting and fortifying the terms of authority." On the contrary, Butler follows Irigaray in explaining that mimesis exposes the exclusions as sites of absence which can be mobilized: "The voice that emerges 'echoes' the master discourse, but this echo nevertheless establishes that there is a voice, that some articulatory power has not been obliterated, and that it is mirroring the words by which its own obliteration was to have taken place. Something is persisting and surviving, and the words of the master sound different when they are spoken by one who is, in the speaking, in the recitation, undermining the obliterating effects of his claim" (*Undoing Gender* 201).

In the overall argument so far, I evoke the fact that although *herstorical* methods are not completely successful, they initiate necessary revisions of such cultural constructs as femininity, spirituality, and the female body (as a twofold locus of abjection and fascination). I have analyzed these narratives as forms of feminist mythology posited as alternatives to the established Western canon and inherently divided between the methodical (logical, reasonable) and the hysterical that is out of the phallogocentric control. As such, they prove effective in removing some of the unnecessary distinctions between fiction and history, licensing, to follow Purkiss's argument, the use of both in terms of "what is needed" rather than "what is true." Daly's *Gyn/ecology* and Dworkin's *Woman-Hating* are examples of such *herstorical* ventures formulated, in my analysis, as a theoretical (and narrative) hysteria, as a textual incongruence between the *history* from which they attempt to disassociate themselves and a *herstorical* determination to identify the origins of oppression. Similarly, Walker's and Gearhart's novels are inspired by "rediscoveries" of the repressed and "forgotten" origins of female "power," although, as Purkiss correctly argues, there is no hard evidence to suggest that the majority of those accused of witchcraft were either healers or midwives. They have been selected here as examples of "matriarchal" narratives subverting the course of patriarchal history, indebted to the identity principle that is crucial to much early feminist work. In blending myth, history, and fantasy, Gearhart's radical ecofeminist and Walker's Afra-American witch figures set out to deconstruct the phallocentric philosophy of sameness by identifying with what has been repressed or underrepresented. Both Gearhart's and Walker's characters of women have been conceptualized as *different* on purpose, connecting with a supposedly "feminine" pleasure "outside" of culture. Resonating with these US-American feminist recuperations of the traditionally negative figure of the witch, Morgner's *herstorical* fantasies in *Amanda* are equally strategic and political, using a withdrawal into the "fantasmatic" as a tool for cultural transformation and a therapeutic way out of a female cultural vacuum. The short stories analyzed in the final section of this chapter, which are to some extent representative of the new wave of popular women's literature in contemporary Germany, provide an explicit example of conceptual simplifications of women's (witches') independence, rebellion, and authority, ending up as an appropriation rather than a deconstruction of sameness.

One of the risks to be negotiated by the radical feminist projects discussed in this chapter is that of merging, intentionally or not, with the patriarchal definitions of women that de Beauvoir struggled to contest, confining women to the mysterious and not quite human other, as a muse incapable of taking responsible actions in the "symbolic." Although significant as radically positive and empowering rewritings of the historical witch into a therapeutic narrative figure, the narratives analyzed here demonstrate how difficult and sometimes risky it is to work against the phallocentric structure, especially once we start to diversify feminist *herstories* across race, class, and political systems. The stigma of the female body, evoked by the radical feminist "we" and projected as the commonness of female experience, proves to be constructive only in a limited way, since the concepts of femininity, bodily empowerments, and spirituality have different implications in Walker's African American proposal of an androgynous ideal, Gearhart's ecofeminist separatism, or Morgner's East European socialist feminism. In this sense, "speaking as a woman" can be seen as "a fact determined by some biological *condition*" and "by a strategic, theoretical position," both by anatomy and by culture (Felman 9). However, if the feminist position of "speaking as a woman" is not a "natural" given, we need to start examining the splits between women themselves rather than between "women" and "men"—between mothers and daughters, to follow Irigaray's example. Employing a feminist psychoanalytical awareness, the narratives considered in the second chapter offer therefore an important expansion of the witch as an archaic figure who does not fit the model of symbolical castration. While disclosing their own versions of women's entrapment in ensnarling maternal territories and their own hysterical erasures, these texts posit the witch both as a phallic mother (establishing the paternal law at the level of the semiotic) and an *om-phalic*, a symbolically inarticulate one.

Chapter Two

Splitting the Feminist Subject

The Archaic Mother and the Semiotic *chora*

The theory and narratives discussed in this chapter shift our attention from the witch as a fantasmatic therapy of a/the woman in culture towards an archaic mother of the semiotic. This archaic figure is of importance here in the context of feminist identifications with the loss of the semiotic mother rather than the loss of the symbolic phallus. The concept of the archaic mother as a continuous separation has been thoroughly explored in Continental European feminist psychoanalysis, notably by Kristeva, Cixous, Irigaray, and Braidotti, who, consequently, link the division of flesh ("sexual difference") with the division of language, and constitute the theoretic framework of the present discussion.

For Kristeva, psychoanalysis proceeds "to the arrangement of new spaces, gratifying substitutes that repair old deficiencies in the maternal space" ("Women's Time" 862).These deficiencies (or psychoses) converge "on the problematic of space, which innumerable religions of matriarchal (re)appearance attribute to 'woman'" and which Plato, recapitulating in his own system the atomists of antiquity, designated by the *aporia* of the chora, matrix space, nourishing, unnameable, anterior to the One, to God and, consequently, defying metaphysics" (862). Following Lacan, Kristeva's concept of the symbolic is a domain of position and judgment: It establishes itself after the semiotic, during the process of the subject's self-identification; known as a "mirror stage" (Campbell 32). This identification presents itself in Kristeva's theory as a metaphorical transfer from chaotic forces to the place of significance (the symbolic). As every transfer however it contains instabilities. The instabilities of the symbolic, which fracture the centrality of the established subject, are rooted in "the prohibition placed on the maternal body," the very body that in culture inevitably constitutes a pre-linguistic space, "a chora, a receptacle" (Kristeva, "Stabat" 14), or, as Irigaray describes it, an "intimate place—which does not collect itself...in specified propositions" (Irigaray, *Reader* 56). Kristeva and Irigaray, delineating the Platonic concept of *chora* (*chōra*, the receptacle; Plato 52), bring us back to an "invisible, formless being, a mysterious, intelligible but most incomprehensible receptacle of all things" (Irigaray, *Reader* 56). While the *chora*'s articulation is both uncertain and, in contrast to the symbolic, lacking position and identity, it is the aim of Continental feminist psychoanalysis, as it was of radical feminist politics discussed in the first chapter, to reexamine the semiotic subjectivities that logocentric philosophy has rendered "mysterious" and "incomprehensible" in the context of sexual difference.

Expanding the Lacanian metaphor of the "abyss of the female organ from which all life comes forth" (Kristeva qtd. in Heath 54), Kristeva speaks of an "abyss" that opens up once the umbilical cord has been severed: the separation between the mother and the child that become inaccessibly different from and to each other ("Stabat" 179). In light of the prohibition placed on the maternal body (as described by Kristeva), identifications with the somatic and psychic traces of the archaic mother are types of gender identification related to the inaccessible Lacanian "real." Posited by Butler as "a kind of melancholia in which the sex of the prohibited object is internalized as a prohibition" (*Gender Trouble* 63), these identifications are yet inescapably the consequence of the symbolic loss of the mother. This mother, as examined by Irigaray, should be carefully given "new life," new form, and the right to pleasure, to *jouissance*, and to passion. Her right to speech has to be restored, "and sometimes to cries and anger...the sentences that speak the most archaic and most contemporary relationship with the body of the mother" (*Bodily Encounter* 43). Thus, Continental European feminist thought extends the Freudian notion of the Oedipal mother to include other faces of the mother: the fecund mother (Cixous's central figure) and the fantasmatic (archaic) mother of the semiotic (Irigaray) both playing significant roles in the formation of subjectivity. Coinciding with two of the principal phenomena in psychoanalysis (the return of the repressed and transference), the *unconscious* formations of subjectivity appear in various forms of repetition (*Daughter's Seduction* 104). These repetitive patterns, according to Gallop, are affected not so much by the frustration of a particular desire but rather by the lack of its very recognition (104). Also, in Mitchell's analysis, the repression of unrecognized desires, the ones prohibited, transferred, and hence made *unconscious*, is never successful "for the tabooed desires...and their unsuccessful prohibition would inevitably return as one symptom or another" (21). The master story of these *unconscious* desires is the Oedipus complex—and its prohibition, which was formulated somewhat later, is the castration complex.

While unveiling the relations between this master story and the feminist emergence of the archaic mother, the Freudian formulations of the *unconscious* intersect unavoidably with the Derridean "alterity of the unconscious" that "is not...a hidden, virtual, or potential self-presence. It differs from, and defers, itself" (Derrida, "Différence" 73). The trace of the archaic mother comes precisely as an intersection, and "makes us concerned not with horizons of modified—past or future—presents, but with a 'past' that has never been present, and which never will be, whose future to come will never be a production or a reproduction in the form of presence" (73). This form of the *unconscious* is linked in my analysis to feminist psychoanalytical narrative tools that work against the phallocentric assumption that female creativity can have no metaphysical sanction (except the Christian model of the Virgin Mary); in fact, against the very concept of creativity symbolically placed in opposition to female procreation. As Irigaray argues, this "lack of a self-representation to venerate, contemplate, admire or even adore" posits the female subject in the field of "the infinite/unfinished" that permanently transgresses the phallic sphere, the Lacanian sphere of "support" without which "the infinite" collapses into an endless "formlessness, into the archaism of a primitive chaos" ("Limits" 111). Although the "fe/male" is a priori inscribed with/through the phallus, she/he is not entirely there; she/he belongs to it, but not really, she/he plays the game, and acts "as if she were belonging" (Clément and Kristeva 59). While discussing the vulnerabilities, or otherwise, instabilities of the symbolic, I turn in this chapter to trace some tabooed and unrecognized desires as well as their symptoms in relation to the mother within and beyond the symbolic. In calling for recognition of the ways in which prohibited desires constitute the indefinable regions of subjectivity, I invest this subjectivity with Deleuzian and Irigaray's (decisively anti-Lacanian) readings of "becoming-a-woman," in addition to Kristeva's more conservative approach. The question for Deleuze and Irigaray alike is primarily that of the "stolen" body that undergoes fabrications of opposable organisms in the process of constituting oneself as a subject. The split from the "primary loss," crucial in the process of this constitution, forecloses access to the maternal, depriving the specifically female subject of ontological grounds for self-reflectivity. This loss, recognizable through symptoms, resonates with the position referred to by Deleuze as "symptomatology," an art of diagnosis based on the cultural readings of bodily symptoms and their implications of the loss of unity of the subject. The multi-layered Deleuzian vision of "becoming-a-subject," a dynamic entity defying the established modes of representation, opens new identifications within the symbolic (social meaning) and is thus of crucial importance for feminist psychoanalysis. Giving priority to issues of sexuality, desire, and erotic imaginary, Irigaray, and later Braidotti, reinscribe the subject as a "becoming" entity immersed both in relations to power and knowledge and in relations to unacknowledged regions of desire. The latter, involving a quest for alternative female genealogy (see Irigaray) calls for the maternal imaginary, that is, for explorations of images that represent the female experience of proximity to the mother's body.

The impact of psychoanalysis on feminist thought, resulting in a radical deconstruction of the subject position, acknowledges what US (radical) feminism did not take into account: the significance of the very split in subjectivity from the supervision of rational thinking. US-American feminism of the 1960s and 1970s, "monopolized by the quarrel over pornography and prostitution," identifies sexuality with issues of violence and domination, "that is to say negatively," leaving "all issues related to bodies, pleasures, eroticism and the specific ways of knowing of the human flesh hanging nowhere" (Braidotti, *Metamorphoses* 30). Drawing on Dworkin's and MacKinnon's antisexuality campaigns as "a specific form of internal backlash and a threat against feminism," Gallop and Braidotti attempt to refocus feminist attention from stigmatized sexuality towards women's capacity for self-determination. The "body," if it continues to speak from the position of "stigma," "cannot be positively associated with sexuality in either the critical or the public discourse" (Braidotti, *Metamorphoses* 31). Following this theoretical divide, materiality, which becomes fundamental in the Continental discourses of psychoanalysis, has little place in Anglo-American political discourse. In referring thus to the split of the feminist subject, Braidotti identifies it as the "transatlantic disconnection" (*Metamorphoses* 28) that made some stopping on the issues of identity, normativity, and power (Wittig and Butler) and some moving toward psychoanalytical "becoming" (Irigaray, Braidotti). The subject itself, no longer identified with consciousness and ratio, opens a range of inquiries both to the separation between the psychic and the social processes and to the complex task of joining them or putting them in a relation, emerging as central to Butler's political project of recasting agency in the subversive mode of performative repetitions. Yet, Gallop and Braidotti, in their radical opening of the intersections between psychoanalysis and critical social theory, remain critical of Butler's reduction of psychoanalytical insight into "erasure of homosexuality by a gender system which invents (hetero)sexual normativity and imposes it on living bodies" (Braidotti, *Metamorphoses* 45). This concept of gender, derived as it is from sociological discourse, is foreign to the discourse on sexual difference that emerges from the Lacanian and post-Lacanian framework. As Butler explains retrospectively, "in *Gender Trouble*, I understood the theory of sexual difference to be a theory of heterosexuality. And I also understood French feminism, with the exception of Monique Wittig, to understand cultural intelligibility not only to assume the fundamental difference between masculine and feminine, but to reproduce it" (*Undoing Gender* 208). Today, as Butler has observed, "to assume that gender always and exclusively means the matrix of the 'masculine' and 'feminine' is precisely to miss the critical point that the production of that coherent binary is contingent, that it comes at a cost, and that those permutations of gender which do not fit the binary are as much a part as its most normative instance" (*Undoing Gender* 42). Similarly, in Gallop's comments, "to refuse authority does not challenge the category distinction between authority and castrated other, between 'subject presumed to know' and subject not in command" (*Daughter's Seduction* 21). No doubt, however, the traces of heterosexuality on us all are undeniable, and it is in this sense of "transatlantic divide" that Braidotti (following Irigaray) returns to "sexual difference" as a positive other: "One can clearly choose to disguise this fact, to avoid all the morphological wrappings of sexual difference, such as a penis actually attached to a desiring male body, biblical-style penetration, fecundation of the ovum via penetration of sperm-carrying penis into vagina. One can sing the praises of masquerades and polyvalence, such as lesbian cross-dressers who pump iron: one can choose to emphasize all kinds of prosthetic or technological alternatives, such as women with strap-on dildos and penis-less men, but that will not suffice to erase sexual difference. A mere shift in the empirical referent cannot alter the somatic and psychic traces of sexual otherness" (*Metamorphoses* 46).

Simultaneously, the feminist split in subject positions opens a quest for interconnections between the psychoanalytical theory of desire and the social practices of enforced normativity (prohibitions and exclusions enforced upon the subject). In view of these interconnections, Irigaray's fantasmatic mother emerges from the semiotic and psychic realm of feminine sexuality that, in psychoanalysis, becomes a form of language, a sexual reflector (*speculum*) in which bodies can speak. To ignore this language is to ignore the multiple possibilities of potential expression still trapped in the phallic representation of desire. Feminine sexuality, as multiple, complex, and ex-centric to phallic genitality, disengages thus, to follow both Irigaray and Braidotti, the question of the "embodied subject" from the hold of Lacanian (and Kristevan) psychoanalysis. It brings the little girl's body back into play: a body as an interface of multiple codes (race, sex, class, age) that refuses to separate the discursive dimension from the empirical, material, or historical one (Braidotti, *Metamorphoses* 25). It also holds the debate about trans/gender in proximity to the presence of real-life women (albeit predominantly of those who occupy Western spaces of culture). Irigaray's political philosophy of the maternal posits the subversion of identity (proposed by Butler) as having sex-specific connotations and consequently requiring sex-specific strategies (rejected by Butler). In the end, what clearly becomes central in this political and conceptual feminist debate is a "task of creating, legitimating, and representing a multi-centred, internally differentiated female feminist subjectivity, without falling into relativism or fragmentation" (Braidotti, *Metamorphoses* 26).

Following Irigaray's objective, also Cixous extends the/a mother's biological ability to produce nourishment into the agency of a feminine voice. It is through the mother's own milk that she can regain her ability to speak against the historical silence: "Voice: milk that could go on forever. Found again. The lost mother/bitter-lost. Eternity: is voice mixed with milk" (Cixous and Clément 93). In an attempt to work out a "deconstruction" of the mother entangled in the Western logos, Cixous proclaims an *écriture féminine*, which, as she declares, "will not let itself think except through subjects that break automatic functions, border runners never subjugated by any authority" (Cixous and Clément 91-92). Defining a feminine practice of writing is as impossible a task as defining the semiotic chora "with an impossibility that will continue; for this practice will never be able to be *theorized*, enclosed, coded" (92). Although the latter does not mean that *écriture féminine* does not exist, it does imply that "it will always exceed the discourse governing the phallocentric system," and in positing the mother "beyond" the symbolic function, it will takes place somewhere other than in the territories subordinated to philosophical theoretical domination (92). Thus, Cixous's rebellious conflation of the semiotic and the feminine is as likely to lead to madness as to recovery, and emerges, in Wittig's, and later Butler's, analysis of the semiotic, as an ineffective subversion of phallogocentric culture. Rejecting the ontological difference between the sexes as heterosexual and capitalist, both Wittig and Butler (following Rubin) posit gender as an activity without substance, rendering "sexual difference" a fundamentally political enterprise reproducing compulsory heterosexuality. Gender, in this performative mode, becomes a process by which women are marked off as the female sex, and men are conflated with the universal, but both remain subjugated to the institution, in Foucault's sense of the term, and to sexual normativity in Rich's sense. Thus, Butler takes her leave from psychoanalytical theories of sexual difference, in particular the transformative power of the semiotic in subverting the representational economy of phallogocentrism. As commented by Butler, the "multiple drives that characterize the semiotic constitute a prediscursive libidinal economy which occasionally makes itself known in language, but which maintains an ontological status prior to language itself" (*Gender Trouble* 80). It is this peculiar location beyond the symbolic that plays a crucial role in establishing the Continental feminist subjectivity of the semiotic, and I explore it in detail in the subsequent parts of this chapter. At this stage, I address several French feminist positions that will continue to frame my discussion of subjectivity in relation to the Freudian/Lacanian *unconscious*.

Evaluating the historical and psychoanalytical concepts of interpretation, Cixous's, Irigaray's, and early Wittig's positions refer to the concept of linguistic oppression, "a confusing static for the oppressed, which makes them lose sight of the material cause of their oppression and plunges them into a kind of a-historic vacuum" (Wittig, *Straight Mind* 22). Contrary to Irigaray, however, who sees the subject position as structurally masculine, Wittig believes that women can enter into the subject position, repossess it, and redefine it for their own purposes. In her *The Straight Mind*, Wittig argues against Cixous's ambiguous view of giving birth to a text, which is "delivered" from the body (Cixous's *Souffles*). Addressing Lacan, and his "blind" followers, Irigaray meets here with Wittig's position: "You refuse to admit that the unconscious—your concept of the unconscious—did not spring fully armed from Freud's head, that it was not produced ex nihilo at the end of the nineteenth century, emerging suddenly to reimpose its truth on the whole of history" ("Poverty" 80). Both Irigaray and Wittig reject explicitly psychoanalytic "science" as the sanctioned object of "theoretical qualifications" while believing that the "singularity" of psychoanalysis "stemmed from the fact that it can never be complete," that it has to remain "interminable." In fact, it can only take place without subordinating itself to the analyst mastery over the analysand ("Poverty" 83). If desire is always "particular," as Irigaray inquires, how "can you force analytic material into a lexicon or a syntax, with schemata, graphs and mathemes which have nothing to do with this particular analysis" (84)? Wittig, however, encourages women to use language to express their own meanings, without falling into the deconstructive complexities of Irigaray's and Cixous's *écriture feminine*. Rather in her quest for an alternative symbolic, Wittig argues against the interpretation of the *unconscious* as an instrument in the hands of a master and his revelation. As a way out of the enslaving cultural vacuum, Wittig asserts the *unconscious* as an alternative awareness of a presymbolic space activated in the literary process. In *Les Guérillères*, she writes: "you say there are no words to describe it, you say it does not exist. But remember. Make an effort to remember. Or, failing that, invent" (89). The archaic mother, for

Irigaray, and Wittig and Cixous for that matter, represents such an invention in response to the failure of memory (and consciousness), and as a locus of repressed female desire she becomes central to "everything" which "must be (re-)invented to avoid the *vacuum*" ("Volume" 56). Clearly, this psychoanalytical identification with the archaic mother works to consolidate feminist collective identity as that of cultural un/belonging. In tracing this un/belonging of the presymbolic mother, both Continental and Anglo-American responses to psychoanalysis accentuate the inadequacies of a symbolic translation (transference) of the maternal experience from the semiotic "mystery," a presymbolic knowledge, into conscious processes of naming. Traces of the archaic mother investigated in the narratives to follow clearly resonate with sexual difference, or more specifically "with a certain binary misreading of sexual difference, the opposition phallic/castrated" (Gallop, *Daughter's Seduction* 124). Drawing our attention to the Lacanian preference for metaphor, and his subsequent repression of metonymy, Irigaray and Gallop compare "the latency of metonymy" to the "hiddenness of the female genitalia," concluding that while a metaphor consists of supplanting one signifier with another, "a metonymic interpretation supplies a whole context of associations. Perhaps this metonymic interpretation might be called feminine reading" (*Daughter's Seduction* 129). This feminine reading (or writing) would thus be a response to "sexual difference" that, both in Lacan's theories and in Irigaray's post-Lacanian critique, "is not a simple binary that retains the metaphysics of substance as its foundation" (Butler, *Gender Trouble* 27). If the masculine subject is a construction produced by the law that prohibits incest and forces an infinite displacement of a heterosexual desire, the feminine is never a mark of the subject. Rather, the feminine is a symbolic signification of lack, "a set of differentiating linguistic rules that effectively create sexual difference" (27). The witch as an archaic figure, or the Freudian/Lacanian *unconscious* that comes to represent her, converges theoretically with Lacan's configuration of hysteria and the language of the *unconscious* as a signifier of "something quite other than what it says" (Lacan, *Ecrits* 155). Precisely this "other" constitutes an important and complex fantasy of gender that can be broken down into a number of subconsciously present figures: a monstrous womb, vampire, hysterical, possessed body, femme fatale, witch, oracle, castrating mother. Of a particular importance is the phrase "monstrous-feminine," as coined by Creed, and emphasizing the importance of gender in the construction of monstrosity. For Creed, expanding Kristeva's psychoanalytical inquiries, the numerous figures of the "monstrous-feminine" have been obscured between abjection and horror on the one hand, and fetish and fantasy on the other. Hellenistic culture provides an important insight into this complex fantasy. Significant for the following analysis is the distinction between the domesticated wife and mother (Penelope) and the untamed monstrous forces (Scylla and Charybdis), the female devouring whirlpools, threatening both to masculine and feminine identities. This split, to follow Creed, has a number of consequences for psychoanalytically based theories of sexual difference: "On the one hand, those images which define woman as monstrous in relation to her reproductive functions work to reinforce the phallocentric notion that female sexuality is abject. On the other hand, the notion of the monstrous-feminine challenges the view that femininity, by definition, constitutes passivity. Furthermore, the fantasy of the castrating mother undermines Freud's theories that woman terrifies because she is castrated and that it is the father who alone represents the agent of castration within the family" (Creed 151).

Following Creed's differentiation, it becomes clear that the archetypes of the archaic mother of the semiotic and the phallic (fetishized) mother are quite distinct: the archaic mother represents a terrifying fantasy of sexual difference, while the phallic mother is a comforting fantasy of sexual sameness (8). Ultimately, the archaic mother falls into an alternating, and therefore ambiguous, fantasy of a castrating/castrated woman, persistently represented in the mythology either as "the tamed, domesticated, passive woman or else the savage, destructive, aggressive woman" (Creed 116). On the contrary, the phallic (fetishized) woman is designed to deny the existence of these castrating/castrated feminine images, reminding us of the delusional character of the child's wish to be the mother's Phallus, marking the subject's capacity to distinguish between fantasy and reality. Likewise, the distinction between the maternal figure of the pre-Oedipal semiotic and the Oedipal mother as object of sexual jealousy and desire has been obscured. As Madelon Sprengnether notes in *The Spectral Mother* (1990), the archaic mother emerges in patriarchal culture as a "shadowy" figure, a figure of subversion, a threat to masculine identity. Never a major theme in Freudian drama of the father-son relationship, the archaic mother has a ghostlike function: "Like the spirit of the mournful and unmourned Jocasta, she haunts the house of Oedipus" (5). According to Sprengnether, this "spectral" appearance of the archaic mother relates to "spectacle," "speculation," and "suspicion," "while its immediate source is the Latin *spectrum*, meaning, simply, an appearance" (5). All these connotations explain and consolidate the symbolic unrepresentability of the semiotic "mother": "In English a specter is a ghost, a phantom, any object of fear or dread. Freud's representations of the preoedipal mother evoke all of these associations. She is the object of his fascinated and horrified gaze, at the same time that she elicits a desire to possess and to know. In her disappearing act, she evades and frustrates his attempts at grand theory at the same time that she lures him, like a fata morgana, into the mists of metapsychology" (5).

The archaic mother thus collapses in the symbolic order into Creed's figure of the *monstrous-feminine*, that is, into "the pre-symbolic or dyadic mother, the mother who is thought to possess a phallus" (Creed 21). As a trace of abjection and horror, as well as of an ambiguous comfort, this archaic mother has been silenced (somewhat comparable with the Lacanian "real" to which there is no access in language), and, in reference to Irigaray's standpoint, it is this silence that perpetuates the most primitive phallocentric fantasies and projections of a woman. As feminist psychoanalysis suggests, her maternal body has not been marked by "symbolic castration" but by "the real incision" evoked by the cutting of the umbilical cord, deferred and perpetuated by the cultural presence of the scar, the navel. The umbilical cord, cut and eliminated, represents desire for the *anoedipal* space (an alternative antidualistic figuration of intersubjectivity; see Deleuze and Guattari). The loss of the cord refers to the "real" loss of the mother, Irigaray's extension of the Oedipus story. Her figure of the passionate Clytemnestra, who "certainly does not obey the image of the virgin-mother that has been held up to us for centuries, will go as far as a *crime passionnel*: she will kill her husband" (Irigaray, *Bodily Encounter* 36): "Why?...out of jealousy, out of fear perhaps, and because she has been unsatisfied and frustrated for so long. She also kills him because he sacrificed their daughter to conflicts between men, a motive that is often forgotten by the tragedians. But the new order demands that she in her turn must be killed by her son, inspired by the oracle of Apollo, the beloved son of Zeus: God, the Father. Orestes kills his mother because the rule of the God-Father and his appropriation of the archaic powers of mother-earth require it. He kills his mother and goes mad as a result, as does his sister Electra. Electra, the daughter, will remain mad. The matricidal son must be saved from madness to establish the patriarchal order" (36). In this order, the figure of archaic mother fuses into that of the Furies: the chthonic, subaltern female forces, the remnants of the maternal who inflict "temporary" madness on Orestes, and, like the ghost of his mother, pursue him in vengeance, haunt him wherever he goes. "They are women in revolt, rising up like revolutionary hysterics against the patriarchal power in the process of being established" (37). On the one hand, thus, the mother's entry into the Law of the Father appears as an incorrect, inaccurate entry marked by the mother's separation and dispossession from culture. The denigration of the patriarchal mother (ascribed to her reproductive functions), is furthermore "endorsed by her," since she "teaches the infant to abhor what she herself comes to represent within the signifying practices of the symbolic" (Creed 165). And, in connecting with the abject as an invisible and culturally discarded umbilical cord, the mother connects with the obscene bodily displacement and a demarcation between the intimate womb/placenta (Irigaray's and Kristeva's *chora*) and the externalized body inscribed with the name of the Father.

Linking this unrepresentability of the semiotic chora with the intimacy of the umbilical cord leads us to the psychoanalytical concept of the navel as cultural category for analysis of the archaic mother. As explored by Bronfen, the navel appears as "the enmeshment between connection, incision, bondage, and negation, that is, the bond constructed over naught" (Bronfen 19). The enmeshment both conceals and discloses the existence of the mother, since the "knotting occurs over a wound, both shielding and constructing a site within which are the remains of the traumatic impact" (19) of separation. The human body, always already the knotted subject, appears thus as "a resilient trace of bondage, vulnerability, and incision" (8); however, to speak of the knotted subject is not only to emphasize "that the subject is split and multiple but how this multiplicity offers a new means of integration" (9). To follow this possibility in the subsequent analysis of the narratives, I employ the witch figure as a particularly resilient trace of the enmeshment converging with Bronfen's psychoanalytical reading of the *omphalos*, Irigaray's *placenta*, and Kristeva's *chora*: all three present a theoretical confrontation of the old subject within the new subjectivities. Central to my investigation is the hysteric strategy of self-representation and self-performance of the witch: her negotiation between what has been split in culture: the *phallus* and the *omphalos,* "the maternal emblem, commemorating the now invisible umbilical cord" (Bronfen 19). As represented in all the narratives selected for discussion in this chapter, the witch of the semiotic chora is a fantasmatic creature of the womb with no other place in the symbolic order but that of un/belonging. I designate her as *om-phalic*, that is, providing a traumatic passage, a type of umbilical cord connecting to the symbolic: Trauma, "not capturable through representation or, indeed, recollection" often renders memory incomplete, "known through the gap that disrupts all efforts at narrative reconstruction" (Butler, *Undoing Gender* 153). The symbolic, attractive and indispensable because of its linguistic potentialities, will be thus reached through "the imaginary," or as Gallop has put it, "by knowingly being *in* the imaginary" (*Daughter's Seduction* 60). Upon scrutiny of the semiotic functions in the language of the narratives, I will also argue that phallogocentric discourse does not employ/enslave the witch in the same way as it employs/enslaves the mother who has entered the symbolic. The witch as a trace of the archaic mother may in fact provide a therapeutic treatment for the "real incision" and the cultural denigration of the mother who, according to Irigaray, is "in danger of being reduced to a fiction" ("Limits" 107). Marking the possibility of the mother's rebirth and reevaluation, the "archaic witch" clearly manifests a desire to connect the semiotic chora with the symbolic. Consequently, the witch comes to represent "the imaginary and the unconscious" in a way that the patriarchal (castrated) mother in her "empty gestures of an enforced everydayness" (107) does not. The psychoanalytical value of the witch draws thus on the limits of the woman in culture, and, in delineating these limits, on the mother in particular. While recalling the phallocentric construct of the witch as a specific trace of the unencumbered woman, the witch will come to represent a ghost of the repressed, uncanny absence of the archaic (rather than phallic) mother. It is precisely the archaic absence, the mourning for the archaic Thing (Kristeva, *Black Sun* 41) that links the witch with the return of what has been eliminated or repressed: the fear of slipping back into the abyss of the semiotic fantasy, of losing ourselves on the way. Here, in agreement with Kristeva's readings of Freud, the term *heimlich* signifies friendly, familiar, and intimate, as well as concealed, deceitful, and malicious; hence the positive term is already marked with its own negation. At the same time, what these narratives also express is our passionate desire of such a frightening return. They serve as examples of positing the witch as disturbing (sick, mad, obsessed, maniacal), and through all this a figure who embarks on new processes of responding to the unfitting model of the Oedipus complex, which, as Irigaray has argued, "states the law of the non-return of the daughter to the mother" and "cuts her off from her beginnings, her conception, her genesis, her birth, her childhood" ("Limits" 105).

The symbolic beginning of language lies thus in the negation of loss. Signs are arbitrary because language begins with a negation of loss that turns into a denial and becomes internalized as the subject enters the symbolic patterns of signification. The contingency of the witch, her scattering across culturally forbidden spaces, the leakage of fluids across her bodily boundaries, and her transgression of the norms of such leakage (Purkiss 81) are central in delineating the ways to trace that irretrievable loss back. The following narrative makes her a symbol of that lost un/belonging, and therefore a desirable maternal space as an effective means of overcoming the primordial alienation. These "critical" or "clinical" narrative encounters, to use Deleuze's notions, are possible by the peculiar nature of symptomatology: unlike "etiology, or the search for causes" and "therapeutics, or the search for and application of a treatment" that are integral components of medical approach, symptomatology occupies a "sort of neutral point, a limit that is premedical or sub-medical... located almost outside medicine...where artists and philosophers and doctors and patients come together" ("Mysticism" 132-34). This space, called sometimes art and sometimes literature, harks back to the imprint of the archaic loss as the very condition of being that haunts us from the inception of subjectivity.

Politicizing Locations of the Hysterical Body

Angela Carter (1940-1991), seen as both representative of and distinct from late 1970s and 1980s feminist writers, has often been criticized for her reactionary style and a language trapped in "conservative sexism" (Jordan 128). Belonging among the most controversial and original British texts, her writings indeed resist conventional encapsulation. There is no doubt that "The Lady of the House of Love" (1975) and "The Scarlet House" (1977), the two short stories to be discussed here, are far from being straightforward in sending their message. However, I agree with Merja Makinen that often it is the critics, and not Carter, "who cannot see beyond the sexist binary opposition" (23). To follow Makinen's inquiry as to whether reactionary forms can be rewritten, I propose an analogous question: Can the fantasy of the castrated/castrating woman be rewritten for the reason of "becoming"? Can she stop speaking as a "hysteric" and transgress the symbolic structures that have kept her half-wild, half-tamed, half-imaginary? In the two stories chosen for discussion here, Carter repeatedly returns to the image of castrated woman, "addressing it as ideological issue, as narrative device, as image" (Wyatt 59). In Creed's vein, she works both with and against this fantasy, disrupting the inherent but artificial opposition between the castrated and castrating vagina. The stories are of interest here precisely in this context: as powerful, although not immediately obvious, revisions of this image.

Both the figure of a female vampire in "The Lady of the House of Love," and Madame Schreck in "The Scarlet House" serve as prototypes of the castrated/castrating woman who produces death instead of life. Her barren womb (alluding to her suspended reproductive function) clearly associates with the tomb and opens several questions pertaining to the denigration of female autonomy in culture. This prototype, proposed in my analysis as an "archaic mother," is no longer of a female but of an apocalyptic, abysmal sex, infinitively poised between the woman and the monster. As with all other cultural attributes of the nonconforming female body, it is defined in terms of hysterical sexuality. Arguing that this sexuality is never expressed in a vacuum, Carter sees sexual expression as bound to the "metaphysics" of femininity (*Sadeian Woman* 11). A reader of Foucault, she formulates her interpretation of power structures and places them in the context of partly abused and partly romanticized female sexuality. Her aim is to demystify the hysterical locations of female sexuality by disrupting the prohibitions placed on the body, a strategy deriving from the conviction that "where there is a desire, the power relation is already present" (Foucault, *History* 83). Following this premise, Carter recognizes the agency of sanctions that appropriately channel and sublimate sex into a "negative relation" with power: "rejection, exclusion, refusal, blockage, concealment, mask....Where sex and pleasure are concerned, power can 'do' nothing but say no to them" (*History* 83). In producing absences and gaps about sexuality, power "overlooks elements, introduces discontinuities, separates what is joined, and marks off boundaries" (83). In this vein, Carter's compelling returns to desire and sexuality have a clearly defined transgressive and therefore political purpose. The critical (feminist) task for Carter is to understand not only how the category of female desire has been historically and socially determined, restrained, and repressed but also how it interacts with the very structures of power. As in Butler's theory, female desire "takes on the meaning of 'repressed' to the extent that the law constitutes its contextualizing frame." The law identifies this "repressed desire" as such, "circulates the term, and, in effect, carves out the discursive space for the self-conscious and linguistically elaborated experience called 'repressed desire'" (*Gender Trouble* 65). Carter proposes, then, to emancipate the repressed through textual psychoanalysis, through repeated returns to various interrelated prototypes of nonconformity (*vagina castrata, femme fatale*, bitch/witch, whore, etc.). Associated in my analysis with the biblical abyss as "a female place of difference" (Pippin 68), it is in particular *vagina castrata* that offers an insight into Carter's textual practice.

As examined by Pippin, the abyss in the Apocalypse represents otherness, disorder, and chaos; it is "a bottomless pit," "the interior of the earth, a place of exile, the original flood waters under the earth, chaos, the primordial goddess, the source of the universe, the underworld" (68). In *Apocalyptic Bodies*, Pippin analyses the fifteenth-century depiction (in the *Hours of Catherine of Cleves*) of the mouth of the abyss, which can signify both female pleasures (castration desires) and their annihilation. Of all these associations, the abyss-as-chaos and the underlying phallogocentric desire to control and rationalize its "disordered" forces are especially important for Carter as defining female sexuality. However, for both Pippin and Carter, "to locate oneself at/in the pit means to be in a place that is no place, no ground, no bottom, no context" (Pippin 65), that is, somewhere outside of the symbolic order. The female abyss can serve here as a reminiscence of the semiotic chora, a trace of the archaic mother, "both a part of earth and a part of the body, the female sexual organs" (70). Simultaneously, the biblical abyss is a metaphor of eternal punishment, "a prison-house for evil monsters" (67-68), a womblike torture chamber, or, as Creed observes with reference to soulless bodies, "a collapse of the boundaries between human and animal" (10). To pause at Creed's analysis, the "bodies without souls" (the vampires), the "living corpses" (the zombies), the "corpse-eaters" (the ghouls), and the robots and androids are "creatures, whose bodies signify a collapse of the boundaries between human and animal, and the witch (one of her many crimes was that she used corpses for her rites of magic) also belongs to this category" (Creed 10). As a container of these categories, the abyss holds vampires, monsters, phantoms, and witches, all of whom project abjection and horror and simultaneously fascinate by their ambiguous status: "The abyss is the black hole in space; what happens when one entered the abyss is still only speculation. Is the abyss where eroticism and death are linked?...As a 'rupture within discourse' the abyss is a hysterical place, when the veil or lid is taken off. Or is it a place of *jouissance*?" (Pippin 74). Such imagery of the abyss as a hysterical mouth with teeth is intrinsic to Carter's exploration of sexuality. "If conditions of power are to persist, they must be reiterated: the subject is precisely the site of such reiteration, a repetition that is never merely mechanical" (Butler, *Psychic Life* 16). Carter's exploration, like Butler's, undermines the Freudian elevation of the father as representing the agent of castration within the family. In "The Lady of the House of Love," Carter's rewriting of the Dracula story, the father and son are long gone and dead, and we are faced with an alienated girl as the only "legitimate" agent of castration. Defined in terms of her paternal license to kill, the vampire (queen) does kill but with a hesitance, and out of somewhat "indoctrinated" obedience. If Stoker's Dracula has been inscribed with the uncontrollable, monstrous paradigm of the Other, and has as such challenged the most sacred phallocentric values (heterosexuality, masculinity, whiteness, or marriage [see Levy]), Carter's figure of the vampire surpasses all these challenges by her monstrous gender transgression. "With the hectic, unhealthy beauty of a consumptive" ("The Lady" 202), she seduces as a female, penetrates as a male, and drains as a vampire, transforming thus into a different species, an abysmal fantasy of the other sex: the uncanny, the unsettling, and the supernatural. Carter's queen, as if Butler's melancholic drag queen in reverse, demonstrates precisely how femininity becomes an ideal that everyone always only imitates. In Butler's mode of mimetic incorporation of gender, Carter's queen, apparently female, succumbs thus into gender mourning.

Following in this respect Braidotti's observation that mourning has acquired a quasi-religious quality in psychoanalysis, Carter is far from idealizing the vampire's condition. Ultimately, the vampire, as a monstrous-feminine, is both sarcastically underscored and potentially liberating. She seems to be mute (or has nothing to say), because as a phallocentric fantasy/fetish she represents "the Other of any conceivable Western theoretical locus of speech" (Felman 9). Moreover, her sexuality is suspended in a vacuum of bodily indisposition: she "has no mouth with which to kiss, no hands with which to caress, only the fangs and talons of a beast of prey" ("The Lady" 206). Following this suspension of sexuality, her monstrosity is displaced, forced into a cultural formula that is incongruent with her particular existence. In Stoker's novel, Dracula lures, consumes, and pollutes in the name of forbidden pleasure (in order to transcend his unfulfilled sexual desires). In Carter's text, the queen lures and consumes without dedication, as if continuing Nosferatu's "tradition" by lack of other choices. Thus, in performing her vampire's duties, the queen is a "drained hysteric," void of all desires except the one to overcome her nature: "In her dream, she would like to be human; but she does not know if that is possible... She loathes the food she eats; she would have liked to take the rabbits home with her, feed them on lettuce, pet them and make them a nest in her red-and-black chinoiserie escritoire, but hunger always overcomes her. She sinks her teeth into the neck where an artery throbs with fear, she will drop the deflated skin from which she has extracted all the nourishment with a small cry of both pain and disgust" ("The Lady" 197-98). Owing to her alienated degeneration, the desires and needs of the vampire represent different patterns of perversity. Rather than a figure of jouissance, she is a psychopathological failure, Dracula's hysterical mimesis, a "cave full of echoes" and "a system of repetitions" (195). Repetition, specifically, is of importance here since it harks back to all the frustrations of unrecognized desire that the queen has buried in her readings of Tarot. She indeed is perverse, but not because of her vampire's nature, rather, precisely because of its lack. Her nightly rites (darkness, blood, oral sadism, bodily wounds, and violations of the law) are of no particular meaning to her since she does not take pleasure but simulates her fate. "The carnival air of her white dress emphasized her unreality, like a sad columbine who lost her way in the wood a long time" (204). This internal landscape suggests an entrapment in someone else's fate from which she cannot extricate herself. And so, the plot she enacts is short and cruel: When she leads her ignorant victims to her bedroom she ratifies the fantasy of orgasmic pleasure. Her victims "can scarcely believe their luck" (204). The pleasure, coming as a result of its internalized prohibition, climaxes in her violent mouth and subsequently causes death. It is in that double role of the castrated and castrating vagina that the queen's sexuality experiences an internal split, a break indicating suspension of meaning and hence suspension of pleasure. Thus, Carter's queen, although powerful through her castrating potential, is a wounded fantasy of gender: displaced, afflicted and consumed by her own contaminating and consuming nature, which makes her effectively "lifeless" in culture. She is "like a doll, or, more, like a great ingenious piece of clockwork...inadequately powered by some slow energy of which she was not in control; as if she had been wound up years ago, when she was born, and now the mechanism was inexorably running down" (204). This lifelessness speaks to some of the key issues raised by Carter as pertaining to suppressed human sexuality and its running against the fascination and liberating power of sadomasochistic fantasy. Although representing different concepts, the *unheimlich* (uncanny) desire and the feeling of abjection (as its result) are brought together in Carter's story in a form of eating disorder that destabilizes identity. The queen has the hysterical body of a dispossessed and indisposed little girl (very much in the sense of a Deleuzian process of becoming). She is weak, "shivered all the time, a starveling chill, a malarial agitation of the bones...sixteen or seventeen years old, no more" (202). She endures a hysterical indecisiveness that suspends her Nosferatu identity between the repressed familiarity of the *unheimlich* that was once *heimisch*, familiar: "the prefix '*un*'...is the token of repression" (Creed 54) and the abjection (repulsion) of her own inability to control her cravings. The moment in which these two concepts converge has been captured by Creed: "abjection is not something of which the subject can ever feel free—it is always there, beckoning the self to take up the place of abjection, the place where meaning collapses. The subject, constructed in/through language, through a desire for meaning, is also spoken by the abject, the place of meaninglessness—thus, the subject is instantly beset by abjection which fascinates desire but which must be repelled for fear of self-annihilation. A crucial point is that abjection is always ambiguous" (10).

In representing this ambiguous desire of self-annihilation, the queen's devouring lips call into mind the entrance to the abyss in Pippin's analysis, and suspend her pleasure in a pain produced by disconnection from the repressed (uncanny) maternal territory. As such, the queen provides an important model for the culturally suspended, but sexually and subconsciously fascinating, archaic mother. She can be castrated (disconnected), but her mouth—as the abyss—is dangerous: "her extraordinarily fleshy mouth, a mouth with wide, full, prominent lips of a vibrant purplish-crimson" (Pippin 202), the morbid mouth of a whore. The disconnected/disconnecting lips converge thus with the abysmal mouth: a hole that leads to the abject leftover after the cut of the umbilical cord. Both are tropes for nourishment, for a connection with the Kristevan "ab-jetted" mother, a relation that has been broken, removed, and sealed. What seems crucial in Carter's story is that the queen represents the deficiency and asymmetrical incompleteness of female sexuality and this incompleteness, according to Carter, has to be reformulated, reinvented. However, the story does not provide us with any explicit reformulations, since the castrating queen insists on her own castration and nothing seems to prevent her from choosing this self-destructive path. The queen's longing for a "savior" (who would bring an end to her melancholic tomb/womb existence) converges with the actual arrival of a young man, who, as a Freudian type of hero, descends into the world of the female uncanny. Coming from the world of the living, this patriarchal figure signifies all that the queen is not: light, life, destruction of the tomb...the stake/phallus, and enforcement of the law (Creed 71). Carter, in particular, draws our attention to his logocentric applications of reason that are of little use when he sees the queen in "a hooped-skirted dress of white...fifty or sixty years out of fashion but once, obviously, intended for a wedding" ("The Lady" 202). In her elusive presence, the rational subject encounters the *unconscious* that seeks to negate "the repressive predominance of 'logos'" (Felman 8), but in Carter's text, comes out as a pathetic failure. The rational abilities presented by the hero are crucial to the queen's fate, since he will recognize her hysterical condition and, inadvertently, erase her contradictory existence. Although there is no room in her drama for this intervention, the queen breaks the set of rituals of the House of Nosferatu, and indeed through an inadvertent improvisation, hurts her finger with the broken glass. In inflicting this very concrete physical wound (a discharge of blood) on her body, Carter's queen initiates a deconstruction of her own vampirism, a "dismembering" that leads to a transformation into a human. "Her painted ancestors turn away their eyes and grind their fangs. How can she bear the pain of becoming human?" ("The Lady" 207). This initiation into the human order represents a momentary fulfillment of the queen's long-suppressed desire to overcome her "nature." But does her dying monstrosity redefine the myth of "castrated woman," that despite local variations, continually "states that women are terrifying because they have teeth in their vaginas, and that the women must be tamed or the teeth somehow removed or softened—usually by a hero figure—before intercourse can safely take place" (Creed 2)? Can she break away from the logic of polar oppositions? Ironically, what Carter depicts in her story is both what we are long familiar with (the phallocentric taming of the uncontrollable forces of the phallic woman) and what comes as a dismantling of that very belief. The phallocentric presumption that he/the doctor figure can actually deliver the cure is demystified by Carter (the doctor virtually erases her heroine), and finally rejected as no option for solving the identity dilemma. Breaking into death, soon after becoming human, the vampire transforms into a dark purple rose, a pretentious gift to the "savior," and a literal trace of her castrated condition. Her death, and especially its transitory character, leaves many questions unanswered. Both unpredictable and inevitable, it clearly has two sides: the political (Carter's demystification of the phallocentric entrapment), and the psychoanalytical (as a liberating act of "return" to the Freudian *unconscious* through the uncanny). In both cases, the presence of erasure (her death) is important insofar as it acknowledges the inadequacy and provisional status of the archetype employed. Alluding to Freudian endeavors to categorize female sexuality through the *unconscious*, Carter comes close to Felman's perception of Freud as an important though inadequate and eventually helpless analyst. In softening the medicalization of the vampire's body (removing her castrating organs), there is no promise of a cure. Instead, the queen's newly attained humanity is devastating: it is a failure resulting from "theoretical blindness to the woman's actual difference" (Felman 9). By demonstrating this failure to recognize the complexity of (female) sexuality, Carter draws on the psychoanalytical (and perhaps feminist) failure to remove female desires (sexuality) from the "symmetrical conception of otherness" (Felman 9). The queen's erasure is most certainly an ironical act, since it can never be accomplished, and she will remain present/absent both in the form of an (archaic) trace and in the form of explicit bodily frustration. Hence, following Felman's "new type of theoretical reasoning" (Felman 9), Carter's philosophy both rests upon and reasserts the importance of different logic that would account for the actual difference.

While "The Lady of the House of Love" examines the subversive and non-compatible zones of castrating/castrated desire, "The Scarlet House" explores multiple female castrations, blurring individual bodies into a plural, repetitive oppression. In this story, Carter's imagery of the Freudian *unconscious* is far more elaborate, as it illustrates her attempt to consider it in relation to knowledge and power and to the organization of gender and its function and structure. In its indication of subconscious processes at work, the story unfolds as if dispersed throughout the deck of Tarot cards. Its elements, speaking in the name of the *unconscious*, could be restored once all the cards are laid out. But the narrator is a wounded fortune-teller, devoid of memory and unable to reveal the details. The "ambiguous unconscious, sometimes an ensemble of repressed libidinal drives, sometimes the face of language as Other, is never anything that could count as a social agent" (Fraser, *Justice Interruptus* 159). In addressing the plural quality of the repressed drives, Carter opens the story with the imagery of a "bordello" and renders it a metaphor of confinement, a prison of enslavement and hysteria. Representing the structures of the *unconscious*, the Scarlet House imitates a violated, abused, and erased memory, recognizable through marginal moments such as slips of the tongue and other odd disclosures. There, women (kidnapped, raped, and drugged) are kept under restraint. The house "embodies" female sacrifice and "annihilation" ("Scarlet House" 421), a monstrous accumulation of indistinguishable female bodies: a bordello and an asylum "built of white concrete...very much like a hospital, a large terminal ward" (418). The master of the house, the Magician of the Tarot (also known as the Count), is "dedicated to the obliteration of memory" (419), to the erasure of women's (personal) memories and lives. As a possessor/professor of the phallus, he represents an omnipotent psychopathic analyst who lives out the fantasy of female fragmentation: "Dedicated as he is to the dissolution of forms, he intends to erode my sense of being by equipping me with a multiplicity of beings, so that I confound myself with my own profusion of pasts, presents and futures" ("Scarlet House" 423). The Count, whose character is embedded in Lacanian theory, recognizes "him/self" as a totalized concept and impersonates the Mirror (Stage), the entrance to the symbolic: "He has methodology. He is a scientist, in his way" (424). The structures of his house, once entered, engulf the captured women and force them into a physical and cultural displacement designated in the story as chaos: "Preparing chaos with the aid of a Tarot pack" (417), the Count/Magician "sits in a hall hung with embroideries depicting all the hierarchy of hell, a place, he claims, not unlike the Scarlet House...Chaos [a type of return to the 'real'] is coming, says the Count, and giggles" (417). In denigrating "feminine" identity, he follows one particular formula in Freudian argument that there is no libido other than masculine: "There is no woman but excluded by the nature of things which is the nature of words, and it has to be said that if there is one thing about which women themselves are complaining at the moment; it's well and truly that—it's just that they don't know what they are saying, which is all the difference between them and me. Meaning what? Other than that a whole field, which is hardly negligible, is thereby ignored. This is the field of all those beings who take on the status of the woman—if, indeed, this being takes on anything whatsoever of her fate" (Lacan qtd. in Rose 27).

Thus, returning to Lacan's central question (who is speaking: I or the language?), Carter questions the illusions structuring the authority of the psychoanalytic critic, and her approach parallels in many aspects the theoretical discussions of Wittig's, Irigaray's, and Baym's rejection of Lacanian psychoanalysis. Exposing the cartography of the power relations that define fantasy while correcting and structuralizing female *unconscious*, Carter puts into question the very representation of the fantasy, of the imaginary constitution of the sociosymbolic world. Subjectivity as a socially mediated process encounters here the loss of the maternal in which specific memories take on the characteristics of formless, intangible, semiotic space—shadows of culture. Like Lacan's laws in Baym's interpretation, the Count's laws are unbreakable, as he seems to be a far less "forgiving" father than Freud (287). To follow Baym, Lacan's "deployment of the castration complex as the basis of the model for the symbolic order into which children—boys—are initiated, takes one particularly 'sexist' element in Freud's rich system (which contains many ungendered insights) and makes it the whole story" (287). This observation is particularly relevant to Carter's story, since it directly alludes to Lacan's pronunciation condemning women to silence: "Lacan's ideas of women belong neither to his realms of the real nor the symbolic, but to his imaginary. Both Freud and Lacan make haste to correct the fantasies of others that their own prevail. Not truth, but power, is the issue" (Baym 287). Carter's story reveals a similar practice of identifying woman with sexuality as a target of power and of structures normalizing what Freudian woman should be, or possibly want to be. Normalized sexuality is, "therefore strictly an *ordering*, one which the hysteric refuses" (Mitchell and Rose 28). This practice, in Carter's story, has long been in effect, and it continues: "Soon everywhere will be like the Scarlet House" ("Scarlet House" 417), a "well-locked (whore) house [maison bien close]" that Irigaray defined as "a matrix coiled back on/in its interiority [that] is not women's. Except sometimes in their maternal phallicism, or their impotent mimicry" ("Volume" 63). Also in *Expletives Deleted*, Carter elaborates on this thought: "my life has been most significantly shaped by my gender...I spent a good many years being told what I ought to think, and how I ought to behave, and how I ought to write, even, because I was a woman and men thought they had the right to tell me how to feel, but then I stopped listening to them and tried to figure it out for myself but they didn't stop talking, oh, dear no. So I started answering back" (4).

The practices of Carter's bordello seem to go hand in hand with the Law of the Father and its phallogocentric institutions, delineated in the story as implementing totalitarian persecution, prohibition, and finally extermination of female desire. The Count is the only authority—the persecutor, the interrogator, the monarch. Again, Carter alludes to a Foucauldian belief that "at the bottom, despite the differences in epochs and objectives, the representation of power has remained" the same (Foucault, *History* 88). This might indicate that there is nothing inherently subversive or even transformative at stake in Carter's erotic depictions of multiple sexual pleasures. In fact, the erotic fascination with power, violence, and sadomasochistic scenarios underpinning Carter's narrative presents itself as a point of contention in the assessment of violence in the sexual representation of the female subject. If "in political thought and analysis, we still have not cut off the head of the king" (*History* 88), then equally a distinction must be made between the authoritarian violence and the transgressive potential of erotic sadomasochism and violence. A distinction that, as Carter suggests, is often difficult to maintain: "When they play the Tarot Game, Madame Schreck sits on a small throne. They bring down the Count's special book, the book in black ink on purple paper that he keeps hanging from a twisted beam in his private apartments; they open it up and spread it out on her open lap, to mimic her sex, which is also a forbidden book" ("Scarlet House" 424). To follow this Tarot imagery, the Count's crucible is reinforced by the presence of the phallic woman, Madame Schreck (German for "horror"), who confirms the illusion of "a comforting fantasy of sexual sameness" (Creed 8): "Madame Schreck waited to greet me in the scarlet splendour of her satin dress that laid open to the view of her breasts and the unimaginable wound of her sex" ("Scarlet House" 421). Trapped in ideological/political and imaginary terms, the cruelty inflicted by this fantasized woman serves its specific patriarchal purpose. It is in and during the cruelty performances, carefully arranged and supervised by Madame Schreck, that the women disappear; their "disembodied voices rustle like dead leaves" as they "stretch out hands to touch one another, lightly, to lay a finger on one another's mouths to assure [them]selves a voice issues from that aperture" (425). Most certainly, reminiscent of Morgner's patriarchal carnival of witches (as analyzed in the first chapter), Carter's carnivalesque performance is not a liberating procedure; its form is symmetrically enclosed in the institutional (sociocultural and linguistic) structure. A deconstructive composure of Carter's text lies thus in a demystification of the structure and its inherent split rather than in a theoretical departure "beyond" or "outside" the structure. Carter's version of the witch, modeled as a *femme fatale*, reproduces invariably phallocentric prohibitions, fears, and anxieties. This figure is still so deeply entangled in the Western metaphor of the terrible mother that she is far from becoming a therapist figure, and equally far from transgressing her subordinate subject position. Trapped within Butler's "matrix of normativity," Madame Schreck impersonates a rapist, a female violator that lives in a "male-dominated society" and "produces a pornography of universal female acquiescence" (*Sadeian Woman* 20-21). She is "Miss Stern with her rods and whips, Our Lady of Pain in her leather visor and her boots with sharp, castratory heels," and as such she represents a distorted fantasy of power: "a distorted version of the old saying 'The hand that rocks the cradle rules the world.' This whip hand rocks the cradle in which her customer dreams but it does nothing else." If she is cruel, it is not "for her own sake, or for her own gratification. She is most truly subservient when most apparently dominant" (21).

In agreement with Creed's theory, the fantasy of a phallic woman in Carter's story provides indeed an explanation as to "why the male might desire to create a fetish" and might want "to continue to believe that woman is like himself, that she has a phallus rather than a vagina" (Creed 116). Madame Schreck is such a fetishized phallic construction designed to negate the complex existence of "woman" as castrated/castrating. "The Count has given her a blue robe to wear over that terrible red dress that reminds us all, every time we see it, of the irresoluble and animal part of ourselves we all hold in common, since we are women" ("Scarlet House" 424). Although not without a subversive potential deriving from her sexual transgressions, a message underlying the story, Madame Schreck is dominated by the presence of the phallus, and cut off from her own pleasures and sexual sovereignty. Her image draws on the symbolic analogy between the female mouth and the labia of the vulva, both holes to be penetrated, hollow body entrances. To be sure, it is not without irony that despite her particular reality, Carter's cruel woman exists entirely as a fantasy figure, more a surface for projections than a real being. Like the vampire's mouth, Madame Schreck's mouth resembles a lascivious surface, and her labia/vulva is part of what makes her abject: "[She] eats small birds such as fig-peckers and thrushes; she puts a whole one, spit-grilled, into her huge, red mouth as lusciously as if it were a liqueur chocolate and then she spits the bones out like the skin and pips of a grape. And she's got other, extravagant tastes as well; she likes to gorge upon the unborn young of rabbits. She acquires the foetuses from laboratories; she has them cooked for her in a cream sauce enriched with the addition of the yolk of an egg. She's a messy eater, she spills sauce on her bare belly and one of us must lick it off for her. She throws open her legs and shows us her hole; the way down and out, she says" ("Scarlet House" 419). Her role is to devour (a phallic fantasy of the vaginal orgasm), not to speak, although it is not her inability to speak that is to be feared but a shift in focus towards the other mouth, that is, towards her unrestrained sexuality. Her "hairy hole" promotes a paradigm of an enslaved, fetishized eroticism to which "we all pay homage as if it were the mouth of an oracular cave" (424). In linking eroticism and death, here again, the mouth alludes to the abyss through which "we must all crawl to extinction, one day; unless it is the way to freedom" (428). This apocalyptic landscape of sexual bodies alludes to the Foucauldian institutional structure in which everyone is caught, those who exercise power just as much as those over whom it is exercised, and where sexuality is always a matter of institutional definition ensuring homogeneity by systematically denying and excluding difference. In this way, Carter's tales are indeed "forms of repetition" (Gallop, *Daughter's Seduction* 104), forms of subversive returns (in Butler's vision) produced by the desire to reveal the semiotic and the suppressed and to place the semiotic in the context of the subliterary forms of pornography, ballad, and dream.

As a nonlinguistic space, the semiotic chora is rendered foremost an illusion, a different form of fantasy in a far-away land of feminist utopian projections. Instead, Carter's attempt to retrieve female sexuality from "imaginary facts" rests on a systematic remembering of the oppressive experience. Since women of the Scarlet House are subjected to castration without knowing or remembering it any more, Carter's message (like Wittig's) is to remember through the *unconscious*. In "Scarlet House," the *unconscious* is symbolized by the hawk as a trace of the narrator's memory about her capture, "preserved as an image, or an icon" ("Scarlet House" 427). Once more in Foucault's vein, Carter's point is not that the social and its collective imaginary is dreadful, but that its power is dangerous, and that the ethico-political choice we have to make every day is to determine the main danger. As Butler puts it, power forms the subject by "providing the very condition of its existence and the trajectory of its desire," and, in this sense, it is "not simply what we oppose but also, in a strong sense, what we depend on for our existence and what we harbour and preserve in the beings that we are" (Butler, *Psychic Life* 2). In Carter's textual images women themselves, physically and violently forced back into conformity with an artificial norm, generate their "misunderstanding of sadomasochistic transgression" (Treut

234). This misunderstanding (from the sexual science of the last century to current collective consciousness) manifests itself as the "lack" of pleasure, of art, and the transgressive thought of the sadomasochistic universe as represented in Sadeian or in Sacher-Masoch's writings (Treut 235). Carter elaborates on the importance of physical transgressions (rape, sadomasochistic devices) precisely by taking into account the submissive role assigned particularly to women: "The whippings, the beatings, the gougings, the stabbings of erotic violence reawaken the memory of the social fiction of the female wound, the bleeding scar left by her castration, which is a psychic fiction as deeply at the heart of Western culture as the myth of Oedipus, to which it is related in the complex dialectic of imagination and reality that produces culture. Female castration is an imaginary fact that pervades the whole of men's attitude towards women and our attitude to ourselves, that transforms women from human beings into wounded creatures who were born to bleed" (*Sadeian Woman* 23). In this elaboration, the opposition between "law" and its underlying heterosexual matrix and "revolt" has been dismissed as artificial. Instead, they appear as politically prevailing tools that come to represent a complex structure of mutually supportive resistances. Subjection, in Carter's understanding, consists in the fundamental dependency on a discourse that is perhaps not chosen, but that, paradoxically, initiates and sustains the agency of the subjected in resistance (Butler, *Psychic Life* 2). Voyaging through this resistance, Carter's "writing the body" undermines the symbolic value of passive affirmation with which "woman" has been impregnated. Her stories do not posit the witch as an archaic semiotic figure, but insist on a dialectical relation between the prelinguistic phase (the *unconscious*) and the order of language. Demystifying mythic, ready-made versions of women and exposing them as devices intended to obscure "the real conditions of life" (*Sadeian Woman* 5), Carter leaves her texts "unfinished," "written with a space for the reader's activity in mind" (Makinen 25). Her insistence on an open-ended structure is a strategic proposal for heterogeneity and plurality of sexual locations. It offers an active challenge to "the myth of patience and receptivity" in which the meaningful semen penetrates "a dumb mouth from which the teeth have been pulled" (*Sadeian Woman* 5). Such a mouth cannot speak and cannot be productive, but only hysterically reproductive. Carter's defence against this silent reproduction is a deconstructive use of irony, activated best if the reader is informed by feminism (Makinen 25). The hysterical displacements of the female vampire, of Madame Schreck, and in particular of the women in the Scarlet House intermingle therefore with political locations, positions from which to speak against cultural and linguistic displacements. This may happen even if the only available language is that of the (Freudian) *unconscious*, as is the case in the following narrative, which continues the theme of the split between mothers and daughters while depicting the phallic mother as the very cause and source of fe/male denigration.

The Defeat of the Maternal Subject

In *Siostra* (Sister), published twenty years later (1996) in the context of postcommunist Poland, Małgorzata Saramonowicz explores similarly problematic traces of the witch as the terrible (phallic) mother. Saramonowicz belongs among the most promising Polish writers of the decade, placed along third-wave-feminist or feminism-informed authors such as Izabela Filipiak, Natasza Goerke, Manuela Gretkowska, and Olga Tokarczuk (on this, see Kraskowska). *Siostra*, a "psychological thriller," offers an exceptional perspective on motherhood within the postcommunist debates on abortion rights. As in Carter's story, the witch figure in *Siostra* embodies the destructive features of the abysmal vagina, and operates in and from the oppressive position of home. In discussing this narrative (clearly articulating a Deleuzian relation between text and clinical psychology), I draw on Juliet Mitchell's psychoanalytical insights into the sibling relationship and connect these insights with de Beauvoir's and Kristeva's theories of the maternal subject. Following such discourse in the light of Deleuzian theory, my discussion focuses on the question of the "stolen" body, which undergoes fabrications of opposable organisms in the process of constituting itself as a subject. This multifaceted vision of "becoming-a-subject," a dynamic entity defying the established modes of representation, opens new identifications within the symbolic (social meaning) and is thus of crucial importance for explorations of images that represent the female experience of proximity to the mother's body. As I argue, this exploration is central to Saramonowicz's narrative, albeit in a twist that turns the maternal subject into an overwhelmingly oppressive and inescapable bodily force.

Placed in the context of a dysfunctional family (mother-son-daughter) living in dilapidated housing conditions somewhere in late-communist Cracow, the narrative unfolds in the form of a fragmentary dialogue, revealing gradually the following key relationships: Marysia is the daughter of an absent (traveling) father, who is pursuing his career in medical science, and an attractive, persistently present (phallic) mother. Marysia's first coma occurs when she is six for which the reasons are obscure. Her mother dies from a brain tumor when Marysia is eighteen and this abruptly instilled maternal death coincides with Marysia's suicide attempt and the hospital's decision to separate her from the family. At this point, Marysia's brother, older by several years, moves to the United States and the further relationship between the siblings is tantalizingly uncertain. As an adult, Marysia becomes Maria, bearing her mother's first name (hence, Deleuzian "becoming-the-subject" and Irigaray's proximity of the maternal), and lives in Warsaw with Jakub, her husband. While writing her dissertation on eighteenth-century French prose, she *becomes* pregnant and undergoes another subject formation, at which point the maternal proximity converts into a physical symptom. How much this symptom is about unreadability (of the *unconscious*) and how much about the subject's resistance to the process of becoming remains at the reader's will to explore, as Maria secretly refines her academic work into "Insects—the motif in literature and art" and locks it in the university computer with an intricate system of passwords. During early pregnancy she experiences another coma and remains in a sleeplike state, first in hospital, then at home, until her "body gives birth" and dies. The sequence of these two bodily enactments is of importance to the very subject of becoming, as the process of giving birth intermingles with dying, such that it is unclear whether Maria's body gives birth in the process of dying or whether the newborn emerges from the body which ultimately resisted *becoming* and, thus, no longer lives.

Jakub (in a way, competing with the reader to make some logical sense of Maria's story) knows very little about Marysia: There are no family pictures, no childhood souvenirs, no connections, except for Maria's occasional but uncertain identification with her father. The reason for her "disease" and the controversial figure of her brother seem to be related in Maria's subconscious flow of thoughts, but the links are vague and contradictory. Is her brother a male hysteric in suspended/unfinished psychoanalytical treatment? Is Maria a victim of his sexual fantasies? Perhaps. The narration is neither from his position (both his and the mother's positions are silenced) nor that of Maria. The entire narrative, opening with Maria's pregnancy while in a coma and ending with her death, speaks the language of Maria's subconscious desire of dying, brought on by *encephalitis lethargica* ("sleeping sickness"), in which life itself has been reduced to a monstrous construction. What comes through the *unconscious* suggests a particular fascination with death as a release from irremediable tension, harking back to the most excruciating wounds of her childhood. Her "sleeping sickness," or *catatonia* (a term coined in 1869 by Karl Kahlbaum) draws our attention to the significance of the symptom. The typical signs are described by Kahlbaum "as a state in which the patient remains entirely motionless...devoid of any will to move or react to any stimuli....The general impression conveyed by such patients is one of profound mental anguish, or an immobility induced by severe mental shock" (Moskowitz 984). The symptom, Maria's bodily paralysis, is thus a reaction, but to what? In this psychoanalytical vein, I link Saramonowicz's disfiguration of the mother figure with Mitchell's analysis of fe/male hysteria in the Freudian context of trauma and death. Analyzing Dora, Freud's female hysteric, Mitchell refers to death and trauma as "crucial to the onset and manifestations of hysteria" (33) and emphasizes the long unrecognized importance of the siblings' relationship in the Oedipus myth. Drawing on this emphasis, I begin this analysis by associating Dora's life history with that of Marysia and argue that Saramonowicz offers a pathological extension of the Freudian case. Although the "mother has been ignored by Dora... there is one even more strikingly buried player in Dora's life history: her brother Otto, older by eighteen months" (Mitchell 100). *Siostra*, as the title suggests, has a similar underlying meaning; it is the story of Maria's, transmitted in the form of a repressed dialogue between the siblings: Marysia, speaking from the position of the female victim, and Piotr, speaking as and representing an aggressive, omnipresent cockroach.

In the *unconscious*, Marysia is reduced to the defenseless, sickening body of a vulnerable child, the yet underdeveloped but already overwhelming body that the conscious Maria hopes to erase from her memory, but that stubbornly returns as a mental anguish, an immobility induced by involuntarily re-enacted scenes of her rape. Moreover, Saramonowicz does not tell us explicitly who, if anyone, has been repeatedly violating Marysia. This parallels Bronfen's suggestion that the hysteric "broadcasts a message about vulnerability...of the symbolic (the fallibility of paternal law and social bonds)...the vulnerability of the body, given its mutability and mortality" (xiii). Hence, there is much more to Marysia's illness than the Freudian assumption about a mother giving all of her attention to her son (in Mitchell's analysis, illness "was" and still "is a standard means of getting more attention when one is jealous of one's siblings" [102]). In my interpretation, precisely because of the vulnerability of the girl/daughter, motherly love in *Siostra* turns into a mother-son conspiracy in search of a forbidden *jouissance*. Like Dora, Marysia tries "her best to remedy this situation by always having the normal childhood illnesses, which she caught...in order to get more attention" (Mitchell 103), especially from her absent father, but her "illnesses" and dreams are to be recognized also as an escape mechanism. The children's rhyme about a carrousel, a recurring motif of a danger that is playful and safe, has been replaced in her *unconscious* by a permanent warning; it is not the carrousel, but "the witch [that] is waiting, calling us from afar" (Saramonowicz 54; unless indicated otherwise, all translations from the Polish are mine). Constant fear of abuse and her alarming awareness of entrapment suspend Marysia in the vacuum of her obsession with the type of mother who does not come to her rescue. This figuration of "mother," a figure disassociated from comforting maternity, forms a persistent narrative resistance to the maternal subject as imposed on women's bodies. The reproductive function, standing for the voracious and violent aspects of the maternal, entirely destabilizes the current illegalization of abortion in Poland, voiding the maternal from all romanticized notions of dutiful and natural female pleasures. On the contrary, the maternal subject in *Siostra* suggests a seductive and manipulative force, which leads to repetitive sequences of trauma. Reminiscent of Freud's argument, the crucial factor determining the repetition of trauma is the presence of mute, disintegrative experience and its lack of access to language. The child's illnesses are illusory escapes and substitutes for security, entailing frequent in/voluntary hospital treatments (un/consciously) facilitated by coma and suicidal tendencies ("Inhibitions" 1953-74).

"So Freud tells Dora: The dream shows 'that we were here dealing with material which had been very intensely repressed'...'the mystery,' says Freud to Dora, 'turns upon your mother.' As the listener to Dora's tales, Freud is not her father but her mother in the transference. Dora not only tells things to Freud the therapist, she talks to her mother" (Mitchell 96). Although Maria does not have the luxury of a psychoanalyst with and through whom to speak, she opens a long repressed dialogue with her mother while communicating with the fetus in her womb. This dialogue recalls (but conceptually also extends beyond) de Beauvoir's description of a "drama...acted out within the [pregnant] woman herself" (521): "She feels it at once as enrichment and an injury; the fetus is a part of her body, and it is a parasite that feeds on it; she possesses it, and she is possessed by it; it represents the future and, carrying it, she feels herself vast in the world, but this very opulence annihilates her, she feels that she herself is no longer anything...the pregnant woman feels the immanence of her body at just the time when it is transcendence: it turns upon itself in nausea and discomfort; it has ceased to exist for itself and thereupon becomes more sizable than ever before" (521). In her transference, especially in the transference to the mother, Maria repeatedly asks the foetus to die within her body. As articulated by the *unconscious*, she speaks to the repressive dominance of "mother," and wants to make this dominance recede. The powerful figure of the mother, alluding to "the unacknowledged foundation of the social order" (Whitford 25), is actually reinforced by the absence of the maternal comfort. The umbilical cord, as a symbolic passage to semiotic pleasures, leads her back to a hollow orgiastic mechanism, a giant maternal cockroach. Addressed as "he" in Maria's *unconscious*, the pronoun can refer to the cockroach brother or cockroach mother, or even perhaps to the foetus in Maria's womb as a symbolical extension of the monstrous semen: "It is becoming claustrophobic. The walls swell with wobbling blackness. Slimy, busy shapes continue to cloy and squeal. I am His. My body is His. There is no salt, no moisture, or the icy cave any more. There is hell. They grunt and whisper there. Scratch, scratch, scratch....But he enjoys this heat. I can hear him laughing at me. The walls have eyes. Thousands of eyes stare at me, following me and you. Little one, he knows that you are here. He knows everything. There is no way out of here" (Saramonowicz 43-44). By refusing to give life to her child, Maria ultimately rejects life as a perennial deferral of suffering because of her (becoming a) mother, "a newly shaped body filled with madness and death. And there is nothing that can stop this" (123). In its obvious premise, I read this rejection of life as an ethical gesture pointing towards a basic human (woman's) right to abortion. But beyond the obvious political aspects of the subject's autonomy, Saramonowicz's account can be read as a decisive rejection of the inherent maternal symbolism engulfing female bodies, a refusal to participate in and endure the "becoming"-of-the-mother. To follow this insight further, I turn to Kristeva's discussion of "primary narcissism": the self-importance and self-absorption of the maternal subject to which "we can definitely attribute existence," and yet, there too, "we are caught in a paradox" ("Stabat Mater" 161). The very discreet presence of the Virgin Mary in both narrative figures, the mother (Maria) and her daughter (Maria), at once consolidates and disrupts the role of a patriarchal mother as a silent agent of reproduction in search of her *jouissance*. Such deconstructive positioning of the Virgin Mary, the only sanctified model of "woman" in the Polish literary tradition, provides a distinct, innovative, and quite daring perspective on the maternal. Although in Maria's *unconscious* the mother is silenced, the projection of silence is not that of a victim, but of a violator. Her violence, linked with her potentially inadequate, uninhibited cultural condition (of being and having "one"), is already implicit, if unexplored, in de Beauvoir's concept of the mother. In *The Second Sex*, de Beauvoir posits the mother as a figure that is both discontented (sexually frigid, unsatisfied, or socially inferior) and through all that threatening to the infant. Once we realize the difficulties in which "mother" is entangled, "how many desires, rebellious feelings, just claims she nurses in secret, one is frightened at the thought that defenseless infants are abandoned to her care" (540). Offering an important expansion of both de Beauvoir's and Kristeva's theories, Saramonowicz discloses her own version of the Oedipus myth in the light of entrapment in the maternal trauma and hysterical erasure of the mother. In linking the mother's narcissism with the symbolic, Saramonowicz grants her an ambiguous position as an object and subject of desire, as someone who not only "is" the phallus, but who also possesses it (an achievement in a collaboration with her son). Indeed, in an attempt to resolve her condition by breaking the Law, Saramonowicz's mother fanatically "seeks to compensate for all her frustrations through her child" (de Beauvoir 540). In sanctioning incest, she unfolds her forbidden desire at her children's cost. The breaking of the incest taboo dividing the universe of sexual choice into permitted and prohibited sexual patterns (see Rubin) results in trauma: "To mother. Even your death does not diminish my hate. I will never forgive you. You are just as much responsible for my persecution...Come to me. Come to me. She calls. The witch. But I keep my eyes shut, and so she thinks that I am falling asleep...She says that Cockroaches only live in the kitchen. And then Baba Jaga captured the children and threw them into the oven. And there it was so hot, so hot, so hot and they were screaming, screaming their wits out and...She hugs me, pulls the cover over...And Baba Jaga devoured Jaś first, and then she devoured Małgosia...I immediately have to open my eyes to look up. Yes, he's there. Ready to jump on me. Lurching" (Saramonowicz 82, 159)

Clearly, the mother's transformation into a devouring monster can be viewed as one of the contemporary avatars of Baba Jaga, a witch descending from the Brothers Grimm's tale, "Hansel and Gretel," about siblings trapped in a chocolate house. Since there are no significant evil constructions of the mother in the history of Polish Christianity, the role of the terrible mother remains vacant. Should the terrible mother be understood as a fantasy, a reminiscence of the archaic, promiscuous, and unencumbered female body, she will be found in the images of stepmothers from the world of folklore and fairy tales. This association is particularly strong, since in the Brothers Grimm's story there is no mother and the witch is an extension of a mean and always hungry stepmother. *Siostra*, however, depicts the witch as a biological mother, and so the bonding with her (as well as the inability to break the process) is therefore culturally sanctioned as "natural." Unlike Gretel in the tales of the Brothers Grimm, Marysia is not able to outwit the witch and fails to succeed in saving either herself or her brother. Subsequently, the witch-mother in *Siostra* slowly consumes her children. Furthermore, the siblings' fascination and fear, as experienced in front of the chocolate house in Grimm's story, have been transferred in *Siostra* into the regions of premature sexuality, divided unequally between sister and brother. As designed by the witch-mother, the sister (an object of desire) and her brother (a figure of the abject and fear) reinforce mutually their entrapment. One experiences the abjection, the other exposes desire: both, however, live out their mother's fantasy of incest. This culturally tabooed fantasy, and indeed, its unthinkable veracity, afflicts the narrative structure. It may be, as Butler would argue, that what is culturally unthinkable "is precisely a fantasy that is disavowed," the horrible act that a parent (mother) was willing to perform, "or it may be that what is unthinkable is precisely their convergence in the event" (*Undoing Gender* 156). But in order to read such a broken narrative structure, one becomes a reader of the ellipsis, the gap, the absence. In reading such absence, as is the case with Jakub in Siostra, we encounter a necessity to rethink the prohibition itself: the incest taboo that sometimes protects against violation, and sometimes becomes the very instrument of a violation: "what counters the incest taboo offends not only because it often involves the exploitation of those whose capacity for consent is questionable, but because it exposes the aberration in normative kinship, an aberration that might also, importantly, be worked against the structures of kinship to force a revision and expansion of those very terms" (*Undoing Gender* 160).

While the Freudian Oedipal analysis results in Dora's "failure to be like, as good as, or just be her brother," it "is the sibling situation that thrusts Dora back on to loving her mother and her father" (Mitchell 103). Dora and Maria attempt to recover by winning the father's attention, and while Dora for a time succeeds, Maria's recovery is deemed to fail. In both cases, to follow Mitchell's insight, the pursuit of the father "is still a part of craving for a mother" (Mitchell 107). In Marysia's case, this craving has been entirely suppressed by her fear of the maternal authority: "Fear became my skin. But fear does not kill. It paralyses" (Saramonowicz 137). Her slipping into coma manifests such a paralysis and indicates a refusal to live and communicate in an oppressive time/space relation. Hence it might be seen as a return to the state of nonspeech, the un/attainable semiotic chora. As some trauma scholars suggest, traumatic experience requires postinterrogation, not only for the sake of testimony, but above all for the sake of cure (see Caruth; Brison). "Piecing together a dismembered self seems to require a process of remembering in which speech and affect converge....The results of the process of working through [the traumatic memory] reveal the performative role of speech acts in recovering from trauma: saying something about a traumatic memory does something to it" (Brison 56). Dora's "desperate, exuberant protests, the labile identifications and demonstrative sexualising of every contact are a way of asserting an existence that has gone missing" (Mitchell 107). If "Dora is trying to find a place for herself" (107), Maria, on the contrary, refuses trying, and her imaginary refuge turns into a hysterical identification with death. Marysia's final refusal of this process, involving her and her baby's physical death, manifests her silent and only available form of protest against participation in the experience of fear. Ultimately, it manifests the defeat of the maternal subject. "Unconsciousness. It is better than consciousness. Oblivion is better. Ignorance is better. Emptiness is better. Non-existence is better" (Saramonowicz 13). In this somewhat concluding part of my analysis, I focus on the Freudian death drive, which monopolizes Maria's *unconscious* in a form of desire or craving for death. In her discussion of the negative therapeutic reaction (resulting in such desire), Mitchell wrote that Freud had difficulties "accepting Dora when she asked to come back in treatment because he knew she did not want to recover" (147). Contrary to Freud's hypothesis of the "death drive as innate and in perpetual struggle with an equally innate life drive linked to a sexual drive," Mitchell "combines the sexual drive with the death drive as well as with the life drive, as maybe innate, but all activated by the initiating trauma of the conditions of life" (139). In setting thus the life drive against the death and sexual drives, Mitchell argues that the "life drive is activated by the presence of caretakers, as opposed to their absence" (147). Since in Marysia's life there are no actual caretakers, the death drive develops into the dominating drive. Maria's identification with her father could be seen here as an initial attempt to endure life, at the expense, however, of the repression of trauma. As Caruth has argued, "the impact of the traumatic event lies precisely in its belatedness, in its refusal to be simply located, in its insistent appearance outside the boundaries of any single place or time" (9). On the contrary, the ability to recover the past "is closely and paradoxically tied up, in trauma, with the inability to have access to it" in consciousness (152-53). Projecting a quasi-normal family life, Maria fails to tell her father what happens during his long absences and learns to maintain her desire for dying as an invisible illness. "They sealed my lips. They had to do it, so that I would not say anything. They want me silent. All of them. Perhaps in the grave. Death is soft, warm and clear" (Saramonowicz 90-91). This particular desire for death is not only a medical diagnosis, it is the victim's pathological identity carefully suppressed in the *unconscious*. It is the absence and presence of the child's hysteria, caused by the rejection and subsequent objectification of the child by the mother (as caregiver). The hysteria, and the exploitable body of the hysteric, renders Maria a passive sexual object of desire. Maria's role is that of a doll, a toy removed from the comforting realm of a little girl's pleasure, and transformed into a passive and speechless instrument of oppression. She fulfills this role in her withdrawal to a biological/physical reflex of motionlessness, typical for insects and certain mammals enacting tonic immobility in situations of danger (Moskowitz 997). Saramonowicz incorporates in her narrative the German scientific term *Totstellreflex* ("death-feigning behaviour"; 25) signposting a posttraumatic stress disorder.

Maria's hysterical lethargy, a particularly strong nervous reaction to pregnancy (as diagnosed by doctors in the narrative), could be also interpreted as "a horrid warning" (Carter, *Sadeian Woman* 124) sent by the mother to the daughter: "If the daughter is a mocking memory to the mother—'As I am so you once were'—then the mother is a horrid warning to her daughter. 'As I am, so you will be.' Mother seeks to ensure the continuance of her own repression, and her hypocritical solicitude for the young woman's moral, that is, sexual welfare masks a desire to reduce her daughter to the same state of contingent passivity she herself inhabits" (124). In refusing and accepting this passivity, experienced through pregnancy and memories of rape, Maria performs a passive/active abortion, not only of her baby but most importantly of herself as an extension or reproduction of her mother. The thought of repetition of her own experience, as projected onto her foetus, is unbearable. In this final retrospection, moving from Freud's phallocentric focus towards the Lacanian metaphysics of *lack*, Saramonowicz endows everybody, including the absent father and Maria's husband (Jakub), with hysterical, pathological predispositions. In trying to find some rational explanation for Maria's coma, Jakub explores the truth, but his attempts are obscured, reminiscent of a cabbalistic initiation, a search for something that is perhaps only imagined. As he believes initially, "Maria, like every other woman, has simply strange whims and fits. Fits are yet to be an illness" (17), or otherwise unattainable, as he begins to suspect that the injury Maria had sustained in her childhood was too painful to share with anyone, an injury she had to hide "deep inside" (72). Mitchell's portrayal of hysteria, and the patient's identification with the dead as a crucial mechanism in coping with hysteria, helps us to measure the depth of Maria's anguish. In hysteria, to follow Mitchell, "the anxiety is so extreme that the subject takes avoidance action" (35). Imitation of death can be brief, but when compulsively repeated, it manifests an erasure of the subject, a drive towards the inorganic, towards annihilation. Indeed, the more Jakub reads through Maria's secret academic research, the more he realizes the significance of the mother in Maria's drive towards death: She is the "reason, the source of evil—the mother, femininity in its entirety, betraying, sly, emotionless. Mother...replaced by the cockroaches [that] took the burden of childish hatred away from her" (77). In configuring the mother as an executioner, an assassin entangled in her own sexual obsessions, and shifting the castration anxiety from a man to a woman, Saramonowicz complicates the feminist standpoint on "female oppression" in the phallocentric structure. The mother is thus present and powerful, but her archaic power, the promise of semiotic pleasures, collapses, as she becomes a monstrous and oppressive substitute for the phallus. As in Creed's definition of the archaic mother, she is the one "who is thought to possess a phallus" (21). This mother is multiplied and confused in Maria's subconscious with her brother, who incorporates the phallus in place of his father. As an eroticized phallic abuser, the mother becomes the source of all evil, embodying a transgression of the ultimate. In breaking the incest taboo, she implies a shift away from the moral sanctions of her daughter's body, and suspends her son in a simultaneous horror (denial) and fascination provoked by her apparent castration. As a result, her son becomes a male hysteric, who "has failed to resolve the Oedipus complex, failed, that is, to internalize a prohibition on parental incest" (Mitchell 21). He "feels catastrophically displaced...because another [the father] stands in his place" (107). The fear of being engulfed in the dark abyss between the mother's legs lives in him as a projection of the violence he performs on his sister's body. The psychotherapeutic conversation, a video recording discovered by Jakub and involving the brother, makes this projection of violence and fear explicit: "I tried to overcome it, but there was something pushing me towards the door of her room. I used to approach her room quietly, surreptitiously, step by step....I saw my shadow move, and I knew that she saw it too. I think that she did not sleep at all. She used to lie there with her eyes open, night after night, and she waited...—Did you beat her?—No, I had never beaten her. I did not have to.—We had cockroaches....I have never seen anybody so afraid of them. If a cockroach was near her, she was ready to do everything. Everything. I did not even have to tie her. Only so that it would not touch her. But they did not obey. They crawled into all possible directions, went into every opening, as cockroaches do. Mother took them away later into the kitchen.—What for?—She used to talk to them" (Saramonowicz 151).

Drawing on the concept of "the peer and sibling as mirror," Mitchell points out that "Dora had a focus for her identification with another child" in her brother (106-07). In Marysia's life there is no space for a similar identification, since she does not seem to have a human brother. The leading image for the brother-rapist is that of a cockroach, an armoured rider—his armour protecting him against unnecessary compassion. However, Maria's compulsive repetition of a childhood trauma, and her obsessive need to analyze every detail of her anguish, indicate her search for a brother-as-mirror. She documents her phobia (her obsession with re/search) in her dissertation, which provides detailed descriptions of cockroaches and their monstrous mutations, their eating habits, and general behavioral patterns. This investigation circulates in her *unconscious* in the intermingling images of her brother's unrelieved sexual cravings and cockroaches penetrating her body. The mother is never activated in these subconscious reminiscences, except through the monstrous *jouissance* of the brother who is speaking to Maria as a cockroach commemorating the moments of her defenselessness. This monstrous *jouissance*, however, stubbornly returns to the unencumbered, engulfing, and specifically female sexuality of the mother. The question thus turns on the relations among memory and desire. As Gallop comments, a "desire must insistently repeat itself until it will be recognized. If satisfaction, the reduction of tension, were the true goal of a desire, it might find a more efficient path than repeated insistence, just as, if the goal of the death instinct were simply the reduction of all tension, it could surely find a quick path to death. Thus repetition...is the effect not so much of the frustration of a desire but of the lack of recognition of a desire" (*Daughter's Seduction* 104). The abysmal and authoritarian body of the mother, beyond which there is no law to refer to, is the underlying repetitive force of Maria's "acting dead," her motionless and speechless states because of omnipresent maternal desire.

In conclusion, I argue that Saramonowicz places the mother deliberately in the context of a Freudian cognitive alliance with the boy, who sees only that the girl's body is penis-less. Yet, if the girl's sexual organs were admitted as the possibility of another libidinal economy, the phallocentric system of sociolinguistic projections of her absence/insignificance would collapse. What the mother communicates to us is that an attempt to subvert phallocentric entrapments can turn into a traumatic experience. As the figure of abjection and horror, the witch-mother indicates permanent displacement; she is first devoured by the (symbolic) abyss, and then taken as its very incorporation. As a displaced, fragmented, or disfigured subject, she is subsequently rejected and erased. The memory of an inevitable distortion of all forms returning to the maternal womb/tomb intermingles both with the belief in maternal comfort and with the fear of the terrible mother. The paradox of the mother, trapped in the biological repetition of life, is that she neither continues nor discontinues, but only suffers, as does Kristeva's mother in her yearning for the Law: "And since it is not made for [her] alone, [she ventures] to desire outside the law. Then, narcissism thus awakened—the narcissism that wants to be sex—roams, astonished.... Nothing reassures, for only the law sets anything down. Who calls such a suffering jouissance? It is the pleasure of the damned" ("Stabat Mater" 175). Equally, in Saramonowicz's account, the mother cannot continue as the origin of life; rather, she incorporates the paradox of the subject in process, drawing our attention to the sociopolitical implications of rejection, loss, and death. Speaking through the *unconscious* against the cult of the motherhood as superimposed on the subject in the social, the narrative confronts us with a concrete, physical collapse of the female body into a grave-mound composed of abject umbilical cords. It thus confronts us with the unexplored and difficult spaces of desire to defeat the maternal. Indeed, the assumption of the mother's phallic sufficiency, her coherent and self-contained identity as an autonomous subject, is disrupted in the narrative by the collective death of the mother, daughter, and subsequently child. This particular synthesis of death, as a form of narrative's conclusion, is the only resolution to the trauma offered—a dissolution, in fact, indicating the collapse of the female subject entrapped in the maternal identification.

I follow these intricacies of the maternal as explored by Sara Maitland in her two short stories, published in the 1980s in Britain. Employing absences, distortions, and slippages of the symbolic, Maitland's narratives continue to speak from the position of the rejected cord (the refused mother). In a resonant parallel to *Siostra*, Maitland draws on the phallocentric force of entry to the symbolic that subjugates the girl/woman's love and desire of and for another woman. This, to continue with Irigaray, throws her into a whirlpool of "a normative hetero-sexuality" (Irigaray, Speculum 54) and results in uprooting her from subjectivity.

The Narrative Fraud of the Phallic Mother

Sara Maitland's narratives, "Cassandra" and "The Burning Times," published in a collection of stories *Women Fly When Men Aren't Watching* (1988), address this suspension of subjectivity in the context of both remembering and contesting the memories of the lesbian/virgin body, its history of cultural incompatibility, and its connectedness with the maternal, semiotic, and fantasized spaces of articulation. The narrative fraud, as I suggest, refers both to the formal structure of the stories (bordering on invented memory and reconstructed history) as well as to their contents (narrative fantasies of a woman who is thought to possess a phallus). In discussing this fraud, I employ Kristeva, Irigaray, and Butler's theories, which all, differently, focus on female subjectivity and its troublesome absence from mainstream Western mythology and history of thought. What Maitland narrates are imagined biographies (*herstories*) about women such as those Irigaray has written about: "uprooted from their subjectivities" and thrown into a whirlpool of "a normative hetero-sexuality, normal in our societies, but completely pathogenic and pathological" (*Bodily Encounter* 44). Similarly to the narratives discussed so far, I examine her texts as forms of feminist therapy posited as alternatives to the established Western canon, and inherently divided between the methodical (logical, reasonable) and the semiotic fantasy that is out of phallogocentric control. In this political sense of absence, the unwritten biographies are reinvented in terms of femininity, identity and language, and critically performed/narrated. As such, they are extremely effective in removing some of the perturbing distinctions between written and unwritten tracks of history, specifically in the contexts of madness and desire, licensing the use of both in terms of what is missing rather than what is true.

Maitland's "Cassandra," a narrative reminder of Christa Wolf's feminist rewriting of Cassandra's story, is a reconstruction of history that might never have taken place, a biography (if Cassandra ever had one) fraught with fantasy of the semiotic and left untranslated. Maitland's Cassandra is a prophetic "madwoman," unable to recognize herself as an autonomous, consciously speaking (and remembering) subject. My reason for choosing this particular story is its bizarre context of the "phallic woman," collapsing into a phallocentric fetish on the one hand and transforming into a threat to masculine identity in the form of a Python on the other. This conflict, to follow Bronfen's insight, crystallizes in the act of Apollo's slaying of the snake Python, who was both Gaia's child and guardian of the omphalos. After Gaia's defeat, and the displacement of her prophetic powers through Apollo's sacrificial murder, "the mephitic cleft in the earth and the omphalos as site of oracle, were maintained. The fetish stone and maternal emblem, however, received a new encoding and were transformed into the sign of the earth's center on which Apollo's monistic faith in a paternal God could be based" (Bronfen 18). In Maitland's account, Apollo "has made love to mortals" and "they have delighted in him" (60). But "who is she, this child, to make mock of a god's desire? Who is she to shame him and despise him? And seeing her as a child, he is more ashamed than ever. And like white heat his anger rises, rises to replace the rising of his genitals which are withered by her rejection" (60). My question, involving the imagery of the "phallic woman," is whether the phallic refers to the Freudian assumption of woman's lack (which in itself is fraught with fallacy) and the subsequent appropriation of phallic discourse by the symbolically castrated woman. Is this appropriated "penis" not perhaps mistaken for a similar, but differently deleted, organ, the umbilical cord, in the form of the snake (Python)? And ultimately, in what relation does the phallic woman stand to the symbolic? Alluding to Ovid's account in the *Metamorphoses*, Maitland describes Cassandra's initial fascination with Apollo, but emphasizes her lack of experience in "sexual matters" and the ease with which Apollo has seduced her (59).

According to Geoffrey Miles, Cassandra's legend, told most famously in Ovid's *Metamorphoses* (Book 14), relates that Apollo "granted the Trojan princess Cassandra powers of prophesy but, when she refused to submit to him, added the rider that no one would ever believe her" (39). Maitland's narrative focuses precisely on Cassandra's refusal to submit her body to Apollo's sexual force, which is incompatible and incommensurable with her desire. Her pain originates in the encounter with phallic desire, with "an" eroticism so different from her own that it violates rather than excites her senses. What we are reading then might be an extended account of Irigaray's "handsome Apollo, a lover of men rather than women, the narcissistic lover of their bodies and their words," who helps Orestes "to recover from his madness" (*Bodily Encounter* 36) and (in Maitland's story) infuses Cassandra with madness:

"When she becomes conscious, she does not remember. They do not understand the long scratches on her face, nor the bruising on her head until she starts having fits. In her fits she murmurs dreadful and dangerous things, lost perceptions that make no sense but are discouraging....Although she is very beautiful they conclude that she is mad. She is often placed under restraint, because of the complicated distortions in all her forms of communication" (Maitland 61-62). I propose that it is worthwhile to investigate the meaning of madness in the ancient Greek context. Following Padel's study, there is a distinction between madness as a physical and mental contamination, and possession as a divine (immaculate) penetration of the fe/male body fertilized by a god: "The key word [to possession] is *entheos*...'with god inside.' It distinguishes 'possessed' from *ekphron*, 'mad'" (14); being possessed implies madness, yet madness does not necessarily mean possession. The connotation of physical pain and erotic penetration establishes the belief "that prophetic possession by a male god involved pain, which the priestess naturally resisted....The entry of god into woman is painful; as, in medieval fantasies about the Black Mass, women's copulation with the evil was painful, since he was very cold" (Padel 14). As the result of an erotic penetration, madness presents one of the main images for possessing a female (soul) that is "a womb-like receptacle for divine intrusion and inner pain" (17). The intensity of Apollo's sexuality, in Maitland's narrative, certainly attests to this, while repeatedly focusing on the violent nature of his paternal intrusion. Cassandra's traumatic refusal, which is too painful to endure, can be thus linked with the unspoken experience of a girl entering the symbolic structure that cannot deliver pleasure but only pain. This child will be punished for rejecting the phallus, and perhaps therefore thought to possess one: Apollo addresses Cassandra, saying: "Since you make a gap between me and my desire I shall make one between your seeing and your saying. You can never leap that gap. It will be a very lonely place" (Maitland 61). This loneliness, bearing a metaphorical sense of a gap, separates the girl from *jouissance* in the act of the symbolic cutting of the umbilical cord.

Wolf's *Cassandra* explores the similar territory of an unwritten biography, and (in the English translation) it takes the form of a "raging desire for confrontation with the poetics" (Wolf 141) of the patriarchal order. Maitland's narrative pursues this confrontation further back to reconstruct Cassandra's punishment as a violent split of the speaking subject, a subject posited as the momentary stasis of homosexual eroticism between mother and child, interrupted by the paternal envy and revenge: "'You're hurting me,' [Cassandra] says, trying to wriggle free. 'I know,' [Apollo] says, without compassion. He puts his tongue on her lips, but now there is no desire, his tongue is like a knife, he runs it up the narrow crevice above her upper lip, very slowly, very coldly....With the force of his chin he bows her head and runs his hard cutting tongue right across the centre of her crown, and she feels the sharp blade cut into her cranium, and into the depth of her brain, a single even slicing and there is intolerable pain, intolerable confusion" (61). Entangled in the impossibilities of language, Maitland's Cassandra remains frozen in nonspeech, in nonstructure, because of her own not quite conscious choice. Her biography is subsequently anesthetized by the paternal language. Further, in a link to Padel's exploration of the divine possession, Cassandra is infused with a distorted form language, with the "real" that, entangled in the umbilical cord, refuses to become symbolic: "She has a knowing that [Agamemnon] will not...that he will wait...that he will...she does not know the word for what it is she fears, for what it is she knows he will not do. Then the next minute it is gone, it is all gone" (55). Cassandra's identity is fragmented like the child's attachment to the mother in Baym's analysis: "The pre-Oedipal mother is rudely rejected when the child discovers the mother's appalling 'lack,' such rejection indicating that...the child was never 'really' attached to the mother, only fantasized such attachment; the 'real' attachment was always to the father" (288), to the symbolic. In psychoanalytic theory, both the pre-Oedipal and the phallic, when referring to the/a woman, articulate her condition in and with reference to the symbolic. Posited, however, at a site of "real incision" (separation from the "wholeness" as mother), Maitland's Cassandra, motherless and childless herself, survives between the semiotic and the symbolic, in a position where the first is unattainable (since there is no return to the mother) and the second is incomprehensible (since she is mad). Her disobedience draws on Lacan's concept of female incongruity with the symbolic function, and provides another interesting link between the imagined biography of the semiotic with the history of paternal desire.

In exploring this link further, I focus on Sissa's analogy between the mouth and the other female *stoma*, "the cervix of the uterus and the labia of the vulva" (5). As Sissa comments, the lexicon of Hippocratic medicine exhibits an early crystallization of this analogy: "the upper and lower portions of the female body are shown to be symmetrical through the use of identical terms to describe the parts of both. The mouth (stoma) through which food is ingested and from which speech emanates corresponds to the "mouth" (stoma) of the uterus. A narrow orifice, the latter is nevertheless equipped with lips that close, just as the lips of the upper mouth are sealed in silence. The image was so apt that it even entered the lexicon of Aristotelian biology, which in other respects was not particularly susceptible to the gastric [but also verbal] connotations of the female apparatus" (53). In a parallel mode, Cassandra appears as a self-sufficient, homoerotic subject in a double understanding of the female *labia*: the uncontrollable lips of the speaking female mouth and the insubordinate unreceptive lips of the vulva: "'I can't,' she cried. 'Stop it, let me go...I don't want it [Apollos's penis]. I don't want your present. I don't want to know the future. I was only joking'" (60). In an attempt to disrupt the symbolic superiority of Apollo's desire, Maitland centers on Cassandra's physical pain and her girlish virginal body. Cassandra's vaginal wound, unarticulated in the Greek legend, inscribes her madness with a lack of sexual joy, a type of *jouissance* that has never taken place. In this sense, Cassandra's punishment for rejecting Apollo's divine semen follows Sissa's argument: She is entrusted/fertilized with the visionary powers that will stay imprisoned within her mouth, unspoken. Just as her vagina refuses the divine power/knowledge, so her mouth is unable to articulate it. Apollo's amatory adventures with humans are even more destructive than those of his father, Zeus (Alcmene, Leda, Io). Besides

Cassandra, Apollo offers the gift of prophecy to Sibil, but faced with the continuous refusal of his advances, he punishes Sibil by making her immortal without granting her eternal youth. Daphne, who may have been immortal herself, actually escapes Apollo's lust by being metamorphosed into a laurel tree. All three are destroyed by Apollo's attention. The nonlinguistic space, in Cassandra's case, has little to do with the semiotic chora as a place of *jouissance*. Similar to Carter's and Saramonowicz's narratives, it is a place of oppression, imprisonment, and paralysis. Cassandra's brain is projected as inherently divided into the conscious and the *unconscious*, the accessible and inaccessible fragments. The signifier and the signified are split between what she knows and what she can/not say. Held responsible and punished for the disintegration of the phallic subject (Apollo's desire), she is split open right between her two disobedient mouths. The gap, the "hemispheric split," accounts for her inability, inarticulacy, and insanity. But what really is "the hell of it," as Carter has put it (and Maitland's story is explicit here), is that the split refers to permanent brain damage inflicted as the Father's revenge (*Sadeian Woman* 5). Cassandra, like the Kristevan Phallic Mother, is the one who is outside the law and the symbolic structure and hence must be annihilated. "No language can sing unless it confronts the Phallic Mother. For all that it must not leave her untouched, outside, opposite, against the law....Rather it must swallow her, eat her, dissolve her, set her up like a boundary of the process where 'I' with 'she'—'the other,' 'the mother'—becomes lost" (*Desire* 191). Disconnected from her mother/herself, Maitland's Cassandra lives in her desire for the whole that indeed, in a Lacanian sense, becomes illusory. As a divided subject, she does not recognize herself as the Phallic Mother, the "unconscious buttress of the laws of the city...apprehended, comprehended, and thrust aside" (*Desire* 192). What the narrative repeatedly reminds us is that Cassandra "cannot leap the gap," and in this sense she is thrust aside with "too many feelings of depression and guilt and euphoria" (Maitland 54). Frozen in her understanding of self before separation, Cassandra "sees what will happen and she tells it and no one can believe her. She cannot believe herself; in each bitter instant Cassandra hears her own truths as spittle and crazed foaming" (56). She is the hysteric, as described by Kristeva, with the phallus that could be the mother, and which "is something often said, but here we are all stopped short by this 'truth': the hysteric, the obsessed, the fetishist, and the schizoid. It is a focus of attention that drives us crazy" (*Desire* 191). And it is this "focus of attention" that is of crucial importance to the fantasy of the/a phallic mother. Her oracular discourse, split and multiplied by the very fragmentation of the phallic structure, carries the scar of not merely the trauma but also the triumph over her fantastic body that is marked by the "real incision."

If Cassandra had not refused Apollo, she would, perhaps, have become (divinely) possessed, and Apollo's semen might have turned her into a phallic oracle governed by the law of the Father. But her fears are stronger than her aspirations; the fear of being raped and turned against her own pleasure simultaneously gives her the right to reject Apollo and denies her the right of entry into the symbolic. The interrupted and denied fertilization of Cassandra deconstructs the myth of the vaginal orgasm (and of the importance of penetration) as ensuring the foundation of the public monopoly of patriarchal society over women. Positing Cassandra as the un/speaking subject, and thus illustrating the dialectical opposition between the semiotic and the symbolic, Maitland's biography of Cassandra re-enacts the experience of a female suffering that both results from and constitutes the opposition between the two. Cassandra's split position is a painful vacuum, a fantasy of suspension of the signifying structure. Drawing on early feminist constructions of the female body as a locus of fear, "The Burning Times" (1988), Maitland's second narrative for discussion here, continues to speak from the position of the rejected cord (the refused mother) and draws on the phallocentric force that subjugates the girl/woman's love and desire for her mother. But is it a memory or a fantasy, or is it both: a historicized metaphor for the split subject, mother and daughter unweaving their destinies, undoing their split? Undoubtedly, what Maitland narrates is again a story of pain, regret, and confusion, perhaps her own testimony, both fraud and fantasy, maintaining traces of a traditional memoir in terms of tone, vocabulary, and its ecliptic fragmentary form. The story is narrated from the perspective of a grown-up daughter (of a lesbian who was burned as a witch) who has now herself become a mother. The mother that the narrator attempts to reconstruct is phallic and therefore fake, either because she acted as if she had a phallus or because she rejected it in ignoring its symbolic centrality. Throughout the story, she and her mother remain nameless, void of reference and location. In this sense of writing about the past (which in Maitland's story is left unspecified and could be anywhere between the fourteenth and twentieth centuries), history is always already suspended, performative, fantastic. Once again, this history proves very useful as a narrative form of biography that reinvents lost authenticity. Supplementing the suffocating atmosphere of her present home with reminiscences from her childhood, the narrator projects her unorthodox childhood cottage onto the omnipotent historical structure of a nearby Catholic church. This structure, ambiguously as well as ironically, becomes the space of the narrator's physical and metaphorical refuge. The church, and specifically its altar of the "burning Virgin," where the narrator spends hours mourning and thereby reviving her past, gains or even usurps the maternal space of the semiotic chora, the womb/tomb of the burned witch-mother. It is in the act of displacing memory into a narrative enactment that the events of her childhood spent with her mother are performed anew. In remembering and reconstructing her mother as a witch, Maitland's narrator enacts a return to her childhood fears: a journey into the heart of patriarchal darkness. The central figure introduced in the story is the agonizing Virgin, conceptualized by the narrator as an absence (ghost, spectrum) of the archaic mother, born of flesh and martyred. The narrator describes the Virgin as a lady "crowned with the sun, aglow with the light from the candles lit by women like [herself]" (133). In the absence of the mother, widely discussed by Irigaray in the context of psychoanalysis, the daughter's prayer is spoken as "a gestural mimesis," in which verbal exchange is useless or perhaps impossible ("Limits" 110). Her words flow into the mysterious desire for the ghost of the archaic mother (Irigaray's "woman"); her desire takes place before speech intervenes and before the authenticity of her as a subject establishes itself in the history (110).

Keeping in mind this prelinguistic space of desire, I turn to explore what might possibly take place in the maternal spaces of the church as narrated by Maitland. First, the memory of the victimized (burning) witch has been projected onto the figure of a sanctified and fetishized Virgin. It is the daughter (as narrator) who focuses on this particular intermingling of the "wild" burning mother (whose body is exhibited, made to be a central focus of the villagers' attention) with the Virgin, veiled and confined to the claustrophobic, restricted space of the church. The two historical/historicized figures fuse into a fraud: a mother, but a phallic one, and therefore not quite a woman. This particular constellation of the (lesbian) mother-virgin who "often seemed on fire" is crucial to the narrator's memory of identity split and alienation, a memory under erasure. Finally, the daughter's fear of historical repetition is intertwined in the story with her personal responsibility for her mother's death: "when I look up at her through the tears and through the candle flames, she seems to me on fire...she is burning, smiling, burning and I scream. Aloud. Dear mother, let no one have heard. But she will not listen to my prayers, because I burned my own mother, I betrayed her and they burned her and I danced around her pyre....And I cannot confess this sin, because they will burn me too. They will torture and break me as they did her. Then they will burn me" (133-34). The daughter, still "alive" and a mother herself, burns thus in a self-imposed penance in front of the Virgin's altar. Accompanied by ferocious images of other burning bodies, her suffering is underscored by the fear that the same thing might happen to her. The frequently repeated "they will burn me, too" motif refers both to a concrete physical fear and to the reoccurring maternal trauma of the "real incision" that keeps "the symbolic castration" intact: "Torn between the sons and the fathers, the stake or sacrifice in dispute between men, she is fragmented into bits and pieces, and therefore unable to articulate her difference" (Whitford 27). It is because of her unresolved erotic difference that the daughter condemns and denounces her mother to the authorities of the village. In burning thus the maternal cord, the narrator appears as a hysteric daughter oppressed by the hegemonic patriarchal structure (she is unhappily married, has three adult sons and no space for herself in the tiny cottage). Possessed and displaced, like Cixous's figure, she becomes "a witch in reverse, turned back within herself" (Cixous and Clément 36), and trapped in the imaginary land of the phallic mother whose desire remains unarticulated. Perhaps only under a different name, a name without identification, half erased, half fraud, a fantasy name. Like Cixous's *Medusa*, Maitland's figure of the lesbian mother refers to the "universal woman subject who must bring women to their senses and to their meaning in history" ("Laugh" 347). To begin with, this subject interrogates the philosophical tradition (Irigaray), particularly from the side of desire. In this link with desire Maitland's mother emerges most prominently as a remembered and remembering subject who "laughed at everyone and at herself" (Maitland 135). The significance of her subversive Medusa-like laugh undermines and ridicules heterosexual hegemony: "Her hair was a great mass of tangled curls, and she would not smooth them down. She was a widow woman, they said, though as a child I heard other things....She did not come from that village, but from another further west, towards the mountains. She never spoke of her childhood, or of what and where she had been before. She was a lace-maker; a very skilful lace-maker, and she loved the work" (135).

Through her daughter's memory, her/story is revived, and her anonymous past, that of a woman ignored by history for centuries, is replaced by the unexpectedly unfolding biography of a peasant artist. In contrast with alienated "madwomen" (such as Cassandra), Maitland's mother emerges as an excellent storyteller, a mouth-dominated, or two-lipped subject speaking from a place that is sealed, inaccessible to her daughter. But nothing, not even her mother's liberatory laughter, can heal the separation and betrayal stored in the daughter's memory. Again, in a parallel to Cassandra's story, the significance of this passage lies in the narrated disconnection between one space, which can be remembered and the "other," which remains unattainable and returns as distorted, collapsed, and incomplete. In what, on the surface, materializes as a "lumpish" attempt to "hush the boys," something else is put out of sight: a broken dialogue between the fantasy that "goes wrong" (becomes fraud) once articulated in the paternal structure: the narrated reality of the daughter who, like Maria in *Siostra*, insists on revising the traumatic past. The question that calls for attention therefore concerns what memory routes or systems she can possibly employ to recreate her mother. How does she remember the unspeaking (remembered) subject that, like Cassandra, refuses to remain silent and is therefore remembering (perpetuating) itself? The narrator remembers her mother as a chaotic, dominant, creative, but also economically self-sufficient woman, assuming the phallic (self-centred) position. Simultaneously capable of maintaining and trespassing against the unwritten laws of the village, the mother is dangerously suspended between both possibilities, perhaps even aware of her collapse to come, as if she knew that her end was just the matter of time and opportunity. Purkiss, commenting on this story, concludes that the mother's lesbian sexuality and the daughter's own unrecognized desire for her mother's lover "lead the narrator to denounce her mother, but plainly this daughter envies her mother at every possible level" (23). This envy for the "phallic" integration, combined with the brutal separation from her mother, repeatedly returns to her in the form of anxiety attacks. The church merely offers a shelter to her body, where in/dependence (her striving for space) is suspended between the archaic images of the unencumbered woman and the domesticated woman bound to heterosexuality. Her body balances between virginity and motherhood, but unlike the Virgin she has no alternative but to be one or the other: "The statue of the Virgin is in painted wood. She holds her son somehow clumsily I feel, having held three of my own. A chance lurch of that serene head and he will fall out of her arms; she should bring him lower so that he straddles her hip....I try to concentrate on that, on that dangerous way in which she is holding the Son of God; and how easy it is for a child to fall out of even the most loving arms" (Maitland 134). This passage clearly links with Kristeva's reference to the maternal attempt "to unite the logic of passion with the order...of the ideal, of the prohibition, of the law" (Clément and Kristeva 114). It is true, writes Kristeva, "that cornering [the Virgin] for her lack of experience with babysitting...is, of course, very funny, but avoids the difficulty of the cunning and, I maintain, splendid construction of the Virgin-Mother-of-God" (114). In escaping to the "splendid" Virgin, the daughter is prey to this "cunning": what she faces is at times her burning mother, and at times a silent stature representing an abstract institution with the omnipresent Father at the top. The imagined dialogue between mother and daughter is broken, divided between the forbidden (homosexual desire that remains unspoken) and what is heterosexual and consciously experienced as knowledge.

This division has been explored by Irigaray in her radical project postulating a female homosexual bond that is required to recompose women's primary narcissism, badly wounded (damaged) by the phallocentric symbolic. The love of another woman is crucial to this process. However, if both the maternal body and the lesbian experience are described "from a position of sanctioned heterosexuality that fails to acknowledge its own fear of losing that sanction," the love of another woman inevitably emerges as already acknowledging its own loss (*Gender Trouble* 87). This argument by Butler has its roots in cultural subversion that not only acknowledges female homosexuality, but also "the varied meanings and possibilities of motherhood as a cultural practice" (*Gender Trouble* 87). Finally, cultural subversion is of concern here since it emerges from beneath the surface of culture, beneath the territory of its laws and prohibitions, from the semiotic possibility of a language and its unwritten track of history. The discussed narratives explicitly draw on these unwritten spaces of cultural subversion and precisely therefore appear as fraudulent, fantasized, and suspended. For various reasons, the relationship with the mother, as described by Maitland, "is a mad desire," a "dark continent" that "remains in the shadows of our culture; it is its night and its hell" (Irigaray, *Bodily Encounter* 35). Although addressing different destinies, these narratives clearly converge in the recognition of the historical debt to the lost maternal identity that, as Irigaray advocated, would free the mother "to become a sexual and desiring woman" and "the daughter from the icy grip of the merged and undifferentiated relationship" (Whitford 77). In deviating from the restorative and liberating spaces of semiotic pleasures, the archaic chora appears as a hole that leads nowhere, an empty barren space, or as a ghostly (spectral) apparition of repressed desires. The texts are thus charged with the repression of the maternal subject that escapes the paternal law but inevitably needs to remain within that law in order to be granted cultural validity. Similar alienation is central to my analyses of Atwood's novel, *Alias Grace* (1996), and, subsequently, Tokarczuk's *E.E.* In both cases, alienation takes the forms of separation and madness infused by the split of one subject (that of mother and daughter) in the process of socialization.

Transcending the Exposures of the Repressed

Mapping the intellectual territory of nineteenth-century Canada, Atwood's narrative reclaims the documented but enigmatic story of Grace Marks, who was convicted in 1843 of murdering her employer Thomas Kinnear and his housekeeper, Nancy

Montgomery, and was subsequently held in the Lunatic Asylum in Toronto and the Kingston Penitentiary. The controversial conviction sparked much debate about whether Marks was actually instrumental in the murder or merely an unwitting accessory. A number of theories were offered as to Marks's psychic state: that she acted as if she suffered from mental illness in order to be placed in an asylum, that she had multiple personality disorder, or that she was possessed by the consciousness of her deceased friend Mary Whitney. Another theory, controversial but supported by some evidence, was that Marks had died, not Whitney, and Whitney had adopted Marks's name and identity (on this see Westwood). As I argue, Atwood explores Grace's estrangement while suggesting a link between a sexually exploited woman and a fantasy of her archaic narcissistic self that refuses to accept the exploitation. Speculating on alternative states of consciousness in a pre-Freudian context, Atwood recreates the nineteenth-century conception of "female difference" that alludes to "the unknown [that] is always more wonderful...than the known, and more convincing" (Atwood 268). Sexuality, the materiality of human reproduction, and consequently the patriarchal household system are central to this exploration. As neurological conditions of possession and hysteria are intertwined in *Alias Grace* with fragments of biblical imagery, superstitions, and, in fact, with demonology, what emerges is an interesting narrative of the female body/sexuality as a contradiction to itself. To explore this contradiction, Atwood follows the nineteenth-century sociological projection of "woman" as deficient and biologically inferior, conceived to assist and support a masculine "consciousness to itself" (Felman 9). Excluded from the patronymic signifier, the "woman" does not possess sexuality on her own, but exists as a relational supplement, bringing something that is missing.

Grace's madness is thus brought into immediate and recurring association with her culturally restricted and exploited body, subjected not only to science and law, but also to the private fantasies of the doctors and judges. Evoking associations with the Derridean "undecidable structure," her sexuality represents the *pharmacon*, a contradictory signification of the *hymen*, both remedy and poison, the fusion of the self and other. It is "an image almost medieval in its plain lines, its angular clarity: a nun in a cloister, a maiden in a towered dungeon, awaiting the next day's burning at the stake, or else the last-minute champion come to rescue her" (Atwood 59). In an oppressively phallocentric structure of knowledge, Grace's hysteria, and perhaps madness, seems to be derived from her connection with the distorted mother of mankind, Eve, who was seduced by the snake and infused with disobedience. Identifying Grace with such disobedience, Atwood narrates a story of her revolt against paternalistic assumptions about Eve's objectification in the face of the Law. This particular identification converges with Cixous's argument, offering a possible key with which to read Grace's madness: "the first fable of our first book is a fable in which what is at stake is the relationship to the law. There are two principal elements, two main puppets: the word of the Law or the discourse of God and the Apple. It's a struggle between the Apple and the discourse of God. All this transpires in this short scene before a woman. The Book begins *Before the Apple*: at the beginning of everything there is an apple, and this apple, when it is talked about, is said to be a not-to-be-fruit. There is an apple, and straight away there is the law" (Cixous "Extreme Fidelity" 134). Focusing on Grace's absence of mind (God, Law) in the moments of her hysterical attacks, Atwood inscribes madness as *mysteria*, a "Western nineteenth-century view, which linked hysteria to a specific version of femininity as itself a 'mystery'" (Mitchell 112): "'Two hundred years ago, they would not have been at a loss,' says Reverend Verringer. 'It would have been a clear case of possession. Mary Whitney would have been found to have been inhabiting the body of Grace Marks, and thus to be responsible for inciting the crime, and for helping to strangle Nancy Montgomery. An exorcism would have been in order.' 'But this is the nineteenth century,' says Simon. 'It may be a neurological condition.' He would like to say *must be*, but he doesn't wish to contradict Verringer too bluntly. Also he is still quite unsettled, and unsure of his intellectual ground" (Atwood 405). To follow this mystery with Kristevan psychoanalytical insight, Grace is left without the social support within the symbolic, without the loving third or access to sublimation. It is within this context that the narrative emphasizes the crucial importance of sexuality in the formation of subjectivity, without which there remains depression, melancholia, and entrapment in the biological body. Indeed, Atwood depicts nineteenth-century (women's) bodies as "meant" to be domesticated, "caged in wire crinolines...so that they cannot get out and go rubbing up against the gentlemen's trousers" (22), just as they are destined to become pregnant in order to preserve their cultural entrapment. This specifically female condition correlates with *hysteria* as a gendered complaint deriving from woman's social role to serve masculine centrality as "a daughter / a mother / a wife" (Felman 7-8).

The parallels between feminist psychoanalysis and Atwood's text are overt. In fact, as I see it, Grace Marks attempts to become one of the many dutiful Daughters committed to the patriarchal system without understanding its doctrine and also unknowingly reinforcing their own subjugation. A witness to her mother's continual pregnancies, Grace is already urged prematurely to become a "little mother." The wish to kill the father who impregnates the mother becomes her part in the Oedipal drama. Her family position is ambiguous, placed between hating the father and becoming a parent substitute, a role she assumes literally after her mother's death but is soon forced to abandon. Her double separation, first from her mother, then from her numerous siblings, reinforces the need for identification with another, which she finds in Mary Whitney, her roommate and a servant like herself. Mary Whitney introduces Grace into the life of a maid, a "respectful" life within the structure of the patriarchal household, contrasted with prostitution as the only alternative. Echoing this juxtaposition, Atwood exposes both household and prostitution as equal products of the Law that encodes nineteenth-century women alternatively as submissive subjects to the system or potentially mad. In Atwood's account, not only the servant, but every woman, independently of her social position, can be "exploited, enslaved, treated as a thing rather than a person" (de Beauvoir 586), and consequently, needs to be analyzed in the context of madness (as inflicted by Law). To return to Felman's formulation, Grace is in "the impasse confronting those whom cultural conditioning has deprived of the very means of protest or self-affirmation" (8). Far from being a contestation, her mental illness is a request for help, a manifestation "of cultural impotence and of political castration. This socially defined help—needing and help—seeking behaviour is itself part of female conditioning, ideologically inherent in the behavioural pattern and in the dependent and helpless role assigned to the woman as such" (Felman 8).

What seems to be crucial in Atwood's reading of the nineteenth-century woman is the imagery of her disobedient (speaking) mouth that in refusing to keep silent destabilizes the Law of the Father/God who "made women with skirts," so they can be "pulled over their heads and tied at the top, that way you don't get so much noise out of them...the only thing of use in them is below the waist" (Atwood 240). As with all other cultural attributes of the nonconforming female body, the mouth is defined in terms of hysterical sexuality. Having a cunning mouth, Grace Marks is fascinating, and then abject, trapped, and imprisoned as she continues to speak. Her stories, like those of the Homeric Sirens, "ought never to be subjected to the harsh categories of Truth and Falsehood," since they "belong in another realm altogether" (377). The realm Atwood refers to is the Freudian *un/heimlichkeit*, correlated by Kristeva with the linguistic suspension of judgment. In this state, the uncanny "is in reality nothing new or alien, but something which is familiar and old-established in the mind, and which has become alienated from it only through the process of repression" (Kristeva, *Strangers* 184). Although Grace's "behavioural pattern" might indeed be "ideologically inherent" (Atwood 8) to phallocentric thinking, it discloses irregularity, slippages of personality, and difference from patriarchal patterns. The violent death of Mary Whitney, in particular, undermines the ideology Grace took for granted or deemed "kind enough" and "usual" (Atwood 308). Her behavioural irregularity begins with a sudden loss of memory and a split in her mind that causes the "other voice, whatever it was" (189) to speak and to act in her name. Grace, left in the room with Mary's body, imagines/is able to hear her dead friend asking her to "*let [her] in*" (179). The shock of the uncanny she experiences implodes both her mind and body: "An auditory hallucination, of course...followed...by an episode of fainting, and then by hysterics, mixed with what would appear to have been somnambulism; after which there was a deep and prolonged sleep, and subsequent amnesia" (189). This particular collapse of Grace's identity could be read as a Freudian *Spaltung* (break, fracture, split) caused by the repetition of an abrupt female "death in blood." In both cases—Mary's, and earlier, her mother's—death is caused by the lack or incompetence of doctors and accompanied by the imagery of maternal bloodshed.

Mary Whitney, victim of an illegal and clumsy abortion, initiates in Grace a sequence of returns to her repressed desires. Returning as the uncanny, unsettling, and supernatural, Mary becomes what Creed calls "the phantasy of the castrating mother," who "undermines Freud's theories that woman terrifies because she is castrated and that it is the father who alone represents the agent of castration within the family" (151). Mary, as the voice of the uncanny, "remarkable for its violence" but "not without a certain logic" (Atwood 406), reveals Grace's *unconscious*, subversive desires, leading her to take on the double task of clarifying and correcting paternal "irregularities" in the name of the loss she has experienced. As she says, "the Bible may have been thought out by God, but it was written down by men. And like everything men write down, such as the newspapers, they got the main story right but some of the details wrong" (459). Thus, what Grace desires, without being able to articulate it, is not a masculine self-identity, but the imaginary semiotic chora, the protective space of the repressed maternal voice. In her somnambulistic trance, she keeps "asking where Grace had gone. And when they told [her] that [she] was Grace, [she] would not believe them...and tried to run out of the house, because...Grace was lost, and had gone into the lake, and [she] needed to search for her" (180). The lake, a watery space, evokes the protective and destructive potential of the mother's womb, as well as the memory of the ocean, another uncanny space that devoured her mother's body during their transatlantic journey to Canada.

In her description of the mother's death, Atwood provides evidence that Grace's mother died owing to the continuous pregnancies that eventually distorted her womb: "There was a hard swelling, and I thought it was another little mouth to feed," although the doctor said "it was most likely a tumour, or a cyst, or else a burst appendix...but there was no way of telling without cutting her open" (120). The distorted womb, suggesting the end rather than the beginning, becomes in Grace's imagination the source of a desire to avenge her mother's and Mary's death-causing pregnancies. As "a token of repression" this womb/tomb imagery disturbs Grace's identity by leading back "to what is known of old and long familiar" (Creed 54), the contradiction of the maternal as an intimate, as well as a concealed, deceitful, and malicious space. In *Alias Grace*, the familiar and the intimate are reversed into their opposites in an analogous way: pregnancy and death are brought together with an uncanny strangeness emanating from the *Unheimlichkeit* of wombs cut open. This strangeness will manifest itself in Grace as madness, although it can also appear to be a "clumsy" defence of the distressed low-class and uneducated woman, or mother (to be), as nineteenth-century medical attitudes suggested.

Locating female madness in the context of a homicide, Atwood shows that the concept of crime is constructed along the axis of masculine presence and female absence, a conclusion drawn also by Creed in her conceptualization of the *monstrous-feminine*. The difference in association between murderer (monster) and the murderess (monstrous feminine) lies in the socially ambiguous status of the female body, both intensifying and suspending the act of murder and its monstrosity. Owing to this unresolved suspension, the female suspect will become a female demon or a witch, and, contrary to Foucault's famous analysis of crime as spectacle, will continue to be publicly displayed. In analyzing the treatment of the condemned in the nineteenth century, Foucault refers to a body that is no longer tortured but caught up in a system of constraints, obligations, and prohibitions: "One no longer touched the body, or at least as little as possible, and then only to reach something other than the body itself" in the form of imprisonment, forced labour, and penal servitude. "But the punishment-body relation is not the same as it was in the torture during public executions" (*Discipline and Punish* 11). Clearly, Atwood's depiction of nineteenth-century imprisonment rituals and interrogation do not attest to "the disappearance of the spectacle" or the "elimination of pain" (*Discipline and Punish* 11): "The reason they want to see me is that I am a celebrated murderess. Or that is what has been written down. When I first saw it I was surprised...what is there to celebrate about murder?...Murderess is a strong word to have attached to you. It has a smell to it, that word—musky and oppressive, like dead flowers in a vase" (Atwood 22-23).

Grace in the asylum and prison is still above all an attractive, celebrated body that forces us to reinvestigate Foucault's claims in *Discipline and Punish*. Although the relation of body to the punishment has changed, and Grace will indeed no longer be burnt at the stake, she remains "a temptation": her body is suspended between the doctor's scientific interests and his physical desires, "if possible to arrange it unobserved" (Atwood 29). Her madness and her monstrosity are simply used here as a medical pretext to interrogate her female organs: "Keep still, I am here to examine you, it is no use lying to me" (32). Contrary thus to Foucault's assumptions, physical pain, in the context of Atwood's narrative, is still "the pain of the body itself," even if "officially it is no longer the constituent element of the penalty" (*Discipline and Punish* 11). Grace's abused body is loaded with the fear of rape, and it is the particular combination of female pain and fear that constitutes "a remarkable aphrodisiac" (Atwood 378) somehow overlooked by Foucault. The disappearance of spectacle as a part of the new "economy of suspended rights" (*Discipline and Punish* 11) is illusory in itself, since Grace's sexuality is put on display and confession is in order: "Confess, confess. Let me forgive and pity. Let me get up a Petition for you. Tell me all" (35). Consequently, in a hysterical spectacle of outrage, Grace re-enacts her initial shock at confronting both death in bloodshed and her own vulnerability, whereby death is displaced/replaced by an "irrational" fear of rape as well as of doctors in general: "of being cut open by them, as some might have a fear of snakes" (30). What is thus transmitted through the fear of being cut open parallels Bronfen's suggestion that the hysteric "broadcasts a message about vulnerability—the vulnerability of the symbolic (the fallibility of paternal law and social bonds); the vulnerability of identity (the insecurity of gender, ethnic, and class designations); or, perhaps above all, the vulnerability of the body, given its mutability and mortality" (xiii).

With the wisdom of the hysteric, Grace remains silent when she is "back to normal" (32), as if in a refusal to assist in perpetuating the experience of mortality: "Even when they are not doing the killing themselves it means a death is close" (27). The experienced shock, as Mitchell explains, converts "the previous pleasure of contact to a desperate, painful excitement, a kind of survival-sexuality kit which could well lead to rape or compulsive, violent sexual encounters. The frenetic repetition is the mark of the death of the 'other' and of his own survival—it is sexuality in the interest of the surviving self" (143). Although Dr. Jordan, a "psychotherapist" pursuing Grace's case, is a liberal thinker, he still unmistakably represents the Law. In analyzing Grace as "one of the negative female variety" (361), he follows what Irigaray has explicitly revealed as the self-sufficient discourse of the masculine subject. Indeed, Dr. Jordan treats Grace's fluctuating identity as a provisional neurological but inherently female indisposition. In linking Grace's amnesia with "the effects of a hysterical seizure," he maps the subconscious as a form of "auto-hypnotic somnambulism, not much studied twenty-five years ago but well documented since" (432). Both idealistic and disillusioned, he resents "the widely held view that women are weak-spined and jelly-like by nature, and would slump to the floor like melted cheese if not roped in" (73). He has dissected enough women to know better; he "has been where they could never go, seen what they could never see; he has... peered inside" (82). Visiting Grace in the Penitentiary, Dr. Jordan approaches her as he would any of the cornered women, but Grace eludes him: "She glides ahead of him, just out of his grasp, turning her head to see if he's still following" (407). The only memory "she seems to have forgotten" is the memory of the crime; "the very plenitude of her recollections may be a sort of distraction, a way of drawing the mind away from some hidden but essential fact" (185). The biblical motifs that Grace interweaves into her story clearly focus on the paradox of primordial sin chasing her memories since childhood. In an attempt to adjust the symbolic imagery to her own understanding, Grace unfolds new spaces within her biblical knowledge, spaces for the archaic mother. Filling in the missing role of the mother as a powerful and autonomous life-giver, this imaginary, dyadic figure connects in Grace's fantasy with a revengeful and angry woman, cornered, like her own mother, and abused like Mary Whitney. Grace, subconsciously identifying with Mary, is now able to laugh at "the curse of Eve [menstruation]" (179), because Mary thought it "stupid, and the real curse of Eve was having to put up with the nonsense of Adam, who as soon as they were in trouble, blamed it all on her" (164). These imaginary and autonomous spaces allow her to keep Dr. Jordan at a distance, and make her suspicious of all his suggestions: "[Dr. Jordan shows her an apple] An apple, I say. He must think I am simple; or else it's a trick of some sort; or else he is mad and that is why they locked the door—they've locked me into this room with a madman....The apple of the Tree of Knowledge, is what he means. Good and evil. Any child could guess it. But I will not oblige" (40).

To decipher this implicitly erotic scene, I turn to Mitchell's analysis of the relationship between the patient and the therapist: "the traumatic shock experienced by the patient becomes the moral shock of the therapist. This is one of the reasons why it should never be the task of the therapist to investigate what actually happened—that task must fall to others. But the shock itself is crucially important" (Mitchell 141). Dr. Jordan follows precisely what Mitchell postulates: He is the first who rejects the necessity to investigate Grace's crime and attempts to define the source of her shock. However, Grace's sexuality constitutes a significant obstacle to his investigation: "With memory blasted, the shock can be sexualised. The shock itself becomes an end in itself" (Mitchell 142). Climaxing in the image of her seductive mouth, Grace's hysterical symptoms are irresistibly fascinating, projected as the abyss, the biblical metaphor of eternal punishment, of a bottomless pit. Dr. Jordan got "the hook in her mouth, but can he pull her out? Up, out of the abyss" (Atwood 322)? What Atwood suggests is that the relationship between the patient and the therapist is broken, or caught in a symptomatological interpretation. Grace, "whose song is sweet but dangerous," seduces him "into deep waters" (423), where symptoms and diagnosis become inseparable, making readable what otherwise cannot be said. In the end, "it comes to him that Grace Marks is the only woman he's ever met that he would wish to marry" (388). Notwithstanding Dr. Jordan's fantasies of her deceitful mastery, Grace remains yet a rather "flat landscape" (388), a good, dutiful Daughter attempting to please the paternal gaze. If we follow this contradiction further, it is not because of her "bad will" but because of her unresolved nucleus of *unconscious* emotions that she cannot be successful in the symbolic order. She has a history of lapses, of dangerous splits of identity that make her the "undecidable structure": "If I am good enough and quiet enough, perhaps after all they will let me go; but it's not easy...like hanging on the edge of a bridge when you've already fallen over; you don't seem to be moving, just dangling there, and yet it is taking all your strength" (5). As the recipient of a shock, Grace is "by definition, passive" (Mitchell 141). Her "strongest prison is of her own construction" (Atwood 361), and her stubborn strength is set to thwart the doctors, to prevent the "recovery." According to Mitchell, violent death, the trauma of separation, and the collapse of identity belong to the most "penetrating" of human experiences and need a long-term psychological convalescence: "When, in the process of recovery, a fantasy is constructed, this fantasy bears the marks of both the shock and the implosion" (141). Placed in the context of such a fantasy under construction, Grace's subconscious projection of herself as Mary can be understood as the protest of a hysteric who cannot define herself in the world. The world is "like a puzzle [she] could not guess" (Atwood 202); it has become for her a place of difference. Because the "hysteric does not remember. An actual trauma... wipes out memory. The hysteric unconsciously models [her]self on this process and becomes amnesiac in order to create a traumatic shock" (Mitchell 141). Thus, Grace escapes to the *unconscious*, so that she cannot remember but repeats and recreates shocks; "these shocks entail the blasting of memory. The broken object, rather than the feeling that caused the breakage, becomes the focus of attention—the feeling can then be forgotten" (Mitchell 142).

In a process of self-therapy for what she has (not) done and in a protest against repentance, she locks herself out of anybody's reach and interrogates herself. Moreover, this self-interrogation expands into an analysis of the doctor "as if it were [the doctor], not she, who was under scrutiny" (Atwood 59). The more she remembers and relates to the doctor, the more energy "she's drawing out of him—using his own mental forces to materialize the figures in her story, as the mediums are said to do during their trances" (291). Finally, approaching the center of Grace's story, Dr. Jordan realizes that the center was always missing, that, in fact, there is no language to describe the center: "'The truth may well turn out to be stranger than we think,' says Simon. 'It may be that much of what we are accustomed to describe as evil, and evil freely chosen, is instead an illness due to some lesion of the nervous system, and that the Devil himself is simply a malformation of the cerebrum'" (80). For Grace as much as for Dr. Jordan, the "area of erasure" (291) cannot be grasped, analyzed, or named. As a result of all the failure to break the inaccessibility of the *unconscious*, Dr. Jordan agrees to hypnotize Grace. This happens in front of the invited audience of experts (other Law representatives) as the doctor agrees to display Grace's body. The hypnosis should constitute advancement, albeit with shocking disruptions, towards remembering the object. In this final attempt to link science with the *unconscious*, the hypnosis ironically becomes a session of modern exorcism. While the re-enacted shock causes an estrangement of Grace's body/mind in the form of Mary's voice, the "area of erasure" turns into a carnival (sabbath), a temporarily liberating force. Mary's voice, representing Grace's *unconscious*, is not prepared for compromises, and in its refusal to speak in the symbolic, it erodes any possibility of scientific understanding. The voice/force actually comes close to "becoming" the semiotic chora, a "place" or a "state" that Grace, with all her "incongruence," is unable to retrieve from linguistic formlessness. Mary's voice represents "quintessentially, the absent or missing body" as part of the collapsed maternal subject, and "it is the terror of the body going absent that drives the hysteria" (Mitchell 221). Rather than providing a therapeutic treatment, Mary gives Grace a therapeutic shock (competing with Dr. Jordan's therapy) that re-enacts (remembers) the death of her mother. Coming against Grace's will, Mary's uncompromising voice initiates an unsettling confrontation between fear and fascination with death. Moreover, her absent body constitutes a misleading, paradoxical factor since, as Mitchell explains, "there is no more excessively present body than that of the hysteric (in hysteria the body is always acting and thereby expressing something)." However, "it is exactly this bodily excess which is dependent on its subjective absence" (222). Tracing this paradox, Atwood grounds the objectification of Grace in the logocentric metaphor of "the inhuman female demon," a woman already marked with the Scarlet Letter, "a foul-tempered witch" (277). The reference here is to Hawthorne's 1850 novel, which provides one of the most memorable images of social stigma, hypocrisy, and punishment set in the early days of Puritan US. In Atwood's novel, Simon "is surprised to find a clergyman reading Hawthorne: the man has been accused of sensualism, and—especially after *The Scarlet Letter*—of a laxity in morals" (192). Placing the figure of a doctor on the other extreme, in the context of an institutionalized confession, Atwood describes him as "one of the dark trio—the doctor, the judge, the executioner," all sharing "the powers of life and death" (82), powers similar to those of the mother's womb. Certainly, Atwood's narrative focuses on institutionalized forms of female madness and on professional doctors who fail to penetrate the *unconscious*. But most importantly, her narrative is about Grace's failure to locate the (*unconscious*) voice within herself. She had been only as far as "the threshold of the unconscious" (412). Owing to this lack of (self-) communication Grace does not succeed in defining herself outside of the symbolic. Upon her release from the prison (as a result of general amnesty), her story converges with the promise of pregnancy, indicating her dutiful return to the symbolic. The return is provisional, because Grace's story refuses to end precisely where Atwood's narrative ends, offering an open (unspoken) conclusion. The pregnancy reintroduces her to the mother's body, which, as a metonymy of female execution, articulates pain that cannot be ignored. Although Grace comes to represent the imaginary and the *unconscious* associated with the mother, she necessarily tries, but eventually fails, to articulate her experience in the symbolic. This confirms Mitchell's division of the woman into a "true" woman "who accepts her 'castration' and the replacement of her missing penis by a baby" and "a false or phoney woman who only pretends to. This phoney woman is the new name given to the hysteric" (187). Without being aware of the consequences (without becoming a feminist rebel), Grace finally evaluates her biblical knowledge, and in fact her world knowledge, as censored and castrated. As she draws towards the end of her (narrated) story, she returns to a household structure, but her sexuality attains a new quality. Atwood depicts her sitting peacefully and making a new quilt (459), into which Grace weaves whatever remains unspeakable and otherwise might interfere with her newly arranged status of wifehood. In this sense, Grace's weaving alludes to the Homeric account of Penelope's un/weaving as a form of un-doing his/story. In itself, Grace's quilt-making is a conservative, conforming activity placing her among the obedient patriarchal daughters, but its pattern (the language) is subversive, stealing the patriarchal myth away in order to rewrite and to revise its meaning. In the absence of valid representations of female sexuality, the dutiful quilt-making merges with Grace's sexuality as a whole. There are no words to talk about it, except mutilating words to the effect of anxiety and "a haunting fear of castration" (Irigaray, "Bodily Encounter" 41). But she finds ways to express the urgency to transcend the repression without words. The quilt-making represents both household stability and sexuality-in-process, a release from the repressed self-consciousness and a strategic protest against the phoney and the hysterical. Her pregnancy, a fluctuating fantasy of pleasures and dangers, creates a space for the om-phalic mother, the one symbolically inarticulate and prohibited (Kristeva, "Stabat Mater" 14).

As demonstrated through my readings, Atwood, like Maitland and Carter, attempts to rewrite the specific histories of paradigmatic boundary figures (Grace, Cassandra, and the female vampire) into biographies of the repressed archaic mother. In an astounding parallel to these narratives, Olga Tokarczuk's novel *E.E.* explores a similar case study underscored by Freudian theory from a culturally different but nevertheless psychoanalytical feminist perspective: "For the first time [Freud] saw his mother naked. Her full breasts must have awoken an anxiety in the child. He desired and feared them at the same time. Her naked body was a knot by which the world was tied" (Tokarczuk 18; unless otherwise stated, all translations are mine). Providing a link to the Freudian geography of the *unconscious* at the turn of the twentieth century in Central Europe, Tokarczuk provides a paradoxical illustration of the enigmatic figure of a hysteric visionary. Equally drawing on the uncanny, Tokarczuk's *E.E.* provides a parallel to Freud's personal discoveries and encounters. Among other narrative elements, she introduces the figure of a six-year-old Freud who travels by night in a train with his mother (the fragment cited above). More importantly, the main character's initials, *E.E.*, bear connections to Freud's work on male hysteria, specifically referring to his neurotic patients (Mitchell 64-65). The narrative contextualizes the uncanny in the hysterical experience of puberty, following Deleuzian implications of the girl's "becoming" as the primordial erasure of her access to the social structure. The uncanny womb is no longer relating "to the literal origin of the subject" or "the experience of separation" (Creed 54), as is the case in *Siostra* or *Alias Grace*. Rather, it transcends the "literal origin" to broach the supernatural, or paranormal, beyond earthly phenomena. Focusing primarily on the puberty drama, the narrative involves culturally somatized figures of mother and daughter, inevitably touching upon Irigaray's notion of "cultural paralysis" caused by "non-differentiation between one woman and another," "enforced rejection or hatred, or at best 'pretence' [faire comme]." In this cultural paralysis, "the girl's earliest pleasures will remain wordless; her earliest narcissizations will have no words or sentences to speak their name, even retroactively" (Whitford 101).

In *E.E.*, set in Breslau and written in postcommunist Poland, Tokarczuk introduces an interesting blend of Polish and German names. *E.E.*, an ambiguous, teenaged Erna Elzner, belongs to the Freudian prototype of an upper-middle-class German family, living in Wrocław under German control in 1910. Erna's father, Fryderyk, spells his first name according to Polish orthography while his surname remains German. Streets, places, and servants' first names are German. The city landscape is a permeable borderland between Polish, German, and Jewish ethnicities. Erna's mother, Mrs. Elzner, a housewife of Polish origin, lives an unexciting life with her German husband, the owner of a textile factory, in a spacious apartment in the heart of the city. Erna is portrayed as an uninspiring, unattractive, perhaps even inadvertently disappointing girl, compared to her younger and elder siblings. Shortly after her fifteenth birthday, during a family dinner, Erna suddenly becomes aware of a ghostly apparition and loses consciousness: "No one paid attention to the man standing in a visible spot and Greta went through him with a bowl full of asparagus" (9) and Erna concludes "that she became ill due to some disease which enables her to see ghosts" (19). This condition remains undiagnosed. As in Atwood's narrative, the status of her illness builds an ambiguous tie between neurological predicaments and supernatural phenomena: "When Dr. Löwe came, Mrs. Elzner closed herself up with him...and told him in a clear and confident tone what, or rather whom Erna saw yesterday during dinner. She also said that most probably Erna had revealed mediumistic skills that were not uncommon among Mrs. Elzner's family members.—'In that case I have nothing to do. You should rather call for some exorcist'—said Dr. Löwe and stood up" (14). To explicate this enigmatic diagnosis, I engage the Deleuzean-Guattarian suggestion of the "originary" theft of the girl's body as achieved through the transcendental organization of her organs into a symbolic form, a receptacle for male desire and progeny. Following Deleuze and Guattari, it is because neither a "girl" nor a "woman" is accomplished socially as (a fully-fledged) subject that "becoming-woman" constitutes an identity-in-process, not an outcome or result, but a transgressing continuum. In reading Deleuze and Guattari with Irigaray,

I propose here that Erna constitutes such an unfinished subjectivity, a passage, or a "line" that is never realized fully. In order to "become," as Irigaray notes, one needs a gender or an essence (necessarily sexed) as horizon; "otherwise the becoming will be only partial or multiple without a future of one's own" (*Sexes* 73). "Becoming" "means achieving the fullness of all that one could be," (73) a process that obviously remains open-ended. In this context, Mitchell's comments on Freud's Dora, referenced in my reading of *Siostra*, are relevant again. Although it "is commonplace to note the patriarchal suppression of Dora's mother to a marginalized position of housewife's neurosis, of making life difficult and of being ill-educated and lacking culture" (Mitchell 96), neither Mitchell nor Kristeva agree with this (feminist) belief: "When Dora came to Freud...at the turn of the century, we can see that mothers were powerful and important figures behind the structures of patriarchy, and that sexuality among the bourgeoisie was rampant and profoundly subject to sickness. It was round this conjuncture that Freud the doctor started to shift his ground to become Freud the psychoanalyst. And hysteria was at the centre, indeed was really the cause, of this shift" (Mitchell 98). Similarly, in her letter to Clement in 1994, Kristeva notes: "Freud wrote that women did not have the capacity for a superego. I am well aware that he was thinking of his Vienna and his protected middle-class women, but that doesn't ring true for everyone, far from it. The anorectic is welded to her superego: hypermoral, hyperscrupulous, hyperdevoted to the Law, to God, to the One—call them what you like. It is because of that rigidity, which both sustains and destroys her, that she has come to me, to ask that I get rid of it" (Clément and Kristeva 116). In Tokarczuk's narrative, Dr. Löwe is rather conservative, pre-Freudian Jewish family doctor prescribing herbal infusions and purges for all types of complaints (61). However, in a case like this, "the scientific word 'hysteria' was the key," and Dr. Löwe, "the same evening when he was called to Erna, remembered that term and held on to it" (39): "In medical science, as in a textiles or furniture, various fashions come and go. Hysteria was an absolute hit, but it was also particularly shapeless, undefined. He sometimes had the feeling that this word was uttered by his collegues when they were covering up their embarrassment" (39). Under this fashionable influence, Erna is diagnosed as hysterical but healthy; her "indisposition" is linked to her biologically immature, "transitory" body (13). During his regular visit, Dr. Löwe concludes that "Erna's nervous system is still developing and at this age she is prone to faints or convulsions, hence the use of made-up diabolical fairy-tales could only upset her already unstable balance" (14-15). To Erna, however, the experience offers a chance to be noticed, while her subjectivity becomes acknowledged in the symbolic order. As an undistinguished sibling, Erna naturally exhibits her greed for love/food in her un/consciously enacted deviances. Her vision takes place in the presence of all the family members (greed for love) at the dining table (greed for food), and provides an interesting parallel to the phobia from which Freud himself suffered, as well as his patient E., as analyzed by Mitchell (65-66): "The motives for being ill often begin to be active even in childhood. A little girl in her greed for love does not enjoy having to share the affection of her parents with her brothers and sisters; and she notices that the whole of their affection is lavished on her once more whenever she arouses their anxiety by falling ill. She has now discovered a means of enticing out her parents' love, and will make use of that means as soon as she has the necessary psychical material at her disposal for producing an illness" (89).

Erna's animated alterity (alienation and distinction in the household) is derived from the fact that her sisters have either already gone through menstruation or are still very young. Her longing for mother, "the old and long familiar," to have her entirely to herself before it is too late (before she herself becomes a woman/mother), turns for Erna into a desire for the uncanny, categorized by Creed as related to the notion of a multiplied object, (a ghost or spirit), "an involuntary repetition of an act" (54). "Whatever it is, let us pretend that nothing happened" (*E.E.* 15) is Dr. Löwe's suggestion, but Mrs. Elzner does not share his opinion, stubbornly insisting on "the easiest method to make a madwoman out of [Erna]" (17). In a narcissistic trance, the mother recognizes herself in her daughter who reminds her of how "she was at that age—modest, ugly, lonesome and strange to the world, as if she did not belong to it" (13). The mother, "imprisoned in the same house with a man, who did not understand her at all, as if they were from different worlds" (17), projects her daughter's talents as her own. Erna's parents do indeed speak different languages: the mother's background is characterized by Tokarczuk as hysterical, irrational, and set in opposition to everything that is represented by her stereotypically German husband. The mostly neutral to entertaining narrative tone becomes at this point sadly ironical. Erna, trying subconsciously to please her mother, becomes the mother's chance to live. The mother's desire to "become significant" (organizing séances, inviting interesting people) signposts her subconscious protest against "housewife's neurosis" (Mitchell 96). Not unintentionally, the mother thus instigates the objectification of her daughter, turning her into a multiple object of desire: her own desire and that of many others, including the doctors, the specialists, and the audience. The narrative pattern emerging from "diagnosing" the girl echoes Irigaray's claim that "desire is connected to madness. But apparently one desire has chosen to see itself as wisdom, moderation, truth, and has left the other to bear the burden of madness it did not want to attribute to itself" (*Bodily Encounter* 35). Already, before Erna "becomes" a woman, she is "the phoney or hysterical feminine" (Mitchell 187), linked by Irigaray and Mitchell alike with the Freudian/Lacanian concept of "femininity as masquerade": "Joan Riviere, a British analyst analysed by Freud...wrote of 'femininity as a masquerade,' indicating a particular type of woman whose femininity was an act, or, I would claim, hysterical. Lacan turned this notion of Riviere into 'femininity is a masquerade' (thereby echoing Freud's mistake of a universal repudiation of femininity instead of a repudiation of the hysterical situation). In this argument one cannot be a 'true' woman, as the woman is defined as being nothing to be—no penis" (187).

In her masquerade, or enactment of femininity, the woman loses touch with herself and "plays" on her femininity: "this masquerade requires an *effort* on her part for which she is not compensated" (Irigaray, "Power" 130). Associated with her immature, not-yet-fruitful womb, Erna's phoniness becomes the abysmal figure of another medium, Teresa Frommer. These two female (but, for different reasons, not quite "feminine") bodies echo each other in the story. Teresa, a visionary marginal character with "an appearance of a very old, wrinkled child," a "hunchbacked gnome from a fairy-tale" (22), bears the marks of the witch and becomes central to the narrative through Erna. Teresa's soul overwhelms and deforms her body (25), evoking cultural associations of the masculine mind/soul in a body that is unfeminine. To follow the Platonian tradition, which continues through Descartes, Husserl, and Sartre, "the ontological distinction between soul (consciousness, mind) and body supports invariably relations of political and psychic subordination and hierarchy. The mind not only subjugates the body, but occasionally entertains the fantasy of fleeing its embodiment altogether" (Butler, *Gender Trouble* 12). Teresa's "huge soul" is thus, to take a cue from Butler, incompatible, rendering her a nightmarish creature of "the imaginary" with no place in the symbolic order. There is no "proper boundary" between her soul (which could be understood as the *unconscious*) and her physical body: "Only with difficulty had she learned how to read, but she bravely performed all the household duties. She talked in an unclear and chaotic manner, however, when she described her dreams, they seemed much more real than reality....Whenever [her brother] managed to convince her to tell him one of her dreams, he was surprised to be able to find, in these fragments, connections with real events, some important like political strategies, catastrophes, conflicts, others banal, like the neighbor's illness, the cat's death or Dr. Löwe's visit" (*E.E.* 22). Teresa's biography is of significance here: As a malformed and slow-witted daughter of a continuously travelling, mentally unstable but fascinating mother, she lives with her brother. Her first and only erotic experience is with Rainer, an ambiguous half-relative who discovers Teresa's mediumistic talents. It is Rainer who inconspicuously informs children of the account of their mother's madness leading to her suicide. In her passing, the mother becomes a familiar stranger, a source of the "uncanny" desire, generating among her children a life-long fascination with death-related phenomena. Teresa "was a medium, she talked with ghosts, but that gift was taken away from her" (23). Now, she participates in the séances with Erna as her silent ally, someone who knows "that all things that happen, are connected, perhaps in a chaotic way, but with no exception" (60). In this role of the Kristevan "another *other*," Teresa represents the shadow of the archaic mother, the om-phalic fragment that refuses to be cut off, thrown out, or wasted. Instead, she emerges as heterogeneity of the "becoming" subject. In concentrating on the beyond, both Teresa and Erna transcend their phoney, un/feminine bodies in an "uncanny" experience, in a momentum of different, transgressive, and metamorphic "becoming." In describing this momentum, Tokarczuk explicitly renders it fluid, bottomless. Their bodies are receptacles for all the *other* dis/connected elements (voices, pictures, apparitions) that are contrasted throughout the narrative with the dominant and acceptable discourse of the symbolic structure within which the medical and spiritual doctors operate. The suspension, or the gap between these two dimensions, is conflated in the narrative with the gap between the *unconscious* and the conscious, or the semiotic and symbolic functions. Erna seems to be living in this suspension and her instability derives precisely from it.

For Teresa and Erna alike, the experience of the *chora* is closing the gap between the living and the dead. They are able to synthesize binaries, polarities, and different "scientific" approaches with the passive amusement of an observer, involuntarily "incorporating" the experience/place in which voices/bodies speak. Precisely as such incarnations, they can be identified with the archaic spaces of the maternal that will be employed, indeed spectacularly "utilized," during the séance. In contradistinction to phallic figures, including Erna's mother, who exploits this experience, Erna and Teresa undergo involuntary metamorphoses of their bodily objectifications. The séance in *E.E.*, like Cixous's "sabbat," is a "reverse spectacle" (Cixous and Clément 10), with Erna's theatrical body as a central object of desire for the "beyond." The guests gather around her and "through" her body take part in the trance, in "the celebration, in which everyone participates, in which no one is voyeur" (10). This type of "audience, ready to satisfy its fantastic desire" (10), calls to mind the spectacular scene of hysteria in Atwood's depiction of Grace Marks's hypnosis, and Cixous's description of a comparable scene: "It is, above all...the circle of doctors with their fascinated eyes, who surround the hysteric, their bodies tensed to see the tensed body of the possessed woman" (10). However, in Tokarczuk's text, the mother is an active agent of interrogation, and her presence is crucial to Erna. The mother is the knot that ties her down rather, as in reference to Freud's encounter with his mother's naked body (130), a knot by which the world was tied. The motherly knot is also the one that Erna involuntarily holds on to in her hysterical, hypothetical "thought delivery" (49). The mother is, in fact, the very secret of the trance, the actual ghost (absence) and the reason for her daughter's "madness." The narrative welcomes all thinkable explanations of the case, including fraud, a secret spectacle of fantasy and seduction. Interweaving the adults' séances (secret gatherings) with the children's secrets, Tokarczuk brings Erna's younger twin sisters into the scene. They act, or imagine they act, as enchantresses, "little witches" as they call themselves. Through their equally seductive but similarly threatening presence, Tokarczuk once more draws our attention to Erna's objectification. In a "secret" performance that is set up to imitate the adults' séance, the twins deconstruct its phallic structure. Their subversive voice both engages and undermines what Cixous has referred to as a "terrifying, immense, and paternal character...as indefinite as the huge shadow of a he-goat haunting the sabbat nights" (Cixous and Clément 12). In Cixous's parallel readings of a secret spectacle, such as the clandestine sabbat or illicit children's games, the involvement of the audience will be saved for later in the scene of punishment, purification, or exorcism: "When the institutional spectators of the Church are in place, when the parents are ready to enforce the punishment—that is the spectacle. For the moment, there is play....The scene will soon take shape. It is a scene of seduction" (12). During this blend of archaic fantasy and phallic seduction, Erna's body and her talents are "returned" to her. The "play," meant simultaneously as a therapeutic act and *unconscious* feminist strategy (in the girls' acting "as if adults"), releases Erna from the entrapment endorsed by her mother's and Frommer's desires.

Ultimately, I read this scene as a strategy to return voice to Erna, who should finally speak for herself. The twins' aggressive presence, as they act against the ongoing denigration of their mother as well as the forthcoming denigration of all their elder sisters, makes Erna indeed perform her "speech" that takes the form of a spectacular hysterical performance, a transition towards becoming a woman. Shortly thereafter, Erna has her first menstruation and enters the sphere of her elder sisters who initiate her into the "feminine" ritual of blood/filth disposal. The final scene in the story portrays Erna's moment of most intense pleasure, one that climaxes in death, or a deathlike condition. Walking through the woods, where she seeks a rescue from the "filth," Erna stops, lifts her shirt and touches the "device" restraining her body. In undoing the cotton loops (187), she freezes and begins to examine the hot, pulsating place with her hand. Her encounter with maternal blood intermingles with orgasmic pleasure, the newly discovered desire of the woman's body. The blood is "nothing new," but in combination with the place from which it issues, it is "uncanny," and Erna separates from it through a deathlike experience, a transcendence of the literal origin. The question as to whether she loses her breath momentarily or whether her ecstasy causes actual death remains open. However, to return to the Deleuzean-Guttarian theory of becoming, her transcendence, or "flight," articulates transformative possibilities of her identity that might or might not escape from the codes that constitute the subject. If her puberty drama is a preparation for phoney "femininity," a masquerade of womanhood, then perhaps it is not meant to be realized in "the symbolic," but in the return to the very first symbolic act, the act of "real incision." To conclude with this insight, Erna does not become a woman, rather, as Deleuze and Guattari would have it, she "is an abstract line, or a line of flight" (*A Thousand Plateaus* 276), a leaping over a logocentric abyss that opens up as a "different" possibility.

The Witch as the Maternal Space of Filth

Shifting the critique from the witch as a source of *herstorical* powers to the properties of the witch as an archaic mother, the narratives have focused on the primary (maternal) loss, depicting cultural constructs of mothers and daughters expelled outside the symbolic structure. As phallic rather than *omphalic* depictions of mothers (*omphalos*, the navel, as the scar left by separation), I view these narratives as both participating in and failing Butler's strategies of subversive repetition. Bronfen's definition of the *omphalos*, following Lacanian and Kristevan discussions of the psychic history of the subject, structures this fundamental loss of the maternal body—"a loss we never own or represent but one that we repeat" and commemorate (19). This reading of the witch as a primal cartography of the body coincides with Kristeva's "precondition for language even though it depends on language, and which suffers and takes pleasures in an other logic, complementary to the logic of linguistic signs imposed and consolidated by paternal laws" (Clément and Kristeva 95).

Subverting the culturally stigmatized cartographies of the body, Kristeva's semiotic unquestionably celebrates the difficult (impossible) separation from maternal authority (95), and further connects with the psychoanalytical intricacies of the navel as discussed in this chapter. In return to Bronfen's visualization of the navel as "a cultural image fraught with reticence," the navel is a common point of connection and severing: "often prominently displayed in sculptures of the human body and frequently a significant detail in paintings of the nude, it yet remains an oversight. Most dictionaries of subjects and symbols of art, or motives and themes in literature and folklore, will ignore the navel or merely include a cursory entry mentioning its multifarious usage as trope for conceptualizations of the center. Nor has the navel been privileged theoretically in psychoanalytically informed semiotic and cultural studies of the body, as have other body parts such as breast, penis, vagina, eye, nose, or foot" (Bronfen 3). Owing precisely to its intangibility, the navel, "an obscene detail that fascinates even as it repels" (3), clearly connects here with the semiotic that is founded on the abject, on what is considered "filth" (Clément and Kristeva 95). The navel, as a reminder of a bodily wound, culturally embodies this semiotic filth. It exists already in terms of culture as "a boundary line that makes the dirty turn into the tainted, since it is then understandable how the ritualization of filth can be accompanied by a complete effacement of the dirty object" (93). In the figure of the witch, the semiotic and the navel converge in the maternal space of filth (placenta, umbilical cord), echoing the old practice of midwives predicting pregnancies by reading the knots on umbilical cords as prophetic signs (Bronfen 4). Definitely, the dirty object, in Clément's and Kristeva's discussion, vanishes when it is transformed, within a particular logic, into "filth" that is "no longer noticed, it no longer smells" (93). This practice suspends the midwife-witch between "symbolic castration" and "the real incision." To distinguish between these two conditions, I propose Bronfen's concept of "denaveling," which "harks back to the traumatic wound at the onset of mortality yet defies any direct representation" (11), and allows me to posit the witch as a negotiator between the phallic and the *omphalic* spaces of culture. The navel, in Mieke Bal's understanding, designates "the other force field constituting the subject," distinct from "phallus" as a gender-specific association in terms "to have it" versus "to be it." On the contrary, the *omphalos* is genuinely "democratic in that both men and women have it" (qtd. in Bronfen 11). Although it emerges metaphorically as the scar of dependence on the mother, unlike the phallus and its iconic representations disseminated throughout post-Freudian culture, the navel is starkly indexical (qtd. in Bronfen 11). Favoring thus the *omphalic* as a source of effective subversion, the witch, in this chapter, like Cixous's figure, "serves to connect all the ends [i.e., loose strands] of a culture that is hard to endure" (Cixous and Clément 8). The narrative representations of the witch embody the instability of culture (symbolic structure), disturbing sexual/gendered identity, and collapsing into a Kristevan abject that designates bodily discharges, excrements rendered alien, to be expelled: "I expel myself, I spit myself out, I abject myself within the same motion through which 'I' claim to establish myself" (*Powers* 3). What is established by the logic of this expulsion are "the boundaries of the body," "the first contours of the subject" (Butler, *Gender Trouble* 133). In linking this specification of the witch with Judeo-Christian associations between the sacred/heretic and feminine/maternal, Kristeva identifies Christianity as the most refined symbolic construct in which femininity meets with "virginal maternality" as a way "of dealing with feminine paranoia" ("Stabat Mater" 180). In a reference to Warner's study (1990), Kristevan Virgin both assumes and overcomes her feminine denial of sex "by setting up a third person: *I* do not conceive with *you* but with *Him*. The result is an immaculate conception (therefore with neither man nor sex), conception of a God with whose existence a woman has indeed something to do," on the condition that she acknowledges her subjugation. "But she succeeds in stifling megalomania [of Church] by putting it on its knees before the child-god" ("Stabat Mater" 180). Exploring intersections of the feminine and the sacred, both Clément and Kristeva posit women's spirituality as a paradoxical crossroad of heretic/sacred and religious experience. The Judeo-Christian concept of virginity or the Roman Catholic doctrine of the Immaculate Conception intersect in their analysis with the historical persecution of Eve-like women stigmatized as witches, heretics, and monsters. As in Warner, whose text is constantly at work in Kristeva's analysis of the Virgin, medieval images of Mary are those of the second Eve, constructed as positive models that supplement Eve's negativity: "The idea of the second Eve, through whom the sin of the first was ransomed, was important to the west, where it inspired the ingenious imagination of the medieval Christian to pun and riddle with a characteristic sense of delight and love of symmetry" (73). Eve, the woman seduced (bitten or penetrated) by the (evil) snake, bleeds every month thereafter. On the contrary, Christian Virgin becomes a locus of female in/dependence, a fluctuating trace of ancient fertility and magic, but representing a body devoid of all her blood and sex.

Diasporic locations of Mary (culminating in Kristevan "paranoia") erase pagan traces of her carnality, but she continues as the (eroticized) maternal body, and intersects in my analysis with the border-locations of the "witch." One of the premises underlying this intersection is Irigaray's notion of the sacrificed state of the earth's fertility, which delineates the cultural horizon of the paternal language and its "forgetting of the scar of the navel" (*Bodily Encounter* 41). The witch as a trace of the presence/absence of the Virgin builds a symbolical counterpoint to the female sex equated with pollution (i.e., the fifteenth-century Virgin, radically opposed to the idea of female carnality and continued to expand over the course of the centuries coinciding with the most severe witch trials on the European continent). The witch's womb, fantasized as "a devouring mouth, a cloaca or anal and urethral outfall, a phallic threat, at best reproductive" (*Bodily Encounter* 41), represent her only way to communicate the body, her only language in fact. "In the absence of valid representations of female sexuality, this womb merges with woman's sex [sexe] as a whole. There are no words to talk about it, except filthy, mutilating words" to the effect of "anxiety, phobia, disgust, a haunting fear of castration" (41). Following Warner, the Judeo-Christian concept of femininity replicates the Greek tradition of equating female innocence with ignorance, and translates virginity as the lack of (sexual) knowledge (185). The same femininity, the "sweetness, submissiveness, and passivity" (that constitutes Levinasian alterity) permits the Virgin "to survive [as] a goddess in a patriarchal society," stigmatizing the nonvirginal body as a locus of abjection. Hence, the witches' condemnation flourishes in countries such as Poland, Italy, or Spain where the cult of the Virgin is particularly strong (Warner 191), and where women rarely act in the public as autonomous subjects, relegated to *other* discursive arenas, mostly within the domestic domain as mothers. In close reference to Warner, Kristeva speculates whether "the 'virgin' attribute for Mary is a translation error that substituted the Greek word *parthenos* for the Semitic term indicating the sociolegal status of a young unmarried woman, which on the other hand specifies a physiological and psychological condition: virginity" (Clément and Kristeva 163). In this twist affiliating the sacred with eroticism, Kristeva's own understanding of virginity differs from the constructions discussed above, since it refers to "a protospace, a timelessness," to a "radical transcendence" of the feminine and the maternal. She writes, "The fact that this nonplace before the beginning has been designated feminine or maternal is not likely to displease me, and it has led me to understand the 'feminine' as something completely different from a symmetrical double of the masculine" (Clément and Kristeva 73). What this "transcendence" allows us to see "are strategies of sense without signification," memories, if you like, but far below language and the signifier" (151). In linking these signifying limits of the body (Clément and Kristeva, Irigaray), I have attempted to reformulate the archaic (prephallic) mother as a therapeutic territory, allowing space for the emergence of resistance to hegemonic, symbolic discourse. This archaic figure, viewed as a pre-oedipal/semiotic mother, in contrast with the phallocentric fantasy of the mother-fetish, serves as a chain of metonymies for a particular (peculiar) space of nullification of the phallic function that fails to represent "all" of the sexes. This turn to the pre-oedipal has taken place "to rethink desire in relation to the maternal," and "engages us, unwittingly, in the resurrection of the dyad: not the phallus, but the maternal, for the two options available are 'dad' and 'mom'" (Butler, *Undoing Gender* 136). Butler's position reminds us of course that there are "other kinds of descriptions that might complicate what happens at the level of desire and, indeed, at the level of gender and kinship" (136). Consequently, the witch, translated textually into a semiotic form, comes to represent the "maternal" part of the Freudian/Lacanian *unconscious*, but is always already unfinished in relation to the "feminine." This feminine no longer coincides with the "maternal" reflection of a dominant subject and takes her departure from these subjectivities. The archaic mother is thus approached as an *unconscious* trace, leading towards the emergence of the feminine as a reconfiguration of language in which the affirmation of the feminine might be accomplished—in fact her morphological metamorphosis, as Braidotti would put it. Irigaray's "transcendental subject" emerges precisely from the place of affirmation: the embodied subject against which multifaceted "feminine" subjectivities can measure themselves "rather than progressing only by taking the place of the mother, the other woman or the man" ("Limits" 112).

Although coming from different cultural contexts, the narratives analyzed in this chapter converge in recognition of the debt to the mother trapped within constructions of phallocentric discourse. This recognition allows the mother to "become a sexual and desiring woman" and frees the daughter from her undifferentiated relation to the maternal. Marking the possibility of the mother's cultural re-evaluation, the archaic witch manifests clearly a desire to connect the semiotic chora with the symbolic. Going beyond the *herstorical* sociosexual victimization of women, the narratives illustrate the multifaceted feminist conviction that women's oppression is not only material and political but that it is established in the very logos connecting "abjection" and "monstrosity" to the feminine libidinal economy of desire. In conveying their own historical reminiscence of a cultural split (in culturally distinct contexts), the figures of women discussed negotiate their positions not in a quiet act of introspection, but in a painful re-member-ing that requires a plural consciousness and fluency in using several systems of cultural understanding. At this point, in contrast to the difficulties encountered in work against the theory of "symbolic castration," another issue is at stake, namely that of a "real incision." This "real incision," with reference to psychoanalytical concepts developed by Gallop, Mitchell, and Bronfen, is posited as a continuous separation from the (archaic) mother, perpetuated through women themselves as carriers of patriarchal ideology. My analysis of the narratives, viewed as feminist configurations of the archaic mother (projected in Western imagery as a figure of horror, monstrosity, and abjection), parallels Butler's belief that the critical task for feminism is not to establish a position outside of constructed identities, but rather "to locate strategies of subversive repetition enabled by those constructions" (*Gender Trouble* 147). The narratives demonstrate this split in subject positions and deviate from the restorative and liberating function attributed by some to the archaic mother. Rather than a locus of semiotic pleasures, the archaic *chora* appears as a hole that leads nowhere, an empty barren space, or as a ghostly (spectral) apparition of repressed, uncanny desires. I recognize the problematic aspects of associating the witch-woman with the imaginary where female desire will be perceived inevitably as a hysterical inconsistency, the signpost of the unspeakable. Designated as the *omphalic* (in distinction to the phallic) mother, she is still so deeply entangled in the Western metaphor of the abject, or otherwise nonexistent figure, that she cannot provide a therapeutic but only a traumatic passage to the symbolic. Deleuzean-Guattarian notions serve here as a device of readability of her trauma, a way of presenting what otherwise cannot be articulated. Surviving from the prelinguistic phase, this *omphalic* creature exists only in dialectical relation with the linguistic and cultural order, assuming therefore marginal (semiotic) positions. To follow Butler, the pleasures of maternity constitute only "local displacements of the paternal law, temporary subversions which finally submit to that against which they initially rebel" (*Gender Trouble* 88). The performances of the witch result thus in a dialectical process of deconstructing the mother in the symbolic. The witch as a semiotic in/disposition cannot exist without constantly challenging the symbolic order (of language), and without being constantly silenced by it. In the discussed narratives, the *unconscious* has a language (voice), and the witch figure constitutes its significant revelation. This language does not represent a position of command, but the more subjective, vulnerable position in which the subject is already exiled from the *chora*. It constitutes an "unsettling confrontation" between two subject positions: one that assumes its linguistic castration and the other that realizes this castration as a gain rather than a loss (Gallop, *Daughter's Seduction* 21). The position adopted involves complex attempts to speak the *unconscious* in the-name-of-the-mother and "to point out some effects, some elements of unconscious drives, some relations of feminine Imaginary to [Lacan's] Real, to writing" (Cixous and Clément 92). Recognizing that the "vacuum" is not only political but is established in the very logos, in the subtle linguistic procedures through which meaning itself is shaped, a new type of linguistic/symbolic awareness of the phallic rape is established. The rape is no longer effected by the father, but above all, by the fetishized suffocating mothers as deployed in the symbolic. Connecting this awareness with the trauma of the "real incision," the narratives install the witch as a variable of the hysterical (displaced) archaic mother and the phallic (devouring) mother-rapist. Emerging from the dialogue established between these two, the witch figure (proposed as a type of return to the *unconscious*) appears in the form of a spectrum of the repressed *omphalic* mother. In this constellation, it remains difficult "to distinguish between incest as a traumatic fantasy essential to sexual differentiation in the psyche, and incest as a trauma that ought clearly to be marked as abusive practice" (Butler, *Undoing Gender* 154). Although not without liberating potential gesturing beyond the maternal, the *omphalic* is dominated by the presence of the phallus, and cut off from its distinct pleasures and sovereignty (e.g., figures dominated by the presence of physicians, judges, and psychiatrists, objects of physiological and psychological explorations). Their subjectivities emerge from victimizing and oppressive positions, unable to resolve the divide. To follow Nancy Fraser, the subject is thus split into two halves, neither of which is a potential political agent. Defined exclusively in terms of transgressing the norms, this subject cannot engage in the reconstructive moment of feminist politics, a moment essential to social transformation (*Justice Interruptus* 164). "Nor can the two halves be joined together," since they rather cancel each other out, "the first forever shattering the identitarian pretensions of the second, the second forever recuperating the first and reconstituting itself as before" (164). What follows is a "paralyzing oscillation between identity and nonidentity without any determinate practice issue" (165).

The suspension of the witch is thus a reference to the culturally inarticulate gap between the radical *fantasmatic* and the archaic mother, a dialogical figure of permanent transgressions. For various reasons, the relationship with the mother, as described in these narratives, maintains a position of a "mad desire in the shadows of our culture" (Irigaray, *Bodily Encounter* 35), from where the strategies of resistance might depart, and what Braidotti would later call "the strategic essentialism of sexual difference" (*Metamorphoses* 34). The final chapter explores the narrative attempts to move beyond the limiting experience of disassociation from "the symbolic," insisting on "the illusion" of identity, which in the end, owing to its paradoxical status, contests and possibly bridges the gap between the semiotic and symbolic types of articulation. In contesting this gap, the witch remains composed of deficiencies, subversions, and historical silences, and through this embraces the essential diversity of the feminine space. But since her essentiality in paternal language continues to indicate absence, the archaic subject emerges as a ghostly, spectral materiality in search of its own (cultural) body. It encounters a type of paradox that recalls Kristeva's *aporia* of the chora: to be approached both as an absent (repressed) and persistently recurring desire for a provocative subversion. If this subversion has any agency, it is opened up by the fact that its constitution was initiated in the social order. That it is contained as a paradox does not mean that it is impossible: "it means only that paradox is the condition of its possibility" (Butler, *Undoing Gender* 3). The subversion, in the end, entails unexpected exposure to new un/conscious and multiple forms of expression. Perhaps the seeming absence, as Dietze has written, is also an opportunity: "Maybe there are no places, systems, or identities where an individual woman can stand phallically erected in order to survey the world. Maybe it is not the place but the journey, not the system but the aphorism, not the identity but the multiplicity from which one speaks. It could be playing with theory fragments, juggling with standpoints on a trial basis, just [like] unabashed eclecticism, that women put to their service" (293).

As I argue in the final chapter, it is the witch's diverse un/belonging, her condensation as a deviant territory that allows her to embark on new processes of responding to woman's cultural "becoming" rather than her denigration.

Chapter Three

The Embarrassed "etc." at the End of the List

Identifications of Subjectivity and the Social

Building on feminist reconstructions of the hysteric and the archaic mother discussed in previous chapters, I set out to examine the conceptual knots that confuse and hold together historical and contemporary identifications of subjectivity with the social meaning of the symbolic. The constitutive and primary importance of "sexual difference" (Irigaray) within the symbolic function and its negative entanglement in the loss of the primary object of desire (Kristeva's "maternal") call for a renewed perspective from which to approach feminine subjectivity. I propose to look at feminist philosophical intersections of femininity and transgressive spaces of race/ethnicity and the social. The *transgression*, in its ethical conjecture, appears supremely incompatible with the hegemonic order of cultural belonging and, by its very reality, makes the limits of that order apparent: transgression as heresy, monstrosity, deviance, in other words, as representable difference of any "constructed subjectivity" that continues to be inscribed with a negative signification (Balibar 190). This notion of "transgression" as negativity goes to the beginnings of European philosophical thought and of Western history in general, culminating in poststructuralist attempts to reframe this model but abstracting from what current transfeminist theory needs to focus on: the social practice and social context of feminist communication (see Fraser). In particular, the post/Lacanian encoding of cultural authority as masculine continues to inscribe "woman" with a disadvantaged place in the symbolic, or otherwise in the putative impossibility of a semiotic sexuality. What remains, at the structure of the social, is a normative symbolic order, with its production of monolithic subjectivities, supporting various channels of nostalgic reassertions of culturally dominant or "pure" identities, racism, and national phobias (see Griffin and Braidotti). In this context, both advanced capitalism and its post/communist locations as new cartographies of power persistently invest exclusionary and phallocentric tactics in areas of sociopolitical significance.

Trans-, either as transition, transformation, or transgression of such historically contingent trappings of dominance (as language, accent, ethnicity, or sexuality), continues as illicit, illegal, or incompatible. Through polymorphic precarious locations that by necessity need to remain peripheral, transgression undermines the conservative preservation and continuous reproduction of boundaries that hold proper bodies and expel pollution and danger. My central concern is to emphasize the renewed necessity to look at *transgression* across the heterogeneity of Western cultures as a concept denoting not only incompatibility with the "proper" order of belonging and identity, but also turning difference into the positive, empowering affirmation of alternative subject positions. Transgression that makes the limits of the proper order apparent in a difference that is long representable and that reflects the current dissemination of cultures in which identities are useful as strategic identifications: either institutionary or with other subjects by the intermediary of an institution. What is changing today, to follow Braidotti, is not merely the terminology or metaphorical representation of the subjects, but the very structure of subjectivity, social relations, and the social imaginary. Braidotti's question—how can we free difference from its negative charge in the social function—is more relevant than ever, but first what do we want to free from what? In elaborating this question, I begin with the Kristevan (Hegelian and, indeed, Lacanian) position on what she names the imaginary "loving third," "the key stone for the capacity to sublimation" and the collateral for the ability to idealize (*Black Sun* 121-22). This third party, according to Kristeva, intervenes between the maternal territory and the child, that is, its subjectivity in process, and emerges in her discussion as a counterbalance to the punishing function of the superego; as a flip side of the Law that recognizes the necessity of negotiating the unbridgeable and is therefore essential to the formation of the subject. What remains if this counterbalance is lacking could be called a masochistic or paranoid construction of subjectivity that believes it deserves punishment due to its instability, and constantly puts itself under the surveillance of the Law. We are returning to the poststructural position of feminine subjectivity that for centuries continued to develop without the imaginary support of the social function. If this subjectivity is to be freed from its negative or ambiguous foundation, it needs to be freed from its entrapment in the abstract position of the "floating signifier": from a "senseless flow that produces its own significance," "impersonal, in short, speaking (in) the name of no one" (*Desire* 190). I continue with Kristeva's terminology on purpose, not only to show how contradictory and antithetical her poststructural theory sometimes appears, but also how difficult it is to posit transgressive practice once and for all. Kristeva's *transgressions* (the abject, the semiotic) certainly give rise to discursive innovations that could subsequently be normalized in the form of modified signifying practices, but the absence of a credible constructive alternative to the symbolic order is part of her theory (see Fraser and Bartky).

Butler's intervention on power discourse is relevant, as power (in Foucault's sense) is precisely what makes the subject possible, "the condition of its possibility and its formative occasion," and "what is taken up and reiterated in the subject's 'own' acting." The subject is formed as "a subject *of* power (where 'of' connotes both 'belonging to' and 'wielding')" and it "eclipses the conditions of its own emergence;

it eclipses power with power" (*Psychic Life* 14). As a conduit, or negotiation, between semiotic drives/affects and words/symbols, "the subject *of* power," in Butler's analysis, is crucial for one's sense of belonging to the symbolic dimension. Denial and loss of the negotiation works precisely against it—if semiotic traces are denied, the subject becomes a prisoner of the "primary loss." The particularities of melancholy, hysteria, depression, or suicidal tendency, returning to Kristevan logic, draw on the denial and consequently on the absence of signifiers of the semiotic loss. The poverty of linguistic activity that marks depression and melancholia—gaps, silences, and the inability to complete verbal sequences—points to the domination of semiotic traces that remain illegible, unrepresentable. In Kristeva's belief, the absence of the interaction between the marginalized subject and culture is followed by the collapse of the psychic space (*New Maladies* 29) that is conceived in a speech act. Reading through this absence, Braidotti might be too quick in rejecting Kristeva's "panic exercises, whether it is in her analysis of horror and monstrous others, of ethnic diversity, and inevitably, of loss and melancholia" (*Metamorphoses* 41). Melancholic returns to the "loving party," crucial to Kristeva's original loss and Butler's notion of desire, derive precisely from the unrealized potential for verbal expression (marginalized identities, sexual, cultural, or social citizenships disenfranchised within the dominant system, are particularly prone to melancholia that work in tandem with processes of social regulation). To read with Butler, in the absence of public recognition or discourse through which a loss "might be named and mourned," melancholia "takes on cultural dimensions of contemporary consequence" (*Psychic Life* 139). Butler's question of "drag identity" interconnects here psychoanalysis with gender performativity and performativity with the subject of melancholic mourning. What might, however, enable the constitution of subjectivity, and the narcissistic structure that supports formation of the subject, is a metaphorical transgression from the place of nonarticulation to the place of social support for the cultural meaning, that is the psychic space of power. In discussing this transgression ("transfer"), I propose to disconnect, theoretically, feminine subjectivity from repression, negative ambiguity, and ultimately depression as the only alternatives to sublimation. Butler, like Kristeva's appraisal of "transgression," seems to valorize change abstractly (change for its own sake) and thereby, similarly, to diminish feminist capacity for progressive sociopolitical action: "Butler's ontology of the subject has some significant conceptual limitations. It does not theorize the relation of embodied individuals, with their relatively enduring dispositions (habitus), to the dispersed subject positions they successfully occupy. Nor does it theorize intersubjectivity, the relations to one another of such individuals" (Fraser 215). Butler and Kristeva rely "on the ontogenetic subject formation by means of abjection," and like Foucault, insist that subjects are constituted primarily through exclusion and elimination. But is it really the case, to ask with Fraser, "that no one can become the subject of speech without others being silenced?" (216). Without "loving" support (recognition) from the Social, the subject is homeless and incompatible with the proper order of belonging, but, on Braidotti's note, this subject is far from being immobilized. There is an immense potential in homelessness and transgression, suggesting ways in which stigmas and recognition are perennially translated one into the other (Balibar 190), in which social order produces modes of reflectivity as it simultaneously limits forms of sociality. Positing nostalgic gesture as "not merely politically conservative," but also "deterrent to serious analysis of contemporary culture" (*Metamorphoses* 41), Braidotti intervenes thus with a discourse of pleasure. Irigaray's "sensible transcendental" is the key to this "feminine" reconfiguration, allowing for new theoretical space between the primary loss and subsequent repression of the maternal body. Braidotti asks: "What if the 'fixer' of the psychic landscape were the over-flowing plentitude of pleasure, rather than the melancholy discourse of debt and loss" (*Metamorphoses* 53)? I return to this question in my readings of the narratives, attempting to disconnect feminine subjectivity from repression and to cut the linearity of the "umbilical cord" once and for all. Not that the cord suggests filth and danger, but that, in its inevitably melancholic posture of mourning over the loss, it demobilizes permutable, plural, and otherwise mobile positions. After all, the cord is not a straight line connecting A and B, but a spiraling, entangling device that connects as much as it flows, persists, and transmutes.

Once cut, the cord does not disappear, but continues to represent desire, which can now unfold in many alternative and unpredictable subject positions. Consequently, the witch employed in the narratives discussed here mobilizes hybridity through her un/belonging. Un/belonging, a term designating both physical location (belonging) and sociopolitical relation with agency (unbelonging), conveys a decentralized but not disempowering cultural topography. As a fugitive from melancholic positions of absence and exclusion, s/he draws on her confinement to the "far away land" of collective myths and superstitions, to her expulsion from the "here and now," and simultaneously her ubiquitous physical presence, her hidden closeness as a neighboring woman, mother, or daughter. But her nonconforming physical appearance is ambiguous, because as a phallocentric projection of the feminine it should be familiar (motherly), but it is not. In fact, as argued in the previous chapter, the diasporic image of the witch's body is marked by the stigma of the monstrous feminine, the castrating vagina, and the witch as a grotesque "unfeminine" figure. Her enforced exile or voluntary flight is from this initially marked gender, as she is caught between, rather than supported by, the various laws and languages of the Father. But eventually the exile inscribes her also with "agency." As Butler writes, "The question of locating 'agency' is usually associated with the viability of the 'subject,' where the 'subject' is understood to have some stable existence prior to the cultural field that it negotiates. Or, if the subject is culturally constructed, it is nevertheless vested with an agency, usually figured as the capacity for reflexive meditation, that remains intact regardless of its cultural embeddedness" (*Gender Trouble* 142-43). Embracing agency involves therefore a discussion of cultural but also social construction. Since today, in a new millennium, Western feminism has accepted that gender in as much as any other bodily identification has become too polyvalent as a concept to be universally accommodating, what remains is to discuss the feasibility of sociocultural "embeddedness." The narratives chosen for this chapter help to illuminate the affirmative rewriting of difference, as outlined by Irigaray and Braidotti, and in particular the shift of the political debate from the issues of difference between cultures and ideologies towards differences within the very same structure of cultural identifications (*Metamorphoses* 14). These new complexities, indeed paradoxes, of difference within the Western condition account for the shifts in theoretical thinking about agency transgression: shifts that defy dualistic, oppositional, and melancholic reasoning. Following Braidotti, what remains if the postures of diaspora and negativity are abandoned is a type of nomadic, multiple existence. Its shifting foundations delineate a very tangible sociotheoretical gap between identity (self-sameness) and difference, a borderline position of philosophical suspension in un/belonging. This formulation of un/belonging converges with a number of theoretical concepts, such as resistance, parody, or subversion, and finally, the emergence of a subculture as a political form of expression. As an experience of self-affirmation that first appears at odds with the social, un/belonging (or nomadism, to use Braidotti's term) permutates and transforms the social structure. It is in this interplay of border positions that resistance, mimesis, and parody take place. I use un/belonging as a key metaphor for a cultural interconnectedness, a common thread in the variety of stories, which are all related, differently, to a clear move away from the psychoanalytic idea of the body. This body, no longer exclusively a map of semiotic inscriptions (Kristeva) or culturally enforced codifications (Butler), is a surface for a nomadic fantasy of gender: of body (and, by necessity, of "embeddedness") as a "bundle of contradictions" in the process of cultural mediation, of becoming-subject (*Metamorphoses* 21). For Deleuze and Guattari, the becoming-woman, embodied in the image of "the little girl," represents the process of becoming-subject, for both, or otherwise, for many different sexes. For Deleuze and Guattari, read in particular with Braidotti, it is the paradox of bodily instability that moves us beyond fixed gender identities and beyond the oppositional arrangement of subject and object. The feminine adolescent is a nomadic subject in a continual process of "becoming," but her becoming-woman is most certainly not the growing of the girl into a woman, but precisely a deterritorialization of this apprehension. The girl, in Deleuzean-Guattarian understanding, and in a flip-side relation to the post/Lacanian "Woman," is an "abstract line," a "becoming" "that remains contemporaneous to each opposable term, man, woman, child, adult. It is not the girl who becomes woman; it is becoming-woman that produces the universal girl" (Deleuze and Guattari 276-77). Narrativity of this theoretical mediation, which I trace in the texts selected for this chapter, is of crucial binding force in this correlation: "a collective, politically-invested process of sharing in and contributing to the making of myths, operational fictions, significant figurations of the kind of subjects we are in process of becoming" (*Metamorphoses* 22).

Various figures associated with, rather than constituting, the witch in the following analyses take a theoretical borderline position between melancholia and pleasure. In this borderline position, particularly relevant as a location that escapes precise definition and needs to be traced under various names and structures, the witch becomes a her(m)etic figure (hermetic and heretical), no longer to be thought of in terms of categories, but in terms of an experience of dissociation, of slipping across borders, of nomadism. The temporal paradox of this figure is such that it necessarily follows Kristeva's, Butler's, and Braidotti's implications of a subject already formed in order to account for its own incompleteness, its becoming: "That 'becoming' is no simple or continuous affair, but an uneasy practice of repetition and its risks, compelled yet incomplete, wavering on the horizon of social being" (Butler, *Psychic Life* 30). Crucial to this process of becoming are issues of other differences, notably religion, nationality, language, and ethnicity, a complex web of identifications arguably constitutive of subjectivities. But to encompass a situated (gendered in as much as political or social) morphology of a subject is indeed an impossible enterprise, invariably failing to be inclusive, exposing the fallacy of "political correctness." Writing of gender and sexual difference, respectively, Butler and Braidotti have addressed this impossibility. For Butler, "the theories of feminist identity that elaborate predicates of color, sexuality, ethnicity, class, and able-bodiedness" are consistently closing "with an embarrassed 'etc.' at the end of the list" (*Gender Trouble* 143). This phenomenon is of course instructive: "what political impetus is to be derived from the exasperated 'etc.' that so often occurs at the end of such lines? This is a sign of exhaustion as well as of the illimitable process of signification itself" (143). Thus, to insist on belonging and self-recognition is precisely to ensure and to intensify a continuing confusion of and about the predicates in question. To follow Gibson, there is an ethical (Levinasian) space in this theoretical narrative of gender and of sexual difference. Butler's "illimitable et cetera" and Braidotti's "embodied becoming" must be understood as a spontaneous and *immediate* desire to escape the limits of identity, a desire generated as those limits are experienced and practiced in their narrowness, even their absurdity: "It is thus a principle of unease within and inseparable from the self that is of a different order to being and more profound than it. Evasion is the ethical impulse towards or openness to the other that effects a release from the confines of the self" (Gibson 37). In this sense, it is impossible to determine our class, gender, or ethnicity once and for all, however much they are assumed, and it is with this recognition that the feminist ethics of un/belonging may begin.

The witch as a boundless fantasy of gender is thus a fantasy of un/belonging opening ways out of limiting significations. Although cross-gender, cross-cultural, and cross-body identifications make subjects politically vulnerable, they allow simultaneously for re-zoning the tabooed borders of stigmatized conditions. As proposed by Braidotti, in particular in her discussion of Deleuzian relevance to feminism, "the challenge that the monstrous throws in our direction is a disassociation of the sensibility we have inherited from the previous end of the century" (*Metamorphoses* 2). Precisely in the face of growing xenophobia, there is a necessity "to think of the anomalous, the monstrously different not as a sign of pejoration but as the unfolding of a virtual possibilities that point to positive alternatives for us all" (2). Thinking through such creative operations, I argue consequently that the witch as a metaphor for cultural pejoration involved in the narratives to follow does not need to invite identification with a lost (semiotic) experience. The language of boundaries that (post/Lacanian) psychoanalysis has involved in elaborating notions of identification and mourning promotes a specific set of assumptions about what subjectivity *is* about, cutting it, in fact, from the plentitude of the subject (Irigaray), "sapping it away into a series of delusional and compensatory manifestations of self" (*Metamorphoses* 54). Instead, Irigaray's position of the *plenum* takes its hold by a proliferation of subjectivities and subsequently permits Braidotti's departure on the status of identity-in-process (in becoming) that derives from multiplicity. This "account of nomadic subjectivity as ethically accountable and politically empowering" (*Metamorphoses* 2) interrupts the problematic discourse of authenticity (and therapy as a result of its loss) at work in narratives as discussed in previous chapters. Gender, for Butler and Braidotti, (and despite their different positions) is always already at an intersection with power (*Metamorphoses* 17) and therefore of a "transgressive" complexity. Equally for both, categories are "open coalitions," alternately affirmed and relinquished according to the purposes at hand (Butler, *Gender Trouble* 16). In this open and hence transitive sense, "power not only acts on a subject" but "enacts the subject into being" (Butler, *Psychic Life* 13). Emphasizing both normativity and the limitations of the category of "woman" (which fails to be exhaustive), Braidotti takes Butler's strategy of performative transgression further and employs it as a nomadic interpellation. Indeed, Althusserian interpellation as a process constituting ideological subjectivity is delayed and expanded in Braidotti's proposal of nomadism in which voluntary acknowledgement of the dominant ideology does not inevitably enmesh subjects in numerous discursive and social subordinations, but first destabilizes this ideology by transgressive enactments of subordination (Butler's position) and then intervenes with the positive difference of subversive spaces: "It would be indeed naive to believe that the mere rejection or destabilization of gender dualism is exclusively or necessarily a subversive position" (Braidotti, *Metamorphoses* 37). The incessant philosophical inscriptions of "difference" with negativity continue to support exclusions and disqualifications of transgressive subjects and their representability within the social. They also unnecessarily imply that the understanding of "sexual difference," as emerging from Anglo-American sociological and anthropological sex/gender relations (e.g., Butler; Scott), is polemically at odds or even conceptually different from the Continental European tradition: "This constitutive ambivalence makes for an interesting case of a location that appears as Eurocentric in the USA and as highly Americanized in Europe," but accounts in fact for two sides of the same coin: a constitution of resistance to the cultural foundations of the patriarchal order (*Metamorphoses* 32).

In a reflection on the phenomena of migration (traveling) and the dissemination of traditions, I take Etienne Balibar's position on identity as an accumulation of stigmas, hyphenated names, and identifications (187). If one of the privileged names of tradition (understood in relation to its conservativism, locality, and institutionalization) is precisely "culture," there remains little sense contained in something as broad as the concept of "identity." For Balibar, there are "only identifications: either with the institution itself, or with other subjects by the intermediary of the institution" (187). Similarily, identity emerges as "a collection of traits, of objective structures (as such spontaneously thought of in the dimension of the collective, the social, and the historical)." As such, identity pertains to the formation of subjectivity "in the dimension of 'lived experience,' of 'conscious' or 'unconscious' individuality" (174). Drawing on these formulations of identity, my analysis focuses on the allegedly free-floating and/or bisexual identities that escape the limits of cultural boundaries, the bonds/bounds preserved by traditional household structures and national frontiers. Precisely because of its subversive potential, the edge (or the margin, taking into account the wide range of geographical/spatial and linguistic images employed in this selection) transforms the nostalgic (reassuring) concepts of "home," "nationality," and "gender" into the blurred areas of cultural un/belonging. As I suggest, following Butler, there is no formula that can predict when or how the historical or traditional identity of the unencumbered woman can be released from its derogatory origins, or can avoid the abjection that persistently echoes in the insulting and proliferating names given to her (witch, hag, slut, bitch, whore). The witch, in particular, as a supposedly imaginary feminine transgressor, seems to be suspended between a traditional cultural structure that she has already been made to abandon, and another, unknown, culturally unrestricted structure that she is about to enter. Transported, she "executes her transit imaginarily, perched on the black goat that carries her off, impaled by the broom that flies her away; she goes in the direction of animality, plants, the inhuman" (Cixous and Clément 8). In crossing the borderline between human and nonhuman, she "endures" in culture as the monstrous feminine (Creed 1993). For Braidotti, it is her association with "the in-between, the mixed, the ambivalent as implied in the ancient Greek root of the word *monsters*, *teras*, which means both horrible and wonderful, object of aberration and adoration" (*Nomadic Subjects* 77). Whether in a narrative spectacle (Cixous) or a narrative ritual (Kristeva, Creed), "the demarcation lines between the human and non-human have been drawn up anew" (Creed 8), or abandoned for politically more empowering spaces in which the becoming transformative subject nevertheless retains her humanity (Braidotti). In negotiating distances, she effectively negotiates with the symbolic by tying a conceptual knot herself rather than remaining entangled in one made to entrap her. And it is the will (and capacity) to negotiate that implies what the process of becoming-subject is about. The critical task for the transformative subject, to follow Butler's formulation, is "to locate strategies of subversive repetition" that are made possible by the narrative constructions of a sexually boundless, or un-bound woman, Irigaray's "volume without contours." Serving as the locus of subversion, this boundlessness is as a construction not beyond culture, "but a concrete cultural possibility" that in the capitalist and neo/capitalist economy of deficit and lack "is refused and redescribed as impossible" (Butler, *Gender Trouble* 77). What remains "unthinkable" and impossible within the terms of this economy "is not necessarily what is excluded from the matrix of intelligibility within that form; on the contrary, it is the marginalized, not the excluded, the cultural possibility that calls for dread or, minimally, the loss of sanctions....The 'unthinkable' is thus fully within culture" but fully excluded from its *dominant* representation (77).

Indeed, in mainstream Western history and religion, witches have been perceived, (re)presented, and depicted consistently as the "unthinkable," peculiar outcasts on the margins of culture (on this, see Sanders). In the absence of any mediation between their peculiarity and the universal norm of a subject, witches have been construed as dangerously polluting the universal "norm." Projected as homeless, they both expose and are exposed to inappropriate and noncanonical bodily forms, through which they mediate their cultural vulnerability. Although specific appearances and connotations of the witch-woman vary from culture to culture, the (projected) peculiarity of her cultural body is common to all the contexts concerned here. Defined as an awareness or consciousness of un/belonging that manifests itself as an openness (vulnerability) to heresy and deviation, the witch comes to represent not what is contained and sustained by traditional identity but rather what is transgressed and therefore eliminated, restricted, or (r)ejected to confined spaces, such as asylums or prisons. In this cultural restriction, then, the witch as a border-crosser and boundary marker opens a new "system of classification" in which, paradoxically, "the negative and borderline values of contaminating objects are reversible, and reverse themselves into omnipotent and positive values" (Clément and Kristeva 92). In Clément and Kristeva's understanding, these formulations of transgression are also effective as a form of sacred disorder: "The sacred shatters the order and introduces a new one...the mystic order, the trance, the transcendence" (113). In this sense, the transgressive potential of the fantasy of gender meets indeed at the crossroads with sexual sameness. Sameness, like difference, is a fantasy, easily disrupted by the politics of location (on this, see Kaplan and Grewal), and in particular its "embodied accounts" (see Griffin and Braidotti). Theoretical positions employed in my study (i.e., Clément and Kristeva, Braidotti, Butler, Irigaray, Kristeva) are interactive in this sense, involving processes of thinking that bring different figurations into light, calling into play precisely a sense of different feminist locations and alternative subjectivities in relation to un/belonging. In the narratives at hand, there is both a tension and a dialogue between the particular/peculiar and the normalized, a dialectic reflecting what Homi Bhabha divided into "culture as the noun for naming the social imaginary, and culture as the act for grafting the voices of the indentured, the displaced, the nameless, onto an agency of utterance" ("Freedom's Basis" 52). In view of the paradox or "illusion of a true body beyond the law" (Butler, *Gender Trouble* 93), the illusion that they often enact, the identities of the "witch" in these narratives evoke certain types of cultural transgression that insert (or smuggle) a nomadic articulation into the collective symbolic discourse. The "beyond" is neither a new (semiotic) horizon on the outside of culture nor a leaving behind of the past, but "there is a sense of disorientation, a disturbance of direction, in the 'beyond': an explanatory, restless movement" (Bhabha, *Location* 1).

Finally, contextualizing the social, there is no going back to the old equality/difference debate in the sense of an exclusive focus on any single axis of difference.

The shift from "gender difference" to "differences among women" and then towards "multiple intersecting differences" remains an unsurpassable gain, although it does not imply necessarily that we should forget the old debate. Rather, what seems to be at stake today is the need for connections between the problematic of cultural difference and the problematic of social equality (Fraser, *Justice Interruptus* 187). Nothing in principle precludes that the subject is both culturally constructed and capable of distance from its own "constructedness," although the subject is itself the product of prior signifying processes, capable of resignification (Butler) and critique (Fraser). I thus propose to view the witch in this chapter as transgressing her "fixed" (stigmatized) identity to produce a range of hybrid and plural literary representations. The notions of hybridity and un/belonging are particularly relevant in the narratives here, in which the distinction between good and evil, that is, what has been culturally sanctioned and embedded as one or the other, is prone to disappear altogether. This textual plurality, however, should not be seen as a universal nihilism acknowledged by Lyotard as "postmodern condition," but rather as a transfeminist acceptance of "difference" that has to be negotiated rather than fought over. Although belonging to different national/cultural traditions, the narrative figures occupy a dialectical position between their cultural abjection and their "porous" bodies, signifying both cultural transgression and gender ambiguity. This dialectical position allows us to see Irigaray's "disruptive excess," Butler's suspension of the category "gender," Kristeva's concept of "porousness," and Braidotti's embodied subject of "becoming" as converging in a common intention to elaborate a theory of a different cultural legality—none of them guaranteeing sexual/cultural subversion per se, but "emphasizing the complex, interactive and power-driven web of relations around the sexuality/sex nucleus" (Braidotti, *Metamorphoses* 33). This multiple system, or legality, does not refer to "woman" as a/the subject or the object of discussion, but "of jamming the theoretical machinery itself, of suspending its pretension to the production of a truth and of a meaning that are excessively univocal" (Irigaray, "Power" 126); it therefore must be seen as a theory of cultural negotiation.

The Sacred May not be the Same as the Religious

Building on the theories discussed, I now explore the transgressive spaces of religion, faith, and sacredness, focusing on Angela Carter's literary constructions of two culturally nonconforming women, Mary Magdalene in "Impressions: The Wrightsman Magdalene" (1996) and Jeanne in "Black Venus" (1985). Carter, a dedicated atheist, deals explicitly with religiously sanctioned values or dogmas, which makes her figures interesting in the context of the feminism-informed subversive potential of the feminine. I begin with the question arising at the intersection of the feminine and the sacred as explored by Clément and Kristeva. What is experienced as "sacred" or as "trance," in Clément's and Kristeva's perception, is "a translation of eroticism into more noble terms" (23). In their post/Lacanian understanding of the subject, "a woman—with or without the trance—is the daily demonstration of ...[a] catastrophic or delicious distillation of flesh within the mind"; she is a subject "capable of giving life," but "a subject whose repression remains very problematic. Rather, she is subject to generalized vapors" (16). As evoked repeatedly in the dialogue between Clément and Kristeva, it is the very intersection, the coming together of the sacred and the feminine, that creates chains of associations between the feminine body, faith, sexuality, and the senses. As I suggest in the following analysis, Carter's figures represent such an intersection; but one that exceeds its post/structuralist premise of repression towards positive reframing of "difference." The figures appear as paradoxical creatures that escape from the limits of cultural boundaries, from the bonds/bounds maintained by traditional structures and religious, national, or gender boundaries. Carter supplies no formula that can predict when or how her figures' traditional identity can be released from their derogatory origins. She seems to be much more interested in delineating what all these evocative categories have in common: the intersection, the borderline, the *cleavage*. Within these permeable categories Carter locates strategies of subversive recurrence made possible by her narrative constructions of a boundless "woman." In this sense, Carter follows Butler's notion of an original or primary gender identity (of a "woman"). This "feminine" identity has been parodied within the subcultural practices of cross-dressing and the sexual stylization of identities in general. And although in hardcore feminist theory, such parodic identities have been understood as degrading or uncritical appropriation of sex-role stereotyping (see, e.g., *Gender Trouble* 137), the parodic identities are, by necessity, more complex. The relation between "gender imitation" and the "original" (*Gender Trouble* 137) is of interest for Carter, as in her narrative framework gender refers specifically to the hetoresexist matrix of power as constituting oppressive social and symbolic representations. As Butler would argue, normative sexuality fortifies normative gender, and hence the politically minded question of how gender hierarchy relates to all kinds of other variables. The point is that Carter's narrative drag is not subversive of gender norms, but that the (gendered) subject lives "with received notions of reality which determine what kinds of bodies and sexualities will be considered real and true, and which kind will not" (*Undoing Gender* 214).

Subcultural parodies are already suggested by Kristeva in her formulation of identity transgressions as part of a "carnivalesque cosmogony" that ignores "substance, causality or identity outside its link to the whole" (*Desire* 78): "This carnivalesque cosmogony has persisted in the form of an antitheological (but not antimystical) and deeply popular movement. It remains present as an often misunderstood and persecuted substratum of official Western culture throughout its entire history... Within the carnival, the subject is reduced to nothingness, while the structure of the author emerges as anonymity that creates and sees itself created as self and other, as [wo]man and mask" (78). However, an inevitable return to culture, its order and sanctions, suggests that these transgressions have an anxiogenic character. Butler, in particular, referring to Kristeva's position, denounces this type of subversion (disruption of cultural form) as "a futile gesture, entertained only in a derealized aesthetic mode which can never be translated into other cultural practices" (*Gender Trouble* 78). We revert to "a primal cartography of the body," representing what Kristeva calls the *semiotic* precondition, "even though it depends on language," which "suffers and takes pleasures in an other logic, complementary to the logic of linguistic signs imposed and consolidated by paternal laws" (Clément and Kristeva 95). In discussing Carter's narratives, Kristeva's concepts of subversion and border transgression, differing from Butler's, might nevertheless appear effective as both unsettled and unsettling, exposing the limits of Lacan's efforts to universalize the paternal law within the symbolic. The semiotic, relating in many respects to Kristevan "abjection," which disrespects positions and rules (*Powers* 4), disturbs the singularity of the identity system. Carter illustrates these types of abjection or transgression as deliberately straddling borders and in a way proposes what Kristeva's, Butler's, and Braidotti's theories might have in common: the transgressions as indicators of cultural negotiating, pointing to a knowledge of when to abandon one particular position for another, "knowing when to let it go, living its contingency, and subjecting it to a political challenge" (Butler, "Discussion" 131). As Braidotti reminds us, the challenge to women's representation today lies in thinking about interconnecting processes rather than singular concepts (2002). Positing both narrative (aesthetic) and political modes as rooted in the social structure, Carter certainly takes on this challenge: Her narrative figures are effective not as temporary escape routes to the outside of culture but concrete (collectively imagined) representations of "women" as ongoing, subversively repetitive alternatives to the dominant order.

Depicted in liturgy, literature, and art as a penitent sinner, Mary Magdalene emerges as more physically "real," more bodily focused than the equally powerful but alone-of-all-her-sex Virgin. Because of the presence of her erotic but penitent body, she answers both to the *phallic* (symbolic, paternal) gaze that accepts her penitence, and to the *omphalic* (maternal) one that identifies with Magdalene's fate and alludes to the presence of the scar, of the navel as a place of disconnection from the semiotic pleasures. According to Warner, Magdalene "was created from unrelated stories in the image of an earlier mould, itself cast in a Judaic tradition" (232). This creation follows the harlot theme similarly to Gomer, the faithless wife of Hosea, who prefigured Israel's stormy union with Yahweh (Hosea 1:2-3), to Jezebel, whose body was torn to pieces and eaten by dogs (2 Kings 9:30-37), and to Rahab, who appears in Matthew's genealogy as an ancestress of Christ (Matthew 1:5). Following Warner, devotion to the Virgin Mary and Mary Magdalene venerates two Western ideals of the feminine—the "consecrated chastity in the Virgin Mary and regenerate sexuality in the Magdalene" (235). In its condensation of physical beauty with temptation and subsequent practice of bodily mortification, Magdalene's prototype mirrors the Christian fear of and the desire to re-form women (232): "The witness of the risen Christ, who, veiled and carrying her jar of ointment, walks up silently to the empty sepulchre in so many early Christian representations of the Resurrection, was transformed in the Middle Ages into a hermitess, the perfect embodiment of Christian repentance. As such, Magdalene was considered a powerful and beneficent witch, a great and beloved saint" (Warner 229). But Mary Magdalene can also be linked with the image of a heretic, anti-religious ("unreformed") woman, incarnating "the equation between feminine beauty, sexuality and sin" (Haskins 3). Precisely because of her feminine but antimaternal potential, the cultural "frontiers" transform the reassuring concepts of "repentance," "faith," and "resurrection" into the blurred space of un/belonging. This space provides, in Carter's story, an intricate passage (a type of umbilical cord) from passion to sanctification, from the symbolically inarticulate and prohibited semiotic *jouissance* to a desire/pleasure, or what remains of it within the symbolic: "Virgin Mary wears blue. Her preference has sanctified the colour. We think of a 'heavenly' blue. But Mary Magdalene wears red, the colour of passion. The two women are twin paradoxes. One is not what the other is. One is a virgin and a mother; the other is a non-virgin, and childless. Note how the English language doesn't contain a specific word to describe a woman who is grown-up, sexually mature and *not* a mother, unless such a woman is using her sexuality as her profession" (Carter, "Impressions" 410).

As I suggest, it is precisely this linguistic gap, the *cleavage*, that becomes the focus of Carter's exploration. Her story, "Impressions: The Wrightsman Magdalene," which gives a commentary on a painting by Georges de La Tour, draws on images of the feminine body as a dividing line, representing both the separation and the tie between symbolic language and *semiotic* ecstasy or *jouissance*. Like Clément and Kristeva, Carter pursues a distinction "between belief and religion, on the one hand, and the sacred, on the other" (Clément and Kristeva 27). In agreement also with Braidotti's thought, Carter's account of transgression becomes a form of sacred disordering and "an account of subjectivity," an "ethically accountable and politically empowering" (Braidotti, *Metamorphoses* 2) process of feminist thinking. Portraying "the fallen woman who through Jesus was able to rise again" (de Boer 8), Carter's narrative extends the image of Magdalene as "the repentant harlot" (Carter, "Impressions" 409) towards the remnants of her voluptuous, "happy non-virgin" existence at the crossroads of sacredness and sacrilege. Carter's understanding of Magdalene's sacredness recalls Clément's perception of the sacred that "shatters the order and introduces a new one...the mystic order, the trance, the transcendence" (Clément and Kristeva 113). The sacred alludes not only to specifically "feminine" traces of (unspoken) jouissance, but also to a politically informed figuration of the subject as a dynamic and shifting entity (Braidotti, *Metamorphoses* 2). If she had been an apostle, Magdalene would have had much to tell, since she "had followed Jesus from the beginning," was "present at the crucifixion and the burial," and was "first to proclaim the resurrection" (de Boer 2). As a "fallen" woman, however, she does not speak but meditates through her feminine body. The fallen and the feminine meet together in her repentant posture: "Mary Magdalene meditates upon the candle flame. She enters the blue core, the blue absence. She becomes something other than herself....She can't speak, won't speak. In the desert, she will grunt...she will put speech aside... after she has meditated upon the candle flame and the mirror ... But something has already been born out of this intercourse...See. She carries it already. She carries it where, as if she were a Virgin mother and not a sacred whore, she would rest her baby, not a living child but *a memento mori*, a skull" (Carter, "Impressions" 413).

The silent archetype of Magdalene, "brought into existence by the powerful undertow of misogyny" (Warner 225), provokes Carter to speak against the association of Magdalene with an antimaternal degradation of the flesh. On Warner's analysis, the Virgin Mary is the only Christian woman conceptualized both as a holy virgin and a holy mother. The concept of a parthenogenetic virgin birth releases the Madonna from hysterical experiences; the Roman Catholic Madonna does not menstruate (is she not fertile?), her physiological integrity in pregnancy and *post partum* is astonishing, her birth pains are never mentioned, and her virginity is never violated. There is no split in her body between the virgin and the mother. Echoing Warner's argument, Carter opens her narrative with an image of Magdalene in a scene that emphasizes her separation from other pious women: "to be a virgin and a mother, you need a miracle; when a woman is not a virgin, nor a mother...nobody talks about miracles. Mary, the mother of Jesus, together with the other Mary, the mother of St John, and the Mary Magdalene, the repentant harlot, went down to the seashore; a woman named Fatima, a servant, went with them. They stepped into a boat, they threw away the rudder, they permitted the sea to take them where it wanted. It beached them near Marseilles....But the other Mary, the Magdalene, the not-mother, could not stop. Impelled by the demon of loneliness, she went off on her own...she crossed limestone hill after limestone hill. Flints cut her feet, sun burned her skin. She ate fruit that had fallen from the tree of its own accord, like a perfect Manichean. She ate dropped berries. The black-browed Palestinian woman walked in silence, gaunt as famine, hairy as a dog" ("Impressions" 409).

There is something about "the other" Mary, in Carter's text, that connects with processes of transition and hybridization, taking place in between nature/biology and social order, in the spaces that flow and connect in-between. Her *jouissance* contradicts the religion she follows and diverges from Christian communion with other believers towards hermetic loneliness, self-denial, and mortification, as she separates herself from the "first" Mary. It is in this separation that Kristeva's suggestion of "the sacred that might not be the same as the religious" meets with Braidotti's "transformative account of the self" (*Metamorphoses* 3). While interpreting La Tour's Magdalene, Carter's narrator experiences a sensation similar to what Clément refers to as a "bizarre feeling" in front of a sacred work. She experiences "the sensation that someone wants to impose a vision" on her (Clément and Kristeva 120): that the religious doctrine leaves no choice of perception, and that precisely this lack of choice provokes antagonism, and a desire for "other" insights: "Mary Magdalene, the Venus in sackcloth. George de La Tour's picture does not show a woman in sackcloth, but her chemise is coarse and simple enough to be a penitential garment...the kind of garment that shows you were not thinking of personal adornment when you put it on. Even though the chemise is deeply open on the bosom, it does not seem to disclose flesh as such, but a flesh that is more akin to the wax of the burning candle, to the way the wax candle is irradiated by its own flame, and glows...you could say that, from the waist up, this Mary Magdalene is on the high road to penitence, but, from the waist down, which is always the more problematic part, there is the question of her long, red skirt" (Carter, "Impressions" 409-10). Although merely suggested, Magdalene's "road to penitence" represents a her(m)etic crossing of the forbidden border towards the knowledge of unexplored eroticism, sensuality, and the body. Whereas Clément argues that the sacred is sexual "because it authorizes the brutal insurrection of the forbidden humors during ceremonies" (Clément and Kristeva 20). Carter explains that "because Mary Magdalene is a woman and childless she goes out into the wilderness. The others, the mothers, stay and make a church, where people come" ("Impressions" 410). The sacred associated with Magdalene's unbound and hybrid sexuality is impossible within the domesticated space of the religious; however, as Carter seems to imply, it is not (culturally) impossible altogether. Braidotti's position on the becoming-subject helps to explore this implication further. In a joint project with Irigaray, Braidotti posits the feminist subject as no longer that of a Woman as the specular other of man but rather a complex, multifaceted "embodied subject" that has distanced itself from the institution of "femininity." This "embodied subject" coincides with positions assumed by the dominant subject, and does so in ways that may no longer be of a particular gender, but of "the subject of quite another story: a subject-in-process, a mutant, the other of the Other, a post-Woman embodied subject cast in female morphology who has already undergone an essential metamorphosis" (*Metamorphoses* 12).

The ecstasy Magdalene experiences in mortifying her body (either feminine or unfeminine, or inseparably both) suggests that it is precisely the intersection of genders that is at work in Carter's story: a merging of oppositions into sensuality that transforms gendered experience into "the sacred." The sacred, in its turn, "authorizes the lapse, the disappearance of the Subject, the syncope, vertigo, the trance, ecstasy" (Clément and Kristeva 30). But Magdalene's earthly ecstatic sins also clearly retain gendered character, or more precisely, Irigaray's "sexual difference" that cuts much deeper to suggest the possibility of a social/cultural etiology. Embodied by the ancient fertility virgin, erased by Christian orthodoxy, Carter's Magdalene suggests constitution and representability of "sexual difference." Until her repentance, she is the trace of an unencumbered woman, the extravagant combination of a harlot and a virgin that to some extent "absorbed the role of the classical goddesses of love" (Warner 235). While the "unspotted goodness" of the Virgin Mary "keeps her in the position of the Platonic ideal" and "prevents the sinner from identifying with her," it is Mary Magdalene who "holds up a comforting mirror to those who sin again and again, and promises joy to human frailty" (235). Is then her scarlet frock, as Carter suggests, only a piece of "left-over finery" ("Impressions" 410)? "Was it the only frock she had, the frock she went whoring in, then repented in, then set sail in? Did she walk all the way to the Sainte-Baume in this red skirt? It doesn't look travel-stained or worn or torn. It is a luxurious, even scandalous skirt. A scarlet dress for a scarlet woman" (410). This passage suggests that Magdalene could also be a hybridized Lilith. Indeed, if the Virgin, the mother-of-god, and Magdalene, the lover-of-god, "together form a diptych of the Christian woman" (Warner 235), the picture remains two-dimensional, incomplete. Magdalene, and this facet of her character is traced by Carter, eventually transcends her feminine promiscuity, turning "into something wild and strange, into a female version of John the Baptist, a hairy hermit, as good as naked, transcending gender, sex obliterated, nakedness irrelevant" ("Impressions" 411): "Sometimes she wears only her hair; it never saw a comb, long, matted, unkempt, hanging down to her knees. She belts her own hair round her waist with the rope with which, each night, she lashes herself, making a rough tunic of it. On these occasions, the transformation from the young lovely, voluptuous Mary Magdalene, the happy non-virgin, the party girl, the woman taken in adultery—on these occasions, the transformation is complete" (410).

In her long-lasting retreat as a hermit, her famished body develops into that of an old hag, and fulfills the third role of the pagan goddess that is lacking in the eternally young Virgin Mary. Thus, Carter's Magdalene reproduces the archaic goddess (in her aspects of the lover and the crone), and she does it in a mould of the monstrous Lilith practically silenced by Roman Catholic mythology. Conversely, has she any choice of "where she wants to be" (as a crone or a lover), or is she "beyond choice," beyond antagonisms, without any other "option but virtue" ("Impressions" 411)? As Carter suggests, there are other traces virtually erased from the popular myths of Mary Magdalene. Donatello's sculpture, also mentioned by Carter, represents Magdalene's repentance and, and as she argues, it borders on masochism, an internalised desire for self-destruction, a nullification of the flesh that, in a way, is a type of choice: "dried up by the suns of the wilderness, battered by wind and rain, anorexic, toothless, a body entirely annihilated by the soul. You can almost smell the odour of the kind of sanctity that reeks from her—it's rank, it's raw, it's horrible. By the ardour with which she hated her early life of so-called 'pleasure.' The mortification of the flesh comes naturally to her....Penitence becomes sado-masochism. Self-punishment is its own reward" ("Impressions" 411). This "odour of sanctity," also discussed by Clément and Kristeva, marks the intersection of the feminine and the sacred with violence and the uneasiness of bodily vapors. In abolishing the physical distance between herself and Jesus, a distance between "the sinful woman and God" constructed by the postmedieval Church (de Boer 71), Carter's Magdalene comes within reach of *jouissance* and returns the divine kiss. To follow Haskins, according to the Apocryphal Gospel of Philip, Magdalene was the companion of Jesus, who "loved [her] more than all the disciples, and kissed on her mouth often" (63.34-35; 3). Similarly, Warner observes that the suggestion of love unfolding between Jesus and Mary Magdalene had been celebrated by the Gnostics in the second century. And this trace of carnal love between the saint and the sinner has been obliterated from the myths of Magdalene. However, an indication that she might have been a visionary entrusted (by the kiss) with divine wisdom is present in the story of Mary from Magdala. As Haskins relates, Mary from Magdala is mentioned among the women who followed Jesus and who "had been healed of evil spirits and infirmities." In Luke, Jesus exorcised seven devils out of Magdalene (8:2). These "seven devils were a focus for speculation amongst early Christian commentators; the link with the 'evil spirits and infirmities' ascribed to some of the women may well have led to their identification with the seven deadly sins" (14). To follow other suggestions, Mary Magdalene "was the best known of the women because her 'healing was the most dramatic,' as the seven demons may have indicated a 'possession of extraordinary malignity.' However, nowhere in the New Testament is demoniacal possession regarded as synonymous with sin. That Mary [Magdalene]'s condition might have been psychological, that is, seen as madness, rather than moral or sexual, seems never to have entered into the considerations of the early biblical commentators" (14). Since Jesus's kisses can be seen as a divine penetration of the female mouth, the Magdalene-harlot receives a sacred gift from her master that purifies her body of the "seven devils." But why then, returning to Carter's story, "has she taken her pearl necklace with her," to the cave, the site of her mortification? "Look at it, lying in front of the mirror. And her long hair has been most beautifully brushed. Is she, yet, fully repentant" ("Impressions" 410)? Here again sacredness, as an odour from her mortified flesh, meshes with her erotic desires; her body in the mirror is not yet fully lost. Secluded in a cave, with long hair covering her nakedness, Carter's Magdalene represents the mutant, the subject-in-process who has undergone an essential metamorphosis (Braidotti): her body is neglected, wrecked, but not abandoned, and claiming in fact a valid position in relation to the sanctioned culture.

Carter had examined a similarly neglected non-mother's body in an earlier story: "Black Venus." Alluding to Greco-Roman pre-Christian religious prototypes of the sacred feminine, Carter's Venus appears as a half-prostitute, half-sacred site of *métissage*. Drawing on the ambiguous figure of Jeanne Duval, one of Baudelaire's lovers, Carter pursues the subject of female identification with strangeness, victimization, and cultural incompatibility, "as if the fatal drama of the primal fruit-theft must recur again and again, with cyclic regularity" ("Black Venus" 231). As a racialized subject, a "woman who makes free use of her attractiveness—adventuress, vamp, femme fatale," Jeanne evokes de Beauvoir's "disquieting type" of woman, who keeps "an ancient fear...alive" (201). Jeanne's fate ironically draws on biblical traces of Eve, who preferred knowledge to virtue ("Black Venus" 231), and of Jezebel, a foreign prostitute. But she also goes beyond these traces, and creates her own paradigm of cultural un/belonging. She reminds us of Wittig's vision of Eve (*Les Guérillères* 1985), who appears as a naked woman walking among the fruit trees in an orchard. Her beautiful body is black and shining, while her hair consists of thin moving snakes that produce music at each of her movements. Also, Cixous's Medusa, a figure ridiculing Freud's idea of female castration, comes into play here: Carter's Venus is, however, enslaved: "This dance, which he wanted her to perform so much and had especially devised for her, consisted of a series of voluptuous poses one following another; private-room-in-a-bordello stuff but tasteful....He liked her to put on all her bangles and beads when she did her dance, she dressed up in a set of clanking jewellery he'd given her, paste, nothing she could sell or she'd have sold it" ("Black Venus" 233). Jeanne resurfaces in the story as "the pure child of the colony. The colony—white, imperious—had fathered her" (238). She knows nothing but the omnipresent Law of the Father; her "mother went off with the sailors" (238). Upon her arrival in Paris, she continues her colonized life as a foreign muse at the service of the poet. Her body dances in the silence of "a kept woman" (241), chained to her "Daddy's" fancies. "Meanwhile, she hummed a Creole melody, she liked the ones with ribald words about what the shoemaker's wife did at Mardi Gras...but Daddy paid no attention to what song his siren sang, he fixed his quick, bright, dark eyes upon her decorated skin as if, sucker, authentically entranced" (233). Following de Beauvoir's concept of the seductive Sphinx deeply anchored in the poet's fantasies, Carter portrays her as a racialized object of phallocentric desire, a witch to be tamed, "deprived of history" (238) and cultural belonging: "Nobody seems to know in what year Jeanne Duval was born, although the year in which she met Charles Baudelaire (1842) is precisely logged and biographies of his other mistresses...are well documented. Besides Duval, she also used the names Prosper and Lemer, as if her name was of no consequence. Where she came from is a problem; books suggest Mauritius, in the Indian ocean, or Santo Domingo, in the Caribbean, take your pick of two different sides of the world. (Her pays d'origine of less importance than it would have been had she been a wine)" ("Black Venus" 237).

The "essence" of foreign womanhood, as incarnated in the figure of "Black Venus," encodes the "second sex" with the colonial experience, in which the subject acts as an object charged with foreign, savage fluids. Thus the fluids in Carter's text attain a doubly transcendental signification: Jeanne's body as an object of desire has something permeable, "porous" about itself; it evokes the vulnerability of the colonized body and a subversive power of rage. Carter refers here to the "the atrocious mixture of corruption and innocence" (235) that transmits its eroticism as an experience of the sacred degradation as if "porous" repentance: "After she's got a drink or two inside her, however, she stops coughing, grown a bit more friendly, will consent to unpin her hair and let him play with it, the way he likes to. And if her native indolence does not prove too much for her—she is capable of sprawling, as in a vegetable trance, for hours, for days, in the dim room by the smoky fire...and dance for Daddy who, she will grudgingly admit when pressed, is a good Daddy, buys her pretties, allocates her the occasional lump of hashish, keeps her off the streets" (233). In both collapsing and reinforcing the boundaries between master and slave, Carter's text moves beyond Jeanne's objectification. The relationship between the poet enchanted by Jeanne's controversial (simultaneously prostituted and unattainable) exoticism and the slave's desire to insult the Law are clearly at play, but also far from resolved. In maintaining this suspension, the narrative collapses the position of object/fetish and its colonized debased nature. Instead, by evoking transitory, in-between conditions, the narrative enjoins the slave and the master in the task to outwit the Law, suggesting a route beyond the poverty of the social imaginary that operates in mental habits of dichotomies. The intersections of the poet's fascination and Jeanne's narcissism designates an always suspended understanding of shifting positions, a continuous deferral of security that is at play in transitory thinking. "Venus lies on the bed, waiting for a wind to rise: the sooty albatross hankers for the storm. Whirlwind!" (239). And this suspended security connects with the Judeo-Christian imagery of sexuality as contained by the Strange Woman. Claudia Camp discusses the relationship between her "strangeness," exogamy, and foreign cults (317) by linking the Strange Woman with "the wife of another," with an adulteress, and, in a broader sense, a "deviation, faithlessness, and the unknown" (311). Accentuating the connection between Jeanne's strangeness and (the flowers of) evil as a specific reinforcement of her foreign status, Carter's text suggests that Jeanne is indeed, as Kristeva has put it, "a stranger to the sacrifice." The odour (scent, perfume) emanating from her body fuses horror and desire into a fluctuating fantasy of pleasures and dangers that need each other as a supplement, as a necessary foil. Jeanne is a foreign fantasy of Eve, even though she is void of Eve's knowledge since, as Carter assures us, "she never bothered to bite any apple at all. She wouldn't have known what knowledge was *for*, would she? She was in neither a state of innocence nor a state of grace" ("Black Venus" 231). Jeanne certainly does not initiate this projection of herself as Eve-before-the-Fall (it is the poet who does so), but she has learned to sell it, to utilize the fantasy, so that the poet "thinks she is a vase of darkness; if he tips her up, black light will spill out. She is not Eve but, herself, the forbidden fruit, and he has eaten her!" (237). In a permanent cultural suspension, Jeanne incarnates evil, "although she wishes to do no such thing" (237).

Pippin's interpretation of the Biblical Jezebel as a punishable object of desire can be used as another parallel to Jeanne. As an extension of the phallocentric fascination with fear, her "evilness" feeds on the metaphysics of deficiency and the supposed uncleanliness of her foreign body. Jezebel, as Pippin suggests, is constructed as a guilty body, the "dying other," an exotic and dangerous femme fatale (186). Jezebel's foreign status might be culturally acceptable, but her "uncontrolled" rebellious womanhood is not. In her accomplishments as an *acting* woman, Jeanne-as-Jezebel incorporates the Strange Woman, "institutionally legitimated as the other woman," and "portrayed as an active creator of her own alien status" (Camp 322). Alluding to the culturally sanctioned "impurity," Pippin's analysis concentrates on Jezebel's dying body, calling it "dung," "the ultimate impurity," Jezebel and her religion are "to be excreted" (38). In a similar environment of carnal pollution, Carter constructs her Venus as a future hag/witch, destined for the unavoidable fate of a polluting and polluted body to be punished, and "rot": "When she was on her own, having a few drinks in front of the fire, thinking about it, it made her break out in horrible hag's laughter, as if she were already the hag she would become enjoying a grim joke at the expense of the pretty, secretly festering thing she still was. At Walpurgisnacht, the young witch boasted to the old witch: 'Naked on a goat, I display my fine young body. 'How the old witch laughed! 'You'll rot!' I'll rot, thought Jeanne, and laughed" ("Black Venus" 235). Her body, infected and punished with syphilis (in Carter's version to be seen as Baudelaire's gift to his "fleur du mal"), makes her conscious of physical borders, those inside and outside of her porous body: "she would have liked a bath...was a little worried about a persistent vaginal discharge that smelled of mice...something ominous...horrid" (236). Her bodily impurities are further linked with the "polluted" language of her granny, who spoke "Creole, patois, [she] knew no other language...knew it badly," and "taught it badly" to Jeanne. In turn, Jeanne "did her best to convert it into good French and started mixing with swells but...her heart wasn't in it.... It was as though her tongue had been cut out and another one sewn in that did not fit well" (239). Creole, projected as an unclean, bastard language of "mixed" race, is Jeanne's mother tongue. Its structure/mixture cannot be "corrected," and will refuse to belong. Her two (female) mouths are mixed too, interconnected in their inadequacy, alienation, and estrangement bound to the stigma of Jezebel. Because of her *métisse* status, Jeanne becomes a double target. First, she is condemned as an adventuress who breaks social boundaries and disrupts the stability of the traditional household, then as "a foreign national, who introduces the dangers of foreign worship" into the community (Camp 312). Carter speculates: "Maybe he found her crying because the kids in the street were chucking stones at her, calling her a 'black bitch' or worse and spattering the beautiful white flounces of her crinoline with handfuls of tossed mud they scooped from the gutters where they thought she belonged because she was a whore who had the nerve to sashay to the corner shop for cheroots or ordinaire or rum with her nose stuck up in the air as if she were the Empress of all the Africas" ("Black Venus" 238). In this role of a double stranger, she blurs/"exceeds" her status of a prostitute: "Had she been a prostitute, the sage's depiction of utter evil would have been undercut, for the professional prostitute does have a place in a patriarchal world" (Camp 322). She, however, is positioned in an unrecognizable cultural structure, a stigmatized vacuum of foreignness encaptured in terms of both race/ethnicity (as black) and of gender (as Venus). Thus to exist in the patriarchal structure, as Carter argues (echoing both Kristeva's and Butler's positions), Jeanne is "in drag," that is "in a duplicitous state of affectation" (Webb 211). To be Jeanne Duval, a strange, weird fantasy of a woman, is to expose this invisible, perfectly reenacted deception in a visibly disturbing un/belonging. It is to be "like a piano in a country where everybody has had their hands cut off" ("Black Venus" 231).

Returning to Pippin's analysis of Jezebel as "a fantasy space" of a foreign culture and religion, Jezebel does not die, she "is the vamp/ire that cannot be killed, who roams through other texts and times and women. She has a future in a different form; she is constantly re-formed in the image of male desire and fear" (Pippin 39). In this sense of continuous "becoming," Carter shows Jeanne as a survivor, an ugly hag, "deaf, dumb and paralyzed" ("Black Venus" 242), while it is Baudelaire who dies in Carter's text: "He told his mother to make sure that Jeanne was looked after but his mother didn't give her anything. Nadar says he saw Jeanne hobbling on crutches along the pavement to the dram-shop; her teeth were gone, she had a mammy-rag tied around her head but you could still see that her wonderful hair had fallen out. Her face would terrify the little children" (242). Carter's narrative does not stop at this bodily collapse. In a metamorphic spirit, it goes on to outwit Jezebel's curse (syphilis), turning its monolithic character into an alternative subject position. With a little extra help, Jeanne-Jezebel will not rot forever, but, indeed, activate her potential in a metamorphosed artificially enhanced body of a crone. Skipping the mother-stage, she moves strategically to le Guin's stage of lost fertility (3). Following le Guin's "barren childhood" as the first "waiting room" to "fruitful maturity," Carter questions fruitfulness/fertility as "the only meaningful condition for a woman" (le Guin 5). This "loss" attains a positive quality, as the "loss of fertility does not mean loss of desire and fulfillment....The woman who is willing to make that change must become pregnant with herself, at last" (le Guin 5). Jeanne is willing, and starts to co-operate. A man "who called himself her brother" ("might have been Mephistopheles, for all she cared") supplies her with artificial teeth; the best wig comes "from the shorn locks of novices in convents." Jeanne is surprised "how much she was worth" ("Black Venus" 243): "Fifty francs for Jeanne, here, thirty francs for Jeanne, there. It all added up....Add to this the sale of a manuscript or two, the ones she hadn't used to light her cheroots with. Some books, especially the ones with the flowery dedications....Later, any memorabilia of the poet, even his clumsy drawings, would fetch a surprising sum" (243). In this profit-making endeavor, Jeanne can afford her metamorphosis and emerges as the triumphant crone who returns to her mother country and her mother tongue. She does it finally to celebrate her cultural un/belonging, her existence as *la mestiza* who learned how to cope with contradictions. Conscious of crossing borders, Jeanne embodies "representable difference," both the heretic (poison) and the sacred (remedy), whose cultural vulnerability begins with gender (trouble), with the "porousness" of her body, and its *disruptive excess* of a foreign race: "In a new dress of black tussore, her somewhat ravaged but carefully repaired face partially concealed by a flattering veil, she chugged away from Europe on a steamer bound for the Caribbean like a respectable widow and she was not yet fifty....She might have been a Creole wife of a minor civil servant setting off home after his death. Her brother went first, to look out for the property they were going to buy" ("Black Venus" 243). In examining the phallogocentric structures of institutionalized religion, imperialism, and colonization as modes of specifically feminine alienation and debasement, Carter's implications exceed Clément's and Kristeva's concept of the borderline between "the animalistic and the verbal." Precisely as a feminine type of sacredness, Carter's borderline in itself represents a process: the becoming of a pagan, illicit *jouissance* in the physiological and cultural *cleavage*. Strategically suspended between the deferred poles of authority, both Mary Magdalene and the Black Venus slip across borders and form their own sub-cultural paradigm of "cultural possibility" (*Gender Trouble* 77). Although excluded from the dominant culture, they provide a valid response to their "fixed" stigmatized identity, at once refused by and initiated within the "indifference" coded as phallic potency and strength. In undoing the conceptual knots bequeathed by laws and prohibitions, they transcend the dominant power-relations, suggesting ways in which stigmas and recognition can be translated one into the other. In evoking the divine (sacred) journeys to the limits, they evoke alternative subjectivities, where the human "becomes" an "embodied subject," where animality, like monstrosity, is an indispensable experience in the process of becoming. It is where metamorphoses as cultural transgressions take place on the threshold of self-annihilation, of consciousness that retains a Kristevan element of "different legality": the presence of the physiological body hinting at the sacred that, in fact, is not the same as the religious. This "legality" is upheld "by a divided subject," a pluralized subject that occupies permutable and mobile places; thus, bringing together in a heteronymous space "the naming of phenomena (their entry into symbolic law)" (Kristeva, *Desire* 111).

The shifting landscape of poststructural submission and melancholy is equally central to the analysis of the next two narratives, emerging as a "different legality," a locus of the transgression and political power of the "maternal." This "legality," pursued by Toni Morrison in her narrative of the subversive household (home of drifters and cultural transgressors), is explored as a sub/cultural resistance to the traditional exclusion of women/mothers from the sociopolitical structures of power. Out of this resistance, the newly established authority of the household negotiates between the sacred and the heretic spaces of culture, shifting the notion of mother fantasy away from the signature of "lack" towards multiplicity and "porocity," the fantasy feeding upon the plentitude of the subject (Braidotti, *Metamorphoses* 54). I now address the political effectiveness of this negotiation in Morrison's proposal of the maternal sacredness that succeeds in reinvesting displaced women with spiritual integrity but in the end takes refuge in the transcendental. "To impose the new order," Clément believes, "one must permit a fierce resistance, an extreme anger, a revolt of pride, to come into oneself" (Clément and Kristeva 29). Both narratives introduce women who demonstrate such types of resistance, pride, and anger, but they also reveal, in Braidotti's sense, their troubling cultural porousness and their alternative imaginary.

Locating Heretic Conditions

In her article "On the Politics of Domesticity," Nancy Armstrong suggests that political power is closely associated with the modern household, rather than with the clinic believed by Foucault to provide "the proto-institutional setting" (918). Home, overseen by a woman, actually precedes the formation of other social institutions, and as a locus of feminine authority and creativity it challenges the phallogocentric sphere of the public. As argued earlier by Douglas and de Beauvoir, a housewife is a transformer of natural products into culture. Responsible for preserving the boundaries between natural and cultural life, she shifts matter out of place into matter in place (Douglas 40): "With her fire going, woman becomes sorceress; by a simple movement, as in beating eggs, or through the magic of fire, she effects the transmutation of substances: matter becomes food. There is enchantment in these alchemies, there is poetry in making preserves; the housewife has caught duration in the snare of sugar, she has enclosed life in jars" (de Beauvoir 476). However, when this process is disrupted by some illegal, culturally abject activity such as witchcraft, "the authority and identity of the housewife are put in question; she can no longer predict or control the processes of transformation required" (Purkiss 97). She becomes a witch, the symbolic antihousewife figure, responsible for disorder, hysteria, and other processes of contamination. Simultaneously, she reveals that the home boundaries were always crossed, while "the notion of the house as a closed container" is at odds with the housewife identity as a member of the community (98). Following Armstrong, once the household "changes into an impenetrable place of magic forces, escaping control of the authorities, every attempt will be made to destroy it" (918). Similarly, Purkiss writes that nineteenth- and early-twentieth-century moralist literature of domestic conduct chains the "virtuous" wife to "house" where she guards "its resources from overflowing or escaping into the general economy....The physical boundaries of property" are thus "identified with the social boundaries of propriety" (98). In order to preserve its access and relation to power and knowledge, the dominant cultural discourse (community, clique) will persecute everything that disturbs and shifts the boundaries of that relation.

This is precisely the case in Morrison's *Paradise* (1998), in which the conservative African American community cannot tolerate "newcomers" who inhabit an abandoned convent at the edge of their settlement: "If they stayed to themselves, that'd be something. But they don't. They meddle. Drawing folks out there like flies to shit and everybody who goes near them is maimed somehow and the mess is seeping back into *our* homes, *our* families" (Morrison 276). For Morrison, the concept of a subversive household counters the traditional exclusion of women from the sociopolitical structures of power. This power, understood as an institutionalized multiplicity of male-dominated discourses, is undercut by Morrison with a narrative of depression, hysteria, and distress. These initially melancholic spaces, which I trace following Kristeva and Butler, eventually unfold as sub-cultural expressions of race and gender. The surfacing of the witch figure as a container for these expressions is at once empowering and incompatible with the dominant discourse: "Something's going on out there...No men. Kissing on themselves. Babies hid away. Jesus! No telling what else...I hear they drink like fish too...Bitches. More like witches...Before those heifers came to town this was a peaceable kingdom. The others before them at least had some religion. These here are sluts out there...never step foot in church and...they ain't thinking about one either" (Morrison 276). The suspicious and transmuting convent "in some desolate part of the American West" (224) was already "entitled to special treatment" (233), since it was previously inhabited by "Catholic women with no male mission to control them." Those who have come now to inhabit the abandoned mission are "obviously not nuns, real or even pretend, but members, it was thought, of some other cult" (11). In fact, the newly arrived women are homeless, exploited, and hysterical daughters, or mothers (to be). In finding temporary lodging in the "recovery" convent, they cross a borderline between the oppressive paternal structures ("what is out there where they come from") and what is "inside" the convent. The unknown inside of the convent reverses the norm by expelling it to the "outside," excluding it from its center. The "inside" promises shelter and rest; it speaks a different language, neither inviting nor rejecting but strategically ignoring and thereby coping with the "outside": "Over the past eight years they had come. The first one, Mavis, during Mother's long illness; the second right after she died. Then two more. Each one asking permission to linger a few days but never actually leaving. Now and then one or another packed a scruffy little bag, said goodbye and seemed to disappear for a while—but only for a while. They always came back to stay on, living like mice in a house no one, not even the tax collector, wanted, with a woman in love with cemetery. Consolata looked at them through her bronze or gray or blue of her various sunglasses and saw broken girls, frightened girls, weak and lying" (Morrison 222).

Consolata, the last "legitimate" convent resident, is introduced by Morrison as a "confused" woman, oblivious to the outside world, suffering from depression and extensive consumption of alcohol. As a nine-year-old, no longer a virgin, she was "rescued" by the Mother, an ambitious missionary, from the severe conditions in Mexico. In the convent's environment of another phallocentric structure, she has been taught to reject the ordinary "feminine condition" as impure. On Kristeva's note, Consolata's inability to express the primal loss (that in Morrison appears as the loss of the maternal culture) has its accompanying affect of a substitution (through the "loving third" of the convent). This substitution, resulting in a suppression of older memories, makes the depressed constantly aware of an "abstracted" loss, all the while unable to name the source of her suppression. The actual loss is not translated into language but is often betrayed by a permeating tone of anguish and sadness. The emphasis is on the evasion—the necessity of resisting the cultural and sociosymbolic processes through which subjectivity articulates itself—rather than on imaginative empowerment. For thirty years "she offered her body and her soul to God's Son and His Mother as completely as if she had taken the veil herself" (Morrison 225). As a "typical Christian conundrum, oppressive and liberating at once" (Warner 77), the convent becomes her home, her element, and a structure that she is not to abandon but eventually, in Braidotti's sense, to transform. Defined by a cultural transgression quite incompatible with the paternal religion, Consolata represents an intermediary figure, exhibiting her strangeness, her irony, and her latent atheism of a foreign national and a passionate lover. Always at odds with the notion of a housewife who maintains the boundaries of home, she opens up her household to the chaotic and disorganized "outside": the lesbian, the bad mother, the hysteric, all types of women "out of control." Suspending the sublime model of the virginal life, Consolata "runs" the convent in a permanent erasure of the nun in herself, in a disabling state of being non-mother, no-body. If she seems depressed, it is because of her alienation, her acknowledgment of the unbridgeable gap between self and the other, self and the "outside." Here, in agreement with Butler, it is not enough to render this "erasure" performative, even if "pleasure" constitutes significant moments of Consolata's subversion. Above all, Consolata continues to live "in a world in which one can risk serious disenfranchisement and physical violence for the pleasure one seeks, the fantasy one embodies, the gender one performs" (*Undoing Gender* 214). Separated from the two people she loved, first from her lover and then from the Mother, Consolata gradually succumbs to melancholy and drinking: "Melancholy is both the refusal of grief and the incorporation of loss, a miming of the death it cannot mourn" (Butler, *Psychic Life* 142). Repelled by her own "sluglike existence," she seems to tolerate the other women's "resignation, self-pity, mute rage, disgust and shame" (Morrison 250). Their experiences connect them, and, in blurring the borders, tell a common story of drift, deception, and cultural displacement. As drifters, Morrison's characters "oscillate" in an oppressive atmosphere between normality and the asylum. Silently breaking the rules and silently being condemned, they end up like heretics "in confinement," in isolation, and eventually "in death" (Clément and Cixous 8). The longer the women dwell among themselves, the more intense and the less coordinated their physical behavior. They are anxious, disillusioned, and obviously uninterested in "proper" housekeeping.

The women's "dwelling" and their bisexuality expand thus into an unbalanced, hysterical condition, which increasingly threatens to break out beyond control; the women are the "go-go girls: pink shorts, skimpy tops, see-through skirts; painted eyes, no lipstick; obviously no underwear, no stockings" (Morrison 156). Connecting hysteria and melancholy, the gradually collapsing convent offers a temporary substitute for security, identity, and representation. Simultaneously, for the town nearby, a Black settlement representing an oppressively ordered and conservative territory, the combination is unbearable: the convent horrifies as it contains secrets in disruptive excess. The convent's "kitchen is bigger than the house in which either man [from the town] was born" (5). In the cell-rooms there is no "proper" furniture, hammocks replace beds, and "strange things [are] nailed or taped to the walls or propped in a corner": "A 1968 calendar...a letter written in blood so smeary its satanic message cannot be deciphered; an astrology chart; a fedora tilted on the plastic neck of a female torso...the series of infant booties and shoes ribboned to a cord hanging from a crib in the last bedroom they enter. A teething ring, cracked and stiff, dangles among the tiny shoes" (Morrison 7). From the settlement's perspective, the convent goes astray, transgresses and transforms into a coven, a den of nonstructure, and "a carefully planned disguise for what [is] really going on" (11). It is a place at the edge of culture, a locus of subversive intention, with no "cross of Jesus," no men, no language (7). Both the co(n)ven(t) and its inhabitants are culturally formless, symbolically embracing the boundless body of the witch, her ability to transform into other bodies, or to change shape and disappear. It frightens by invoking uncertainty about the witch's identity, her intention and her course of action: "Scary things not always outside. Most scary things is inside" (39). As a metaphor for unspoken feminine *jouissance*, the convent's "inside" epitomizes an impenetrable maternal womb. The sphere is ambiguously transmutable, and seductive, suspending "the notion of the house as a closed container" (Purkiss 98). Its self-contained, maternal character echoes the earlier days of the convent, when self-sufficient nuns made sauces and jellies and European bread. The luring, transformative capacity of the convent increases after the collapse of the missionaries, and in offering shelter to the exploited it threatens to seduce the patriarchal daughters away from their traditional gender roles in which women's "identity rested on the men they married" (Morrison 187). And it is above all the independent status of the convent that endangers the carefully re-enacted hierarchy of the conservative African American community. The road connecting the town with the convent represents an umbilical cord connecting the phallic children with the maternal space of filth; it has an explicitly feminine character since "it was women who walked this road...[b]ack and forth, back and forth; crying women, staring women, scowling, lip-biting women or women just plain lost...out here where the wind handles you like a man, women dragged their sorrow up and down the road between Ruby and the Convent. They were the only pedestrians" (270). Moreover, the unpredictable inside of the convent connects all the culturally suspicious activities: the stillborn babies, abortions, alcohol, wickedness, and filthy music: "And in the Convent were those women" (11). Morrison goes on to narrate the story of their extermination, the cut of the umbilical cord resulting from the community's fear of losing its masterfully attained racial/cultural identity. Perhaps, "somewhere else they could have been accepted...[b]ut not here. Not in Ruby" (157), where nine "handsome, utterly black men murdered five harmless women (a) because the women were impure (not 8-rock [pure black race]); (b) because the women were unholy (fornicators at least, abortionists at most); and (c) because they could—which was what being an 8-rock meant to them and was also what the 'deal' required" (297).

Morrison clearly deconstructs the traditional concept of household as a stable phallocentric structure that would continue as a result of the cut. In morphing the mother from various dislocated elements, transitory states and marginalized positions, her narrative re-enacts a political act of cultural un/belonging, whereby Consolata, unaware of the 8-rock conspiracy, undergoes a metamorphosis, a type of spiritual and bodily awakening. Encouraged by the "practicing" woman from Ruby, Consolata, a gifted healer, begins the practice of "stepping into" people's souls. While transgressing and transforming the paternal cult, she thus succeeds in finding "another sacred space" (Clément and Kristeva 64), another cultural, or rather subcultural, possibility within the paternal. Nostalgia and depression, as Kristeva believes, are indispensable in this process, since it is "only in mourning the old seductions and beliefs of our ancestors, in exhausting their artificial spark in the accounting of a sober meditation that we can move in the direction of new truths" (Clément and Kristeva 142). Consolata's extensive mourning in the cellar indeed leads her out of depression and into the "discovery" of a state that has a specifically transgressive character. It rests on the meditative interconnectedness of all cohabitants of the household and requires therefore a substantial change in their behavior, allowing for the imaginative empowerment that would take over grief and mourning: "I call myself Consolata Sosa. If you want to be here you do what I say. Eat how I say. Sleep when I say. And I will teach you what you are hungry for" (Morrison 262). What Consolata manages through this summoning is the completion of two parallel tasks: that of a mother (a household figure) who introduces order into the scattered home structure and that of a healer who provides that structure with a social support. There is a feminist political passion involved in both, following Irigaray's project of the alternative female genealogy, and there is no sentimentality involved in this reappraisal of the maternal/material feminine. Maternity, positioned as a "resource" rather than a biological indisposition or necessity, transforms into a capacity "to explore carnal modes and perception," a resource of empathy and interconnectedness that surpasses the phallogocentric economy (Braidotti, *Metamorphoses* 23). This "maternal/material feminine" is clearly "linked to the political project of providing symbolic representation for the female feminist subject" (23), and, in Morrison's work, becomes the very reason for the convent's success and its subsequent drama.

Although scared by the unexpected transformation of the woman they learned to ignore, none of the inhabitants leaves the convent. Their quest seems to be ending at its collapsing doors, while the convent itself, with its persistently reoccurring maternal quality, becomes a metaphor for the *omphalos*: the navel as the scar of dependence on the mother. Favoring the *omphalic* as a source of effective subversion, Morrison's "mother" (Consolata) negotiates as such between the phallic and the (om-phalic) spaces of religion. The latter, composed of cultural splits/fissures, remains unarticulated in the paternal cult. Consolata is thus rendered a spiritual negotiator, mediating between the "symbolic castration" that denies her the right to speak the symbolic and the "real incision" that draws/lures her back to unspoken semiotic pleasures. Therein, confined to her household, Consolata transforms the place from within, and these (magic) transformations connect her with one of the most interesting aspects of the historical witch, the healer figure who "belongs to the private sphere, from which the rite stems, even if it is collective. Initiation, ritual, healing, love itself have to do with individuals" (Clément and Kristeva 176). In a "mixed" language difficult to follow, a meditative trance rather than an organized grammar, she manages to formulate her spiritual message to the half-frightened, half-amused listeners: "Hear me, listen. Never break them in two. Never put one over the other. Eve is Mary's mother. Mary is the daughter of Eve" (263). In consolidating all the "abominable" conditions of a neglected, dark, and moist household, the cellar becomes the central place of their meetings. It evokes the remoteness of the womb, as a windowless room, a closed container, and a sealed, her(m)etic space. A locus of Consolata's erotic desires from the past, it is a secret crossroads, a place of coming together of the broken, depressive, hysterical and the inarticulate, semiotic: "First they had to scrub the cellar floor until its stones were as clean as rocks on a shore. Then they ringed the place with candles. Consolata told each to undress and lie down. In flattering light under Consolata's soft vision they did as they were told. How should we lie? However you feel....When each found a position she could tolerate on the cold, uncompromising floor, Consolata walked around her and painted the body's silhouette. Once the outlines were complete, each was instructed to remain there. Unspeaking. Naked in candlelight" (263). The "predisposition for the sacred," as referred to by Clément and Kristeva, "better accommodates itself to naked rebellion, insurrectional heroism, the enthusiasm of the moment, in short, to the gaps in social time" (55). These gaps or fissures tie in with the transgressive structure as the cultural practice of suspending the order. This suspension, associated with momentary "gaps in social time," has a different resonance in Morrison's text, since it refuses to be momentary, casual, or orgasmic, and functions as a newly established order for the secret/sacred practices in the cellar. It also challenges the overexcited body of a hysteric, since the sacred experience comes as a result of the cure (treatment) of pathological symptoms. The women's desires, pains, and sorrows intermingle with their newly established spiritual household, and the reversed "system of classification" (Clément and Kristeva 92) in which all are taken care of. "In loud dreaming, monologue is no different from a shriek; accusations directed to the dead and long gone are undone by murmurs of love. So, exhausted and enraged, they rise and go to their beds vowing never to submit to that again but knowing full well they will. And they do" (Morrison 264). The carnivalesque carelessness of their "freedom" is gone, but rather than returning to the phallocentric order, the household prevails as a strategically independent structure.

As initiated by Consolata, household tasks and specifically maternal/material desire (incorporation) intermingle, connect and disconnect, becoming a spiritual practice of renewal, a subculture within the symbolic system of restrictions. Feminine desire, intensified by spiritual and bodily transformation, transcends the stereotypes of race, but not "sexual difference." As in Morrison's earlier work, the reader is never given any final opportunity to distinguish the women's skin color: the racial identifications are ambiguous, exchangeable, releasing the operations of race in the feminine from obligatory references to skin color and its subsequent cultural connotations (Abel, Christian, Moglen 102). By replacing the conventional signifiers of (racial) difference and by substituting for the racialized body a series of disaggregated cultural parts, Morrison exposes the unarticulated (racial) codes that operate at the boundaries of consciousness: "They shoot white girl first. With the rest they can take their time. No need to hurry out there. They are seventeen miles from a town which has ninety miles between it and any other. Hiding places will be plentiful in the Convent, but there is time and the day has just begun" (3). Apart from Consolata's stated Indian origin, the racial indications are few and confusing, almost absent. Their absence directly challenges the Black community's obsession with racial purity that is no longer "the sign...they had taken for granted" but "a stain" (194), a historical repetition but in reverse, as a vengeance. The convent's impurity is projected both as feminine and as not (entirely) black; it reopens and pollutes their grandfathers' wounds. As in Creed's analysis of the horror setup, "the house that offered a solace ultimately becomes a trap, the place where the monster is destroyed and/or the victim murdered" (56). For the nine men on the mission, the place constitutes the ultimate danger of annihilation, of being engulfed by the witch's monstrous and invulnerable womb. Its invulnerability "works to license violence against her, violence tinged with the terror of the maternal. Her hard body is a pretext for violence against her invasive magical power, itself an extension of her body" (Purkiss 127). Inevitably, the subversive power of the convent has to be challenged by the centralized phallic power, believed to be wrong in order to be destroyed. "I know they got powers. Question is whose power is stronger....They don't need men and they don't need God. Can't say they haven't been warned" (Morrison 276). The impenetrable inside threatens life, and is therefore "radically excluded" (Kristeva, *Powers* 2). The subversive household, a condition that gradually supplements the absence of the phallocentric discourse, has the transitory, metamorphic character of a trance that is healing/becoming, and it is this process of growth, restored to its symbolic and economic functioning, that is abruptly ended by the phallic interference. In the brutal murder performed on the women, the men expel their anxieties to the margin of the community, and project a deeply familiar contradiction to everything they believe they stand for. The convent in the end becomes for them a place of disconnection, of separation from anxiety, impenetrability, and vulnerability—from everything that the "unknown" (mother) comes as a reminder of.

The ambiguous maternal pleasures, opening for the women as they transcend life, emerge from the fertile, reproductive spaces of the convent's garden. This garden/paradise offers another transgression of symbolic restrictions as the differently cultured realm of unspeaking Piedade, a transgression that converges with the "sacred body of a woman...at the crossroads of love" (Clément and Kristeva 105). The garden serves as a locus of the specifically feminine trance (order) that contrasts directly with the (disordered) brutality of the men who leave the mission unconvinced of the results they have accomplished. As Morrison suggests, it is the spiritual path of the restorative maternal powers, rather than institutionally sanctioned religious structure, that serves as a strategy for women to cope with the phallogocentric culture. However, as a space of "eternal refuge," Morrison's posthumous paradise fails to protect women within culture. In transgressing into semiotic pleasures beyond culture (beyond body), the paradise simply offers a return to the protective womb. As such it runs the risk of appearing as "a futile gesture" (Butler, *Gender Trouble* 78-80), unable to solve the problem within the social structure, its laws and prohibitions. The political power of the cellar/womb is left unarticulated, enclosed with other secrets behind the convent's walls, and sealed with a scar/meaning that cannot be deciphered. It is in this sense, perhaps, that Morrison's sacred space (as a source of subversion) becomes politically problematic, since it is not "maintained within the terms of culture" (80). Simultaneously, the after-life paradise originates from and maintains its firm connection with/in the convent, where the women, just before being shot, were in the process of "becoming," undergoing metamorphosis. This connection, misunderstood or never taken into account by the self-victimized oppressors from Ruby, is posited by Morrison as an attempt to formulate the space of libidinal character within culture. This attempt converges in fact with Irigaray's project of the "sensible transcendental": the space of unspoken cultural territories that have not been acknowledged as negotiable, and therefore neither strategic nor political. Although a great deal of the political project of "different legality" aims at postulating a sociocultural contract by and for marginalized women (boundary figures, cross-borders, and drifters), it also contains the powerful transcendental value of refusal to be constricted/restricted or categorized, once and for all.

Metamorphoses and New Orders of Significations

Published in 1998, the same year as Morrison's *Paradise*, both *Dom dzienny, dom nocny* (The Day House, the Night House) by Tokarczuk and *Złodziejka pamięci* (Thief of Memories) by Krystyna Kofta expand the concept of a subversive household into a transnational dis/order that abolishes borders between domestic (national) and foreign structures. The notion of foreignness, evoked in these texts as a contingency of disorder and confusion, implies the need for a new classification, in fact, a new order of signification that permeates the structures of the national home. Negotiating race, gender, nationality, and religion, these narratives, and Tokarczuk's in particular, demonstrate the formations of the new positive subject that Braidotti has strived to mark with recognition: the subject of becoming. In Szczuka's account, and in those of other poststructural feminist critics in Poland, Tokarczuk represents "the most important contemporary myth-writer, searching for literary images of religious, unconscious and archetypal structures in spaces of 'minor' and borderline plots" (Szczuka, *Cinderella* 20). In analyzing various poststructural feminist developments, Szczuka places Tokarczuk among authors exploring transgression and the metamorphic potential of the feminine subject, such as Emma Tennant, Jeanette Winterson, and Angela Carter.

Marta, Tokarczuk's figure of the crone blurs a boundary line between the usual and the unusual, or feasible and unfeasible, forms of behavior ascribed to an elderly woman living in a cottage by herself. According to the narrator, Marta's nearest neighbour, she has "nothing to say about herself," and acts "strangely," unpredictably, out of context: "As if she had no history. She only liked to talk about other people... also about those who probably did not exist at all—later I found some proofs that Marta liked to make things up," fabricate places in which she puts people, like plants (*Dom dzienny* 10; unless indicated otherwise, translations from Polish are mine). In winter, Marta's cottage is dark, moist, and cold, while its mysteriously "fragile" inhabitant (her hair is "all silver," her skin is "dry and wrinkled," she is missing some teeth) simply disappears "like everything else here...Out of the window...I can see Marta's house. For three years now I have been wondering who Marta was...always saying different things about herself. Every time we spoke she mentioned a different year of birth" (9). In summertime Marta visits the narrator frequently, but seems to be distant, neither listening nor worrying about the consequences of her own talking. She is indifferent, even somehow cruel, for instance when she feeds her cocks, and then kills and devours them all over two autumn days (12). In her extravagant habits, Marta confuses the binaries of day and night, warmth and coldness, life and death. In integrating polarities, she undermines the structure of traditional concepts of linear time, amount, or degree that are "proper" and "well balanced" (day is for work, night is for rest, hens are kept for eggs, etc.) and develops her own sovereign morphology within this traditional structure. In a metaphorical extension of night into winter, Marta "sleeps" through winter, and like everything else about her, Marta's hibernation is extreme, deathlike, crossing the border into the "forbidden" and unthinkable. Her resting body lies in the dark cellar, carefully stored in the midst of apples and potatoes, suspended in time and language. Half animal, half human, Marta "wakes up around March" and gradually returns from her womblike winter retreat to her "day house" routines. Again, the passage along the umbilical cord seems to be reversible, reiterated, carrying the freshness of the original experience back through the layers of obscurity, repression, and habit. It connects and redefines the ambiguous semiotic spaces within the cultural (or at least, culturally recognizable) structure: "First she sensed the cellar—its moist and safe scent, the scent of mushrooms and moist hay. This was the reminiscence of summer. Her body was awakening from a long dream, until she found out that her eyes were open....And so on, piece after piece, she called into life her entire body" (12). By advocating this bodily transcendence, Tokarczuk's narrative ineluctably moves towards Irigaray's insistence to disengage the feminine, in particular the maternal, from the one-dimensional picture of phallogocentric objectification. Marta, in a link to Braidotti's postulate of "incorporeal materiality" that defines the body "not only as material, but also as a threshold to a generalized notion of female being, a new feminist humanity" (*Metamorphoses* 58), is explicitly rendered transcendental. To put it differently, Marta implies rethinking of space, time, nature, materiality, symbiosis, and mucosity. The circulating, flowing, and transgressive nature of eroticism that codes Braidotti's incorporeality as feminine meets in Marta's particular morphology of desire with Kristeva's "feminine sacred" and Irigaray's "feminine divine." Marta's peculiar way of coping with the seasons undermines the stability of her household as well as her (human) body, which would normally need to be taken care of, whatever the season. On the contrary, dismantling the permanence and continuity of a "kept" household, Marta reveals some metamorphic and incomprehensible capacities of adjustment to the conditions and manifestations of sociocultural causalities: "I didn't understand Marta and I still don't when I think about her. But do I need to understand Marta? What would I gain from the discovery of her manners, or the sources of her stories? Why would I need her autobiography, if she had one at all? Perhaps there are people without biographies, without a future or past, who appear to others in a sort of permanent present?" (*Dom dzienny* 12).

With all the physical transmutability of her body, her origin and substance, we can trace Marta back to the "ghost" of the pre-Oedipal mother, a phantom of the "speaking subject" as emerging from culturally forbidden spaces. I return to Sprengnether's pre-Oedipal mother and her "effect of the spectral" (5) in order to elucidate Marta's articulation of her cultural validity as related both to a "speculation" ("spectacle," "suspicion") and "appearance" in the face of the semiotic that does not speak or read the symbolic. In a way, Marta's language as well as her circular biography can be associated with a "feminine plotting," defined by Szczuka in the Polish cultural context as the "weaving, intriguing, or gossiping" of an uneducated, "simple" woman, very often a housewife ("Spinners" 69-70). In spreading gossip about other people, Marta is spreading silence about herself. "After all, to plait, or to weave," in Szczuka's association with feminine modes of speech, "indicate time spent in an uncreative manner," time that elapses unproductively. This type of plotting is often linked with incomprehensible or incomplete utterances, such as babbling, jabbering, or talking nonsense, characteristic of marginalized but culturally present linguistic spaces: baby talk or language appropriate to a mentally disordered, delirious, or sclerotic person (Szczuka 70). Echoing Felman's and Irigaray's deconstructions of the feminine manifestation of symbolic language, Szczuka refers specifically to aphorisms and generally adopted axioms in the Polish language, such as women's ability to "grind" or to "mince" with their enormous tongues, or to "wag" their tongues and gossip. With Marta, however, these feminine manifestations are reversed or suspended. Instead of plotting, Marta is unplotting her story. Thus, rather than negating herself as the subject, as Szczuka has envisioned the gossiping woman, I see Marta as continuously "becoming": manifesting her presence against time as a category of passing and creating new orders of signification. In Tokarczuk's text, the "feminine plotting" is moreover linked with women's hair, since Marta, earlier a wig-maker, continues to preserve some of her tresses and occasionally wears them when she visits the narrator: "Whenever I asked her to tell me something about herself...she changed the subject, turned her head towards the window, or simply continued to cut the cabbage or plait her own or not-her-own hair" (10).

In occupying this multiple subjectivity, Marta, the incongruent and un/plotting "subject," evokes the borderlands as interlaced with dialogical sites of language: where "subjects are constituted in language, but...language is also the site of their destabilization" (Butler, "Discussion" 135). Marta's (and the narrator's) village represents a crossroads inscribed into constant transformations of culture, and therefore, a destabilization of time. The settlement is placed in-between geographically "authentic" and imaginary spaces: in the vicinity of Wambierzowice and Nowa Ruda, a nationally ambivalent territory (Polish in its current status), adjacent to the German and Czech borders, and fusing culturally different historical traces. This trans/national dynamic of location reconstitutes tradition as a fluid continuous concept-process, projecting the village as a space of Marta's etiology and reinforcing the narrator's addiction to the archaic mother. Collecting the different stories of people inhabiting this equivocal territory, the narrator is a "dispersed" figure, a cultural negotiator maintaining her integrity by developing a metamorphic tolerance for contradictions. In fantasizing about Marta, the narrator evokes the "porousness" of her own homeland and attempts to keep up with its configurations and changes that are simultaneously acknowledged and symptomatic of memory loss. In suggesting different types of Marta's death (128), and subsequently, of her various resurrections, the narrator repeatedly evokes the reversibility of the journey along the umbilical cord. Marta, in fact, can be seen as a negotiator between the phallic and the *omphalic*, mediating (or "denaveling," to use Bronfen's term) between the "symbolic castration" that denies her the ability or right to speak the symbolic language and the "real incision" that draws/lures her back to semiotic pleasures. In depicting Marta's negotiation "with her entire past and present" (10), Tokarczuk herself becomes a gossip-writer, closely resembling an inventive but ambiguous fortune-teller whose predictions develop into the intrinsic model of her narrative, a metaphoric picture of her own methodology. Configuring thus marginal, apparently trivial and inconsequential fables and legends, the narrator manages in the end to threaten the dominant cultural discourse by imposing a new one. Marta's fabrications (wig- and myth-making) connect both with the transcultural stories told by Lissie in Alice Walker's narrative and le Guin's concept of the menopausal crone who becomes "pregnant with herself" (le Guin 5).

As a multiple speaking (becoming) subject, Marta represents a crossroads of identifications that, according to Butler, are carried precisely and inevitably by language ("Discussion" 135): "I should have known where Marta came from. Why she wasn't there for us in winter, why she appeared again in spring time" (*Dom dzienny* 26). Hinting at unspoken territories, Marta is a "ghostly apparition," a site of recurring subversion that introduces a new plot (both as an intrigue/subversion and as a subsequent development of the story) and disrupts the traditional order (by killing all cocks at once).

Most significantly for my further reading, it is Marta who draws the narrator's attention to a peculiar statuette in a wayside shrine and who comes up with the story of the medieval, sacred/heretic, and transcultural figure of St. Vigilance. A popular saint venerated by people on both sides of the Polish-German border, St. Vigilance is also known as Wilgefortis [Wilga], Święta Troska, or Kummernis von Schonau. As a fictitious narrative figure, Wilga represents a peculiar fantasy of gender, blurring all culturally sanctioned boundaries at once: nation, religion, body, and the illimitable process of signification itself. What operates at the level of this illimitable fantasy refuses to dissociate from the ways in which material and metamorphic processes of life intermingle: "On the cross was a woman, a girl, in such a tight dress that her breasts under the paint cover appeared naked....There was a small shoe sticking out under the dress; the other foot was bare, and this is when I realized that a similar statuette was in the wayside shrine on the road that led to Agnieszka. That one had a beard though, that's why I always thought that it was Christ in an exceptionally long robe. The inscription underneath read: "Sanc. Wilgefortis. Ego dormio et cor meum vigilat," and Marta said that it was St. Vigilance (*Dom dzienny* 53). Her life story unfolds in Marta's un/plotting via yet another account: written by Paschalis, a gender-confused monk of German origin, "under the patronage of the Holy Ghost and the superior of the Benedictine Cloister" (54). The legend can be read both as a manifestation of a "sacred transvestism" (Clément and Kristeva 31) and of the bodily heresy that abandons gender for an experience of the sacred outside of religious structure. As a site of cultural transgression, Wilga-Kummernis-St.Vigilance performs at once a gender spectacle and a transmutation of significance, deviating from singular patterns of control and order. Born a daughter, Wilga was already "born somehow imperfect" in the eyes of her father, a knight and a devoted warrior (*Dom dzienny* 54). Her feminine body, as if trying to compensate for this inaccuracy, develops, under the care of Wilga's beloved stepmother, into a medieval ideal of femininity: "Those who saw her admired the miracle of creation in silence" (55). The continuous absence of her father, (frequently participating in the crusades) and the unexpected loss of her stepmother (dying of a hemorrhage) contribute to the gradual decline of Wilga's home in Schonau. Shortly after his second wife's death, the father gives all his other daughters away in marriage, but Wilga, the youngest, is temporarily sent to a Convent (56). The nuns, in Paschalis's account, "accepted the girl with joy, and it soon became apparent that her physical beauty equaled her spiritual beauty, and was even surpassed by it...and even a dark chamber appeared full of light, and her speech was exceptionally wise for her age, and her judging was mature. Her slim body discharged a balsamic scent, and roses were found in her bed, although it was winter. Once placed in front of a mirror, a face image of the Son of God appeared on its surface and remained there until the next day" (57). Wilga enjoys her life in the Convent genuinely, a refuge eradicating her unwanted sex.

The Judeo-Christian concepts of the virgin and the mother are installed in the narrative as suspended between the virginal body and its self-destruction (transformation) in pregnancy. Legalized sets of rules govern this historical feminine body: if a virgin, a woman must remain so until she marries; otherwise, she is a harlot. If a wife-mother, she must obey her husband and remain faithful; otherwise, she commits adultery, often penalized by death. If she chooses to retain her virginity, her only refuge is in nunhood, and she must experience the vocation as becoming the bride/servant of the great Father. Either way, she remains imprisoned in the polluted body of Eve. Subconsciously identifying with a creature "beyond sex," Wilga attempts to resolve the dilemma of a Christian woman caught in the dichotomy of Eve-versus-Mary. This dichotomy is particularly strongly projected in the Polish tradition of feminine patriotism, which draws on the model of Maryja (Mary), whose miracles save fortresses and convents surrounded by enemies, such as the Convent of Częstochowa under the patronage of the Black Madonna. Wilga identifies with the Virgin, "who triumphs where the first Eve failed, who refuses where the first Eve was tempted" (Warner 245). While participating in her "novitiate," a "preparation time for giving oneself to the Master" (*Dom dzienny* 57), she imagines herself the bride of the divine Son, "void of" her physical body, and joined with him in "the moment of ecstatic union" (Warner 129): "But the father was relentless and did not want to hear about giving his daughter away to the nuns for good. There, he believed, she would have become something separate, un-utilized, as if fallow. In giving her away in marriage to Wolfram von Pannewicz, he would almost give her to himself, in other words, to the male kind that he represented through God, so as to rule and watch over the creatures of God" (*Dom dzienny* 58).

Wilga's persistent refusal to leave the convent transforms her virginity into a rebellion that nullifies the Law of the Father, as well as (his) God, as "an effective instrument of feminine subjection" (Warner 49). In attempting to resolve her particular entrapment, Wilga successfully demonstrates that what is at stake is her relationship to the law. Like Cixous's model of Eve, Wilga "is not afraid of the inside, neither her own, nor that of the other" (Cixous, "Extreme Fidelity" 134). Her relationship to the law mirrors in fact "her relationship to the inside, to penetration, to touching the inside" (*Dom dzienny* 115). Wilga's pregnant "inside" is linked to her feminine body imprisoned within the *parthenos*, a Christian shield against physiological and psychological contamination that now turns into a weapon against the Father's will. Virginity, thus "one of the most powerful imaginary constructs known in the history of civilizations" (Kristeva, "Stabat Mater" 163), becomes a cynical armor protecting her autonomy, her right to choose between the two sanctified modes of marriage: "So the father told her: 'With your body you belong to the earth, and there is no other master than me.' To that his daughter replied: 'I have a different Father in heaven and He is preparing a different bridegroom for me.' These words made the baron angry and he said: 'I am the master of your life, He is the Master of your death'" (*Dom dzienny* 58). Given no choice, Wilga escapes to the woods, and abandoning both the secular and the religious order, lives in a cave as a hermit, a version of Mary Magdalene, the embodiment of Christian repentance. There she spends her days in meditation and fasting. Like Carter's Magdalene and St. Catherine in Kristeva's commentary, Wilga "undoubtedly draws great satisfaction from that mind game, by mortifying herself. But the same game builds up her moral being...and her capacity to overcome every privation, every ordeal, beginning with disgust—the oral ordeal. Catherine refuses to get married, devotes herself to Jesus, and stops eating. The fast begins at age sixteen—she allows herself only bread, raw vegetables, and water" (Clément and Kristeva 118). As villagers discover Wilga's ability to "work miracles" (59), she becomes popular as a powerful and beneficent ascetic. With the name Kummernis (the German word *Kummer* means grief, sorrow, and mourning), she "heals the maladies of the soul and sufferings coming from the emptiness of the heart" (60), and is frequently called "to those who were dying to guide their souls through the labyrinths of death" (61). The word of her fame spreads and, as Paschalis's account continues, Kummernis is eventually kidnapped by her father and imprisoned (63). Forced to marry Wolfram, she seeks refuge in meditation, concentrating on the figure of Christ, the redeemer. Paschalis's story reaches its climax when Wilga's father opens the door of her cell to finally make his daughter fulfil her earthy duties: "Kummernis stood in a windowless chamber, but it was not the woman whom everybody knew. Her face was covered with a silky beard; her loose hair was falling down her arms. Two naked girlish breasts stuck out of her torn low-necked dress. Her dark but soft eyes followed the inquisitive faces and stopped at the baron. The maidens began to make the sign of the cross and knelt down one after the other. Kummernis, or whoever it was, raised her hands, as if she wanted to clasp all of them to her breast. She said quietly: My Master saved me from myself and bestowed his beard upon me. The same evening the baron ordered the chamber to be walled up with the monster in it. Wolfram mounted a horse and left without a word" (65). Following this passage, Tokarczuk makes us believe that to achieve her goal, Wilga has to outwit the Law of the Father; to sacrifice her feminine body, mark it with some negation of the sanctified feminine, and commit a cultural slip towards sacrilege, heterodoxy, and deviation. Her metamorphosis into a hybrid figure, a gender-crosser, connects her with the mystic tradition of "moving from one sex to the other" mentioned by Clément as "common currency in the history of mysticism" (Clément and Kristeva 31). The oddness of Wilga's experience lies, however, in the fact that "the mystic does not stop at that difference: he passes beyond....And, although one has the right to scream, to stammer, or to sing, it is forbidden to articulate. To fix the sacred outside the instant is sacrilege" (Clément and Kristeva 31). In fixing the sacred outside the instant, Kummernis, like Consolata in Morrison's story, commits a heresy, and reaches the limits of logic that connects the saint with the heretic, the Virgin with the witch. In imposing a new order, she passes to the logic of another comprehension: that the subject is indeed becoming, remaining forever imperfect, and conferring flexibility and energy to communicate the limits.

Wilga also incorporates Kristeva's sacredness as bound to sacrifice: "to succumb to duty, to immolate oneself for a tyrannical ideal, with all the jouissances that mortification procures, but all the uneasiness as well, even unto death" (Clément and Kristeva 120). Moreover, in her commentary on Saint Teresa of Avila, Kristeva refers to the sacred as involving "a suggestion of disbelief" (37) as well as a familiarity with "the 'other' logic." Like Teresa's, Kummernis's "intense and evasive body" (above all, her face covered with the miraculous beard that continues to grow) turns her "religious experience" into "a confrontation with abjection" (37). Her experience with "the sacred" is different from paternal religion, since it takes place in a dimension that eclipses linear modes of spacing. The sacred "*passes* in a boundlessness without rule or reservation, which is the trait of the divine, while the religious installs a marked access road, with meditations provided for the difficult cases." The sacred "erupts in its time, or rather in its instant, since its nature is to turn the order upside down" (30). Although sentenced to death, Kummernis continues to "rewrite" the female model of Eve by her distorted ("upside down") femininity. Shortly before her execution, Kummernis, as a fantasy of gender (a creature that is part Jesus, part Eve, and part Mary) re-enacts simultaneously two scenes of temptation, those of Eve in Eden and Jesus in the desert. In resisting the seductive promises of the devil, who appears in her cell, she resists the paternal speech in the Name of her/the Father: "'You could have loved and been loved,' [the devil] said. 'I know,' she replied. 'You could have carried a child in your womb, you could have heard it from within, and then you could have given it to the world,' he said. 'Betrayed it to the world,' she said. 'You could have bathed, fed and caressed it. You could have watched it grow; its soul and body becoming so much like yours. You could have given it to your God'" (*Dom dzienny* 66). Her dialogue with the devil permits a heretic resistance, and allows Kummernis to continue becoming; to "resist," as Clément believes, "would be the word befitting the sacred" (53). As an extension of the father, the devil represents the symbolic order of the "community" that, like the Cloister, is a site of support and oppression. The devil explains: "Your stubbornness here, in solitude, with a face of a stranger instead of your beautiful appearance, makes no sense. You are not Him. He poked fun at you and now he does not care. He forgot about you, went to create worlds...left you to face the stupid folk who want you to be sanctified or burnt at the stake just the same" (66). Kummernis's resistance against this community is a revolt that blurs the demands of secular and religious institutions of the social order. Her gender crossing, in this religious context, suggests more than the suspension of her sex: in involving the figure of Christ as actively participating in Kummernis's transition, and therefore sabotaging the patriarchal order, Tokarczuk destabilizes the religious system of signification as a constant and monologic structure. As a border-crosser, Kummernis devalues the symmetricity of signification, fluctuating and altogether weakened by the charisma of her virginal/maternal body. The archaic authority of the "mother," several times signaled by the presence of Kummernis's open breasts, is ultimate in the scene with the devil: "'Look at me,' said the devil. She clasped him harder to her breast...caressed gently his smooth skin. Then, she took out her breast and positioned the devil to suck it. The devil struggled out of her embrace and disappeared immediately" (66).

In this role of the nursing Madonna, Kummernis/Jesus brings into play the "one natural biological function...permitted the Virgin in Christian cult—suckling" (192). In her attempt to nurse the devil, Kummernis transfers Madonna's milk into a fluid charged with semiotic power, neither directed against nor supporting the Father, but an all-encompassing power of life. This particular fluid conceptually resembles Irigaray's *fluid* "which is not a solid ground/earth or mirror for the subject" but "is mobile," arousing phallocentric fear (Whitford 28). Like Kristeva's Virgin in "Stabat Mother," Kummernis "obstructs the desire for murder or devoration by means of a strong oral cathexis (the breast), valorization of pain (the sob) and incitement to replace the sexed body with the ear of understanding" (Kristeva, "Stabat Mater" 181). Designating maternal power as "the spasm at the slipping away of eroticism" translated into tears, Kristeva suggests that we "should not conceal what milk and tears have in common: they are the metaphors of non-speech" (174). The breast has indeed the final word in Kummernis's conversation with the devil, who takes flight from it as if from holy water. It returns and consolidates the powers of the material subject of becoming, its undeniable corporeality that communicates "sexual difference." In the process of subject formation, Kummernis dis/connects with various figures, with death and life, with the demonic sexual rites of witches, and with the excessive spiritualization of her body. Which one perseveres is to be verified by her father, who carries out her crucifixion: "If God is in you, you should die like God" (*Dom dzienny* 68). Kummernis's violent death resembles again the death of Jesus and makes her a beloved local saint. The eccentricity of the female martyr, deriving from "sexual difference," speaks, however, against her official sanctification. In turn, Paschalis, who devoted years to composing Kummernis's biography, is also an interesting figure of in-between gender. With a beautiful face of a girl, "he was born [like Wilga] somehow imperfect, because as long as he remembered, he did not feel well within himself, as if he made a mistake at birth and picked out the wrong body, the wrong place and time" (*Dom dzienny* 74). Paschalis's dilemma is his gender perplexity, which he attempts to resolve by inhabiting the "pleasant spaces" of the same female Convent in which Wilga once lived. The biography, at first his only pretext to stay among women (who make him feel like one), gradually becomes the object of his intense although "vague" desires. Kummernis herself, although long dead and physically distant, becomes his messenger of an unexplored eroticism, a new order of signification. Later, on his journey to plead for Kummernis's sanctity, he meets a woman prostitute who puts a dress on him. The process of new subject-formation requires thus a preemption of his sexuality, a prohibition of cross-dressing that eroticizes the law (Butler, "Subjection" 245). In linking the prohibited desire to the law, Paschalis follows Kummernis: as gender-crossers, both have realized that the act of crossing "works through compelling eroticization" and through "making the law and its prohibitions into the final object of desire" (245). Kummernis, with her bare breasts and beard, and Paschalis, in a dress and stockings borrowed from a prostitute, are "compellingly eroticised," but therefore also alienated and rejected. Paschalis is eventually told by the bishop that his account "is not finished"; like his sexuality, it is unclear, heretical: "'It is not finished, son...or this': 'No matter what I do—it is love for you, and loving you, I have to love myself, because what is alive in me, what loves—is you.' 'This sounds really heretical'...Paschalis understood that everything was lost and took the last argument out of his pocket—a wooden cross with a half-naked body of a woman with the face of Christ. 'You can buy it everywhere,' he said. 'Believers go on pilgrimages to Elmendorf to receive her blessing.' What a tasteless oddity, the monk made a wry face" (*Dom dzienny* 161).

Paschalis's identity as "being in drag" is distinguished thus by a movement towards the other (the "tasteless oddity"), a practice of reversal in which identity and its supposed unity is precisely evaded and abandoned. Drag is the fantasy in which gender is doubled up and exaggerated, in which identity is fissured. By that token, drag is also an ethical representation of gender as a fantasy. Paschalis not only fails to persuade the bishop in Glitz (not to mention the Pope, whom he never encounters) that the thoughts and conduct of Kummernis were in conformity with Catholic doctrine, but, apparently, he allows himself to be subjugated by a heretic woman. This woman, in the multicultural context of Marta's story, resembles Gloria Anzaldúa's figure of *la mestiza*, who continually walks out of one culture (gender, nationality) into another, because, paradoxically, she is "in all cultures at the same time" (Anzaldúa 77). As a type of *mestiza*, conscious of crossing borders, Kummernis represents an un/belonging woman, both the heretic and the sacred, whose cultural vulnerability begins with gender (trouble), with the "porousness" of her body and its *disruptive excess* of femininity. Like Carter's Mary Magdalene and Morrison's Consolata, Tokarczuk's Kummernis translates the abject into a sacred disorder that shatters the dominant culture through transgression. In exposing the artificiality of fixed identity, she negotiates the stigma of "feminine imperfection" that is no longer an essence "lying unchanged outside history and culture" (Hall, "Cultural Identity" 213). In this cultural negotiation, the artificially projected linearity of the umbilical cord has been effectively diffused, and, as demonstrated in Kofta's *Złodziejka pamięci* (Thief of Memories), its diffusion unfixes the origin to which no absolute, final, or nostalgic returns are possible.

The Stigma and the Paradox of the Navel

In Kofta's novel, the traditional concepts of home and community are suspended in persistent returns to a floating, continually rotating past which needs to be "retold, rediscovered, reinvented" (Hall, "Old and New" 58). What structures this relation is the fantasy of un/belonging, coming into play in the stylization of the embodied subjects. Bodies in Kofta's narrative are not inhabited as fixed molar entities. On the contrary, they are "aging, altering shape, altering signification—depending on their interactions—and the web of visual, discursive, and tactile relations that become part of their historicity, their constitutive past, present, and future" (Butler, *Undoing Gender* 217). Braidotti's and Butler's transfigurations of subjectivity are captured in this narrative as a momentum of their theoretical convergence: as a type of subject reconstruction through memory, fantasy, narrative, and through all these processes, as a "becoming" subjectivity that continuously points towards new horizons, and when it is embodied, it accommodates the new. My discussion of this reconstruction centers on the figure of a grandmother, Sabina, whose existence, similarly to Marta's in Tokarczuk's novel, offers a refreshing way of reading the stigma, the mark of negativity engraved on the subject. One of the central narrative figures, Sabina strategically ventures into the cultural margin, from where she is consistently supplying her granddaughter Bogna (Kofta's narrator) with paradoxical identifications, inconsistencies, and difference.

Bogna, a writer attempting to reconstruct the ambiguous past of her family, lives in Warsaw with her husband (temporarily away), her son, and her lover. In fact, she represents a typical female protagonist in contemporary Polish women's writing. Following Kraskowska, the most important element of postcommunist women's writing is that the protagonist constitutes the opposite of the stereotypical literary heroine. In fact, with all her everyday dilemmas as well as her "biological" fate, which mirror many other biographies of women, apparently there is little substance in her life for a novel. The typical protagonist is in her forties; her age connects with the specificities of a "female process of identification" and the crises involved in this process (207). Precisely the case in Kofta's narrative, which recounts the processes of Bogna's "becoming" (her various identifications), the crisis of the subject intermingles with that of the cultural structure, weak and hybrid in itself, primarily represented by Bogna's politically suspended and altogether suspect father, and her grandmother, Sabina Schönmyth, the alienated, marginalized woman labeled as a witch. Bogna's initial discovery, that both her parents' and her grandmother's homeland (as a source and grounding for the subject) is irretrievably past, makes her dwell in continual confusion of her already unstable, provisional identity: "Grandmother Sabina...minor witches could have been trained by her; I remembered what my father said. When I first saw this fragile woman proudly standing in her black dress down to her ankles, my mother had to repeat: say hello, this is grandmother Sabina, come on, Bogienka, what's wrong?" (*Złodziejka* 150). In imposing an imaginary coherence on her experience of disintegration, Bogna imagines herself collecting and storing various fragments of past conversations: moments that, as her mother assures her, she cannot possibly remember. In particular, attempting to disrupt the silence surrounding her origin, Bogna returns to the earliest moments in her life through the prism of postmemory, the memory stored and passed on by her mother. In trying to fix and identify with a culturally incoherent construct, she begins to understand, however, that her morphology is contaminated by an explicitly foreign, incompatible idiom: "It is a beautiful September day....A woman is pushing a stroller in a street. German soldiers look at her. The thoughts and the woman and the soldiers converge in a question of when the war will end. A small girl in a round hat is sitting in the stroller talking all the time. She comments on everything she sees. A German soldier asks the woman about the child's age. She will be one in December, the mother answers in fluent German. The soldier shakes his head in disbelief. The girl doesn't stop talking, asking and answering to herself. People turn their heads and laugh, as if there was no war" (*Złodziejka* 50). In this deconstructive and reconstructive re-membering, the pressures of cultural obligations are suspended in fluctuating geographies of German and Polish nations. Contradictory traces (German soldiers, mother's fluent German, little girl's speaking Polish) reorganize and reshape each other mutually, displacing the center/periphery within the other and within oneself. Homeland, in fact, appears in vague references to "patriotism," which stops at Bogna's denial of German identity, and obliges her to reread the binaries as forms of cultural translation, "destined to trouble the here/there cultural binaries for ever" (Hall, "Cultural Identity" 247). Bogna's grandparents and parents were German citizens of Polish descent, who, like many other Polish families, returned to an independent Poland around 1920. Their diasporic consciousness, silenced during the communist period, lives, to quote James Clifford, as "loss and hope as a defining tension" (257). In postwar Poland, Bogna's father is not only still German but also a remnant of the dispossessed capitalist class. Bogna recalls her father saying, "patriotism is when you come back to the worst place" (*Złodziejka* 114), but she never understood his claims to Polishness, since for him "it was no return, [he] was born in Berlin" (116). The mutually permeating positions of two antagonistic cultures, traditions, and languages haunt her memory, rendering reminiscence into a site of continuous becoming, and voiding it in fact of melancholic mourning. The post/memory she has been continuously "stealing" from her parents allows her in the end to break through the cultural invisibility of her past.

In the continuous process of cultural translation, claiming the memory of all those who have passed away, a middle-aged Bogna in her forties invites them back to life as ghosts, apparitions, reminders of the past, inevitable loneliness that "consists of what she desires and what she simultaneously rejects" (36): "My desire is constantly aroused, it lures, tempts, promises fulfilment. It reappears in strange moments...suddenly, it is a coffin, coal black with little golden twigs. I feel pain. My left hand is stiff with pain. The shooting pain behind my sternum intensifies" (292). In this psycho-symptomatic disclosure, Bogna conveys the metamorphic character of her regression that does not end in the melancholic stupor that afflicts her, but moves on into creating new orders of signification in remembering, reinventing, and "becoming memory." It is above all her mother's ghost that pays her regular visits, usually accompanied by her grandmother, Sabina. Her father appears separately, but "it is difficult to figure out what is happening there" (199). In taking on the multiplicity of the past but recurring subjects, Bogna lets them "drag behind [her] everywhere," a simple task since "she inherited this precarious pleasure of contacting ghosts from her grandmother" (17). Lying in bed with her much younger lover, Bogna sees her grandmother's ghost passing above their naked bodies. An image of the other bed, that of the dying grandmother, "intermingles with the lovers' mattress" (16). This "precarious pleasure" links with Bogna's earlier fascination with incomprehensible German words; both relate to her persistence in diagnosing her identity as a narcissistic wound that refuses to heal except in connecting with other members of her family, her private mafia, as she believes: "My father's name was Wegner, but just like grandfather Franciszek, he considered himself the truest, the most Polish of all Poles, although he went to schools in Berlin. To German schools, you must admit, Bernard, my mother used to respond, when he reproached her for the church Sunday school. He explained over and over again that the Wegners lived in Berlin, because there was no Poland. But as soon as the country became independent, grandfather Franciszek immediately began to wind up his sewing business and moved his company Wegner & Sohn to Poland. He packed up...sold the factory buildings, except for the Singers which he took along as they were the best. He also took two German seamstresses for the beginning, so that they could teach Polish dressmakers how to sew properly" (161). This memory, in particular, constitutes a confusing interference with the increasingly phallocentric and persistently German structure of Bogna's universe. The constant return of paradoxes (Braidotti's internal idiosyncrasies) instill the insecurity of a child that meticulously reconstructs her primal instability. On her sixth birthday, when she receives *The Tales of the Brothers Grimm*, Bogna collapses upon detecting somewhat smaller letters under the big imprint of the Polish title: "translated from the German": "It seemed as if we were all German. Not only the wolf was German, but also grandmother, perhaps like Sabina Schönmyth. Red Riding Hood and Cinderella were also two small German girls. The stepmother and her daughters were German all right, because they had awful characters, like the German witch who locked Jack and Jill in a gas chamber. All are German. The Wegners, the Schönmyths, the father, the mother, and myself, we're all German. I was in despair, I solemnly...promised myself that I would never learn German" (162).

During the early stage of her linguistic discoveries there is no language to face up to her father's strong, although not always rational, talk. In particular, the father's hatred of Sabina Schönmyth, Aniela's mother, is rendered emotional, underscored by class and gender prejudice, and perpetuating in the end his own fear of cultural unbelonging. His hatred suggests a loss that cannot be recuperated, and that leaves an enigmatic trace of stigma on his subjectivity. Sabina becomes in fact his personal "witch hunt," a way of refocusing his own diaspora. In conversations with her father, Bogna gradually learns to answer back, using words of a refined quality, and inventing words to refresh their context. She refuses in the end to listen to her father reciting the dreadful "King Olch" poem, and "covers her ears, since all she can hear is "hajlihajlohajlihajlo," an echo of documentary propaganda films she watched with her school in the theatre: "I saw that my father had stopped now and rebukes me...because my behavior was not up to the Wegners' level. Only Schönmyth children, uncouth village yokels, were so badly behaved....You said yourself, father, that Szotka returned to die in Hitler's country" (157-58). The memory dynamic at work is to conjure her mother (and therefore her origin) into existence; to recreate herself in a maternal memory that she also wishes to relive in the present. However, as the memory is obsessively "replayed," it instigates the involuntary incursion of traumatic loss (of mother, identity) and, as Caruth has argued, it possesses the victim of loss (3-12). "Finally I start to cry, I feel surrounded...they are everywhere, I hear Hitler's language...it is also my parents...who are speaking German, when they want to keep things secret" (112). The penetrating (not-quite-her-own) memory of Jews, Hitler, and Stalin is partly responsible for Bogna's recurring state of serious depression, resulting from her past and present inability to defend herself against massive historical trauma and her own private anguish: "Although I didn't want it, I understood more and more. My inquisitiveness, untamable but well hidden, made me catch the meanings of foreign words immediately. Angry, I called myself 'Deutsche,' I showered slander on myself, Deutsche Schweine, but my German dictionary was expanding with new concepts" (233). Bound to this process of self-accusation, Bogna reminds us of Consolata's posture that under pressures of shifting borders begins to consolidate patterns of resistance. Their vanquishing of a depressive moment, indeed a closure to grief, derives precisely (and becomes possible) at the crossroads of significations. To elucidate the possibility of such closure, I return to Kristeva and Butler. The suspended signifying structure (which I trace in Bogna's anguish) informs Kristeva's psychoanalytical departure on the status of the semiotic as a transgression seeking to displace and subvert the paternal constitution of the subject. Butler, referring to Kristeva's position, denounces this type of subversion (disruption of cultural form) as a doubtful strategy depending upon the stability/reproduction of the "paternal metaphor" (Lacan, *Ecrits* 8). In my discussion, however, the Kristevan transgression of borders, and in particular the intermingling, relational subject positions involved in its practice, are ultimately effective as disturbing identity and order (Kristeva, *Powers* 4). To reject Kristeva's notion of transgression is perhaps too facile. Rather, I posit its significance in an attempt to distinguish two moments that are in constant danger of collapsing—one assigns stigmatized minority to the negative place or mystification within the dominant culture; one questions this minority (as resulting from fantasy) breaking against itself and beyond the system. The latter, I believe, is the case in Kofta's narrative, effectively exposing the limits of the paternal law without conceding that (as Butler understood it) the semiotic is invariably subordinate to the symbolic.

Besides Hitler and Stalin, the symbolic paradigms of good and evil that Bogna "brings from school," a new figure begins to emerge as a site of fascination: the evil woman of Jewish folktales told by her Jewish neighbor. Pandavid, who survived the war miraculously "hidden behind a wardrobe," spoke Polish beautifully, better than they did (*Złodziejka* 96). The tales, unwearyingly depicting a woman as a messenger of Satan, and Rabin Urele or Szolem as correcting paternal figures of the Law, provide her with a key to her mother's "mystery of permanent indecisiveness" (256). Bogna's mother—read with Kristeva—suffers from the inability to represent her affective states, an inability that either results in "psychic mutism," or expresses itself in a barren, sterile language that the subject experiences as "artificial, "empty," and "mechanical" (*New Maladies* 9). Aniela's family, distributed on both sides of the border and bearing the names Schönmyth, Szejnmit, or Szyjmit, is ridiculed continually and humiliated by her husband. Her marriage is a disappointment, making scarcely any difference between the taste of cultural alienation and that of home oppression. Coming from a poor family, a home full of "crying children," Aniela dreams about a peaceful place, like a cloister. But for reasons that remain unknown to the reader, she "gave up her childhood plans," decides to "marry rich" (117), and succumbs to a different type of silence where desires remain unspoken. Plunged into this family puzzle, Bogna remembers her parents stubbornly defending their families against each other, her father in words and her mother in tears. And although a provisory, strategic balance has been established between her parents, there is no balance between them and Sabina. Bogna's need to identify reasons for her mother's as well as her grandmother's degradation is persistent, penetrating: "I knew that my mother would allow nobody to humiliate her as my father did. My mother was no Cinderella. My father did just what she wished; he married her, because she was beautiful" (117). The evil woman, the mother, and the grandmother intersect in Bogna's post/memory with the subject of illicit power that, as Butler has argued, connotes both belonging to and wielding, and eclipses the conditions of its own negativity (*Psychic Life* 14).

The emergence of an alternative subject position, accompanying this process, coincides in Bogna's remembering with the increasing awareness of her aging body, her craving for sublimation, and her detachment from bodily folds, wrinkles, and flabbiness. Sleeping with a cover over her head, she submerges herself in the cooling water of the bathtub, stubbornly attempting to recreate the moisture and warmth of prelinguistic safety, conflating the symbolic with the semiotic: "I left a woman locked in a cube of restlessness on the outside. She fled away like a soul from a dead body. I breathe through my bronchi, lightly, with relief. I am dangling. I am not afraid of being old. It can be like a caress devoid of eroticism, a pure pleasure of unconscious babyhood, a return to the hot springs, an existence without a convulsive shudder" (33). Bogna also remembers the mirror as the "stage" of sudden anger, jealousy, and separation from her mother's body. Lacan's "mirror stage," providing the ideal grounding for the child's delusions of self-sufficiency and omnipotence, meets here with Bogna's desire to transform (transgress). Coinciding with a yearning for the irretrievable semiotic chora as well as a constant struggle against depression, the memory of the "stage" initiates precisely what Kristeva rendered impossible: feminine sublimation. Changing forms and appearances cunningly, depression is sometimes a woman-vampire who salivates at her sight full of devouring desires (47). Sometimes it is her godmother, a gloomy fairy-tale figure who touched Bogna at her birth with her poisoned magic wand (27). Emerging in Bogna's fantasies as a castrating/abject figure (vampire) and a sacred form of the feminine (godmother), depression "performs" on her (body) a different ritual (baptism), a sacred/secret sacrilege, like the Sabbath of religious discourse. When the priest uttered his Christian formula, "I baptize you in the name of the Father, and the Son, and the Holy Ghost," the godmother/depression whispered into her ear: "you will carry the second name after your godmother who loves you and will always be there for you; then she kissed my forehead with her burning lips" (27). As if following Irigaray's suggestion, the "proper" naming of a child appears thus in Kofta's text as a secondary replacement of "the most irreducible mark of birth: the *navel*. A proper name...is always late in terms of this most irreducible trace of identity: the scar left when the cord was cut. A proper name, even a forename, is slipped on to the body like a coating—an extra-corporeal identity card" (Irigaray, *Bodily Encounter* 39).

Echoing Bronfen's reading of the navel as "a willfully unexplored part of the human body" (3), Bogna's depression harks back to a different type of discourse; that of "the scar left when the cord was cut" (3). In exploring this scar, she revises her identity in relation to her family, in particular her grandmother, who, like the depression-ghost of the archaic mother, refuses to disappear, even when dead. In this intractable negotiation, the alternating processes of identification converge into an aporia of origin, an illusion of the subject's beginning. In other words, the normative symbolic order (power), with its production of monolithic subjectivities, is clearly eclipsed by another power: an alternative subject position deriving from the paradox of the subject's autonomy (Butler), indeed, the paradox of the navel. "For although the navel is open to the exploration of the touch, its most intimate point remains impenetrable to the eye, already inside the folds of the body—though it is separated as well from the actual body interior by a piece of knotted skin" (Bronfen 4). This paradox of autonomy, impenetrability of origin and formation, "is heightened when gender regulations work to paralyze gendered agency at various levels. Until those social conditions are radically changed, freedom will require unfreedom, and autonomy is implicated in subjection" (Butler, *Undoing Gender* 101). In her resistance against these paralyzing contradictions, Bogna craves for "a cold composure, even death," but knows that these are transitory conditions, that to imagine death to be composure is "a self-deception" (47). Death, as she learns from her grandmother, is a type of life; the border between death and life is at once permeable and intangible, like the borders between nations. "Sabina Schönmyth dragged the dead behind her always and everywhere. Day and night, untiring, the procession followed her....She believed in after-life, but not the same way the parish-priest wanted it in the small church next to the bus-loop" (212). Sabina's resistance against the "proper" community is a revolt that blurs the demands of secular and religious institutions. Like Consolata and Kummernis, she is always already slipping across borders: "Grandmother Sabina emerged as a terrible but fascinating person from bad fairy tales. Such creatures had snakes and toads in their service, ate worms and were evil to all who came into their clutches. But they had power and were strong...when I first saw grandma...smiling with her hair neatly bound at the back, with a parting in the middle....I wandered whether I could give her my hand without fear that she would tear it off" (209).

Suspended in Bogna's memory between the "weird" mother's mother, the other woman (foreign, forbidden to be visited), and the witch (as referred to by her father), Sabina willfully resists her stigmatization. Later, reinscribed as a "fragile apparition," Sabina does not identify with any permanent structure, but dwells on the edge of a communal integrity in her own complex relationship within. In this strategic un/belonging, Sabina demonstrates both her resistance and her "troubling porousness," alluding to her "ghostly" body, a site of transitions and foreign elements: "in a cover of permanent mourning, in transparent black stockings through which her bones were shining, she was an intermediary state between life and death. She walked gently on the pavement. Old shoes were slightly distorted....She was afraid of wind, because everyday she was lighter, her flesh and bones were...losing weight. At some point she will fly off, and her permanent widow's veil, the plural memory of all her husbands and other men, since my father was sure, she had lovers; well, the veil will be flowing in the sky...and then rise shattered by the wind of memories" (217). Embodying an impossible cultural adjustment, Sabina continues to live in a suspension of identity, in the feminine syndrome of being in a minority. Discouraged rather in defining a distinctive but endorsed position in the context of her displacement, Sabina creates her own heretical fraction, a conspiracy against the rationality and plausibility of the dominant discourse. Her hut "built right after the war from the bricks of the ruined house of the Schönmyths" (168) symbolizes a crossroads of antagonistic structures: a secret/sacred place of refuge for the mother, marking each return with maternal authority, and of pleasure/fascination for Bogna. Designed as to exclude the compulsory (postwar) assignment of people to available housing spaces, the hut was a one-room place; its walls upholstered with wine-red velvet: "the hut built of red German brick, soaked, according to father, in Polish blood. When I approached the door, my mother beside me, I quickly licked the brick. It was hard to tell the taste" (207-08). There, Bogna meets Szotka, Sabina's even more peculiar sister, who "could not say properly a single Polish word," murmuring "some German names of long forgotten relatives...if only my father knew who taught me German!" The trips were a sweet secret between mother and daughter (159). Belonging and cultural authenticity, detectably underscoring the purpose of these trips, remains unresolved (since neither of the sisters is "truly German"; 160). Bogna's identity, already hyphenated by difference, increasingly disintegrates under Sabina's refusal to belong. In its pretense to a spontaneous self-affirming act, or a posture of a monolithic identity, authenticity collapses into a paranoid reaction to the dominant group, the authority. As if "added" to the Polish landscape, Sabina represents Irigaray's "other woman," a woman "without common measure" who exceeds attempts to confine her within a theoretical system. To ignore her (the way Bogna's father ignores Sabina) implies a persistent awareness of her presence as the other, and a simultaneous will not to name the other except by an insult.

It is from Sabina, whose "natural state was motherhood alternating with widowhood" (257), that Bogna learns not to be afraid of what Cixous refers to as the relationship to the law, to the social ("Extreme Fidelity" 134). Bogna admits that she "loved grandmother Schönmyth because of her gift of true life and congenial dying" (330). In her continual desire to identify herself with the eccentric figure of her grandmother (249), Bogna associates her deviations from normative structure with the "porous" nature she inherited from Sabina, the "ghost" of the pre-Oedipal mother, a phantom of the "speaking subject" chasing Bogna's biography: "will you remember your grandma Sabina?—my grandmother asks, sitting up in her bed. She takes three gold wedding rings off her fingers...holding them on her palm, she gives me a sign to come closer. She takes my hand and gives me one of the gold circles. The other two go to my mother" (245). Accentuating continuity (process) within the structure (of the Law), Kofta's narrative connects the fates of all the female characters in a metamorphic relationship to one another. The importance of continuity stands in relation to the mother as a sacred/secret figure, "the goddess with her divine daughter that was always missing in the Holy Trinity" (296). Continuity, both in its flowing, prelinguistic and its "speaking" form, appears in a connection with the kinship structure (law), as deposited and memorized in feminine rituals: "I straighten up the lace of the pillow under my mother's heavy head, like an old experienced woman watching over a dead body. Many times I have seen women sitting at their neighbors' coffins....Every next woman was guarding the one who passed away before her. Continuity, not relationship...is stored in my memory" (255). This continuity, representing transitional sequences and circularity of experience, suggests that the memories converge at the point of unexplored, and perhaps inexplicable climax, a paradox of the navel. Consisting of phases, (old age, maturity, childhood, womb), the female characters/memories are "brought back" into one small room (the navel), in which they contemplate the paradox: "grandmother resigned, reconciled with death, belongs to the past; mother, reconciled with life, represents the present time; I am owned by the future" (343). This metamorphic trinity, translating for Bogna the otherwise indigestible identifications with hybridity, suggests a porous but also sovereign affirmative subject position. "Every child is born of a woman, like a little god, like a divine son or a divine daughter....The conception is always immaculate, because no reasonable...woman believes in the connection between what one does in bed and the birth of a child" (240). The Christian doctrine of the Immaculate Conception, significant in defining and assigning the social function to a "woman" in Polish culture, is recreated by Kofta as a "curable" split. In her reference to the Immaculate Conception, Kofta attempts to bridge the gap between women and the Virgin Mary by merging their experience of a sacredness that is to be located beyond religious doctrine. This formulation is particularly significant in the context of Bogna's discovery that Bernard Wegner was not her natural father, and that there is yet another German "messing up" her biography. Even worse, "that German was [probably] an SS-man" (320), "a tall blond man in a black leather coat" (330), detected in a photograph carefully hidden at the bottom of her father's wardrobe. While absorbing her newly discovered nondigestible context, she holds on to her memory as a source of knowledge, of flow and continuity, rather than of oppositions, "cohesive, yes, yes, no, no, this is bad, this is good. Monolithic like paranoia" (341). Her biography/memory becomes such a transgression, deliberately violating borders, and hence appropriating cultural dispossession as a strategic un/belonging.

Both Tokarczuk's and Kofta's narratives speak about processes of cultural identification as transgressive and paradoxical sites of un/belonging. Although beliefs in coherent identities (which these texts repeatedly question) are imaginary, these processes of identification are not (as such) imaginary, but rooted in the vulnerability of the characters and narrators entrapped in their stigmatized hybridities. It would be more precise to say that their contested identities transgress the culturally privileged discourse of tradition, passing into sites of new identifications either with the institution (law, religion) itself, or with other subjects, by the intermediary of their common desire to abolish the institution. In unplotting their biographies, the protagonists resort to a conceptual fluidity of home and community that is "composed of distances, relationships, analogies, and non-exclusive oppositions" (Kristeva, "Desire" 78). Both narratives can be seen as authographies with an inherently subversive structure that builds new relations and therefore new resistances to culture. As a distinct and dislocating experience, writing thus becomes a provisional, performative, and strategically feminist structure in process. This relational, transgressive cosmogony disrupts the "imaginary," repressed, and persecuted zones of culture, setting up a new frontier, where signifying structure, contrary to Kristeva's belief, does not collapse despite its *transgression*. I conclude with my earlier argument that the witch as an aesthetic (literary, narrative) figure is not a temporary escape route to the outside of culture but a concrete (collectively imagined) representation of woman as an ongoing, subversively repetitive alternative to the dominant order. Adopting ambiguous, provisional positions in between (dramatic) performance and religious ritual, the female figures discussed here express their cultural presence (rather than absence) in fantastic structures of culture, the idea of fantasy being both licensed and illicit. What this form of fantasy offers, in contradistinction to *herstorical* celebrations of "orgasmic freedom" and identifications with the semiotic loss, is the enticing promise of how things might look if we altered the confining conditions of the dominant culture. Defined thus as a strategically provisional form of cultural subversion, the fantasy emerges above all as a site of negotiation between competing spaces in culture. In shifting our attention to differences *within* the very same structure of cultural identifications, the fantasy points towards continuous change, and in embodying this change, towards processes of embodied cultural mediation.

Towards Feminist Passions and Fantasies of Gender

What I attempted to illustrate in this chapter was a hypothesis that the witch, as a fantasy figure of identity transgressions, points to the primary importance of "sexual difference" (Irigaray) as the specific symbolic domain of the feminine. This feminine, contesting its own metaphorical representation (Braidotti), suggests a new theoretical framework for explicating the transgressive locations within the feminist philosophical and narrative discussions of the social (identifications with a particular culture, kinship, religion, system, nation, or home). Equally important to my discussion was to ask how we might use these emerging complexities of location (and of the feminine, in particular), to mobilize multipronged, constructive responses across trans-Atlantic and trans-European feminist divides. How might "femininity" as a fantasy of gender be strategized and embodied for a broader feminist purpose? Either as a transgression of phallocentric agency (Braidotti), or as a constituted subject that "eclipses power with power" (Butler), it seems crucial to keep this feminist purpose in check, so as to create broader coalitions within the social fabric of existence. The call for a renewed perspective from which to approach femininity intersects with the shifts in the political debate from the issues of difference between cultures and ideologies towards differences within the very structure of a particular identification (Braidotti). In tracing these intersections, I discussed transgression in its ethical conjecture, as a manifestation of incompatibility with the hegemonic order of belonging and as the representable difference (Balibar) of any constructed subjectivity that continues to be inscribed with stigma. I suggested, following Braidotti, that we look at transgression both across the heterogeneity of Western cultures and across new complexities of difference within the homogenous clusters of culture.

The discussed narratives and theories equally account for the shifts in theoretical thinking about agency transgression: shifts that defy dualistic, oppositional, and melancholic reasoning. Defined as an incongruity with the normative gender, or alternatively, as a fantasy of gender, the historical and, by necessity, performative concept of femininity stands in an unnecessary tension with "sexual difference." What Butler, in *Gender Trouble*, has questioned *in terms of* and *as* "gender," she also questions in *Undoing Gender*, transferring the very same defining logic from "gender" onto "sexual difference." Like gender, "sexual difference" for Butler "is not a given, not a premise, not a basis on which to build a feminism: it is not that which we have already encountered and come to know; rather, as a question that prompts a feminist inquiry, it is something that cannot quite be stated, that troubles the grammar of the statement, and that remains, more or less permanently, to interrogate" (*Undoing Gender* 178). Detecting, in particular, Butler's framework of defining through conceptual negation, I have turned to Irigaray's project of converting "sexual difference" into an empowering affirmation of alternative subject positions. In a remarkable extension of this ongoing project, Braidotti's concept of "sexual difference" is of particular importance, as it denotes movement and "becoming" as well as permanent interrogation without suspending the subject (as Butler often does) in a vacuum of aesthetic significations. For Irigaray in as much as Braidotti, "sexual difference" is a figuration of the future, one that would assume the multitude of the subject not only as value but as the very condition of its existence. Braidotti's reading of "sexual difference" cuts in fact much deeper to radically shift our attention to the process of the subject formation, to the continuous trans/positions that the subject inhabits while producing new sites of transformation, new ways of "becoming." Crucial to this process of "becoming" is the inexhaustible context of difference, a complex web of identifications (subjectivities) that makes it difficult to posit transgressive practice once and for all.

In discussing transgressions I propose to disconnect theoretically feminine subjectivity from repression, negative ambiguity, and ultimately depression as the only alternatives to sublimation. Kristeva's *transgressions* (the abject, the semiotic) and Butler's performativity of gender certainly give rise to discursive innovations that could subsequently contribute to modifications of signifying practices, but the absence of credible constructive alternatives to the symbolic order are felt on both sides. Melancholic returns to the "loving party," crucial to Kristeva's original loss and Butler's notion of desire, deriving precisely from the unrealized potential for verbal or otherwise culturally valid expression, interconnect psychoanalysis with compelling acts of gender performance and performativity with melancholia. Butler's concept, like Kristeva's appraisal of transgression, seems to valorize change and transformation for its own philosophical sake, diminishing thereby feminist capacity for its concrete social and political manifestations. These significant limitations of theories that remain imprisoned in the ivory tower suit the phallogocentric purpose to interpret "transformation" as reducing and even overcoming of "sexual difference," and thereby to obliterate specific historical feminine configurations of gender (Braidotti). What remains at the structure of the social in the face of such obliteration is a normative monolithic subjectivity that uses the diminishing value of "sexual difference" as a pretext to reinstall phallocentric forms of authority and reasoning. Theorizing the relation of embodied subjects with their enduring dispositions in the social dimension, Braidotti's political proposal of "ethical passions" offers a new perspective on the feminine configuration of gender. What derives from a politics defined in terms of ethical passions (a project inspired by Nietzsche, and read with Irigaray and Deleuze) is a political economy of desire, allowing both for a theoretical space between the primary loss and subsequent repression of the maternal body, and for concrete culturally specific manifestations of the plentitude of pleasure as encoded in the feminine (*Metamorphoses* 53). This combination of feminism, psychoanalysis, and politics enables us to add "a dose of suspicion" concerning the motivation and intentionality of the subject, without immediately condemning the subject to a nihilistic void, or relativism: "On the contrary, by injecting affectivity, self-reflexivity and joy into the political exercise, it may return political beliefs to their full inspiration" (Braidotti, *Thinking Differently* 178). Instigated by this reasoning, the narratives selected for this (inter)relational context were discussed in view of "transcendence" as evoking forms of heresy and sacred disorder, alluding to or recognized as specifically "feminine" traces of *jouissance*, a rejection of binaries on theoretical and political grounds. Formulated by Cixous and Irigaray as transcendental forms crossing the illicit border towards bodily context, eroticism, and sensuality, feminine traces have been further located by Clément beyond (Western) religious and symbolic structures. In these figurations, the feminine is no longer perceived as a symmetrical opposition to sameness (operative in the *herstorical* narratives), but as a system of "different legality" (see Clément and Kristeva), a permutation of her(m)etic *jouissance* and a strategically provisional discourse of pleasure (Irigaray, Braidotti). The witch figure, emerging out of these theoretical discussions, constitutes an affirmative and transgressing subject position, not a feminist given but a project under construction, a metamorphic continuum that violates symbolic restrictions and makes the limits of these restrictions compellingly political.

Throughout the narratives, the witch comes to present forms of heresy, stigma, and cultural provisionality that undermine the very structure of subjectivity, social relations, and collective fantasies that are maintained by these forms. Radically neither a word nor a concept, but rather a condition of possibility and move, the "witch" as a subject is continuously departing from Western logocentric models, and continuously "becoming" in its cultural intelligibility. If Irigaray has diagnosed the strategy of a self-conscious mimesis as the subject of a feminine future, Braidotti suggests that this future is already with us, and, in this vein, the narratives I discussed, as the domain of the contagious imprint of this subject, turn up as witnesses to and explorations of it. But what this subject also narrates is an experience of its incommensurability. As an overlapping cultural trait (of language, system, or geography) or a moment of crossing or transgressing culture, the experience is charged with tension, instilling constant changes in subject value. This topography of the witch, radical in its persistent desire to transcend the hostilities of the dominant structure, interferes with that very structure and transforms its foundations. A key difficulty with respect to this interference, and, in due course, with respect to the "transformation" of the social, rests in the Western logocentric understanding of the "undecidable structure" (Derridean *pharmacon*, Kristevan semiotic) that simultaneously reinforces and loosens the various forms of subordination to the symbolic. Revising, in this sense, the reminiscence (trace) of the historical witch as a culturally "undecidable structure," the narratives irrefutably trouble the Western logic of the other and its passive philosophical constructions fixed in the inaccessible. Braidotti's proposal of "becoming," as a system of "logical" or linear inconsistency, reads dissolution of the reflexive (passive) subjectivity precisely as a possibility to subvert phallocentric entrapments in which the "feminine" and, ultimately, "sexual difference" have dwelled for centuries. If we accept this paradoxical positioning of the subject, with its cultural "undecidability" on the one hand, and its metamorphic potential on the other, the restrictions imposed on deviance and its assumed lack of cultural heritage provide us with the potential for a conceptual shift.

I understand this shift as an emergence of subculture, of "in-between spaces" that Rajchman has addressed in reference to history. The "critical experimentation within society shows that history is not linear or progressive, any more than it is circular or cyclical. It shows that if history is a 'web,' it is one with many gaps and holes which allow it to be constantly rewoven in other ways, and that it thus always carries with it the sort of 'in-between' time and spaces" (ix). It is precisely this location of "'in-between' time and spaces" that comes forward in the narratives as a subversive form of un/belonging, a complex mediation of gender, ethnicity, and social positioning, and a strategic wavering between incongruent cultures and philosophies. Whereas in the radical feminist construction of the witch discussed in previous chapters there are still traces of opposition, with nature, femininity, or the semiotic on one side, and culture and the social structure on the other, the witch figures discussed here blur the nature/culture boundary, rendering the very production of its meaning an artificial designation. Simultaneously, and again, in a significant contrast to the narratives of the herstorical and archaic figurations, these narratives explicitly evoke awareness that (cultural) transformations are never complete. Far from being logocentrically accomplished, the protagonists mark new cultural territories, new ways of pronouncing a collective reappraisal of "sexual difference." In a decisive cut from the sexual politics of compulsory heterosexuality (or the heterosexual matrix of power), "sexual difference," as emerging from this theoretical and narrative discourse, points toward the singularity of each subject position and the complexities of its transgressing experience as a fantasy of the feminine. The feminist fantasy of the feminine is both about transgressing and surviving. To follow Butler's insight, "The struggle to survive is not really separable from the cultural life of fantasy, and the foreclosure of fantasy—through censorship, degradation, or other means—is one strategy for providing for the social death of persons" (*Undoing Gender* 29). Gender, as approached by Butler and Braidotti (and despite their different positions), is always already at the intersection with power (*Metamorphoses* 17), and therefore of a "transgressive" complexity. Equally for both, categories are coalitions "alternately affirmed and relinquished according to the purposes at hand" (*Gender Trouble* 16). In this sense, the transgressive potential of Braidotti's "feminine" meets indeed at the crossroads with Butler's definition of the body as never free of an imaginary construction. Butler's response to Braidotti's position opens precisely as a coalition: "There is transatlantic exchange at work between us: we both cross over. Can we return to the bipolar distinction between European and American with ease?" (*Undoing Gender* 203). As a (motivated) fantasy, governed both by politics of location and its "embodied accounts," the "feminine" does not exclude or reject the social (the culturally sanctioned) body. It builds upon this body, defines its limits, makes these limits apparent, and, as a result, subverts their traditional symbolism encoded and fixed with particular values. In revisiting its relation to "gender," this "feminine" constitutes "a subversion from within the terms of the law, through the possibilities that emerge when the law turns against itself and spawns unexpected permutations of itself" (*Gender Trouble* 93). Fantasy is part of these permutations, as a space of rezoning and articulation of possibilities, it moves us beyond the sanctioned and acknowledged territories of culture. The "beyond" is neither a new (semiotic) horizon on the outside of culture nor a leaving behind of the (historical) past, but a sense of disorientation, minoritization, and a disturbance of linear reasoning, of a fixed direction. There is an immense potential in transgression, suggesting ways in which stigmas and recognition are perennially translated one into the other, in which social order produces modes of reflectivity as it simultaneously limits forms of sociality. The witch as a boundless fantasy of gender is thus a fantasy of un/belonging opening ways out of limiting significations. Although cross-gender, cross-cultural, cross-body identification makes subjects politically vulnerable, it simultaneously allows for a rezoning of tabooed borders and stigmatized territories. In her borderlessness, the witch conveys a permanent deferral of meaning and of linear development of thought; she communicates a paradox of the navel, autonomy engraved with subjugation that is at once refused by and initiated within phallocentric culture. My formulation of fantasy as un/belonging, situated theoretically in the transgressive condition of the feminine subject, converges with a number of theoretical concepts, such as resistance, parody, or subversion, and finally, the emergence of a subculture as a political form of expression. As an experience of self-affirmation that first appears at odds with the social, un/belonging (or nomadism, to use Braidotti's term) permutes and transforms the social structure. In my discussion, I used un/belonging as a key metaphor for a cultural interconnectedness, a common thread in the variety of witch-stories, which are differently but all related to a move beyond the psychoanalytic idea of the body. This body, no longer exclusively a map of semiotic inscriptions or culturally enforced codifications, is a surface for the nomadic fantasy of gender: of body (and, by necessity, of "embeddedness" as "bundle of contradictions" (Braidotti, *Metamorphoses* 21) in the process of cultural mediation. The critical promise of such bodily fantasy, "when and where it exists, is to challenge the contingent limits of what will and will not be called fantasy. Fantasy is what allows us to imagine ourselves and others otherwise. It establishes the possible in excess of the real" (*Undoing Gender* 29).

The lines drawn by fantasy, as every fantasy has a concrete outline and limits to itself, are best understood as invitations to cross over, and that crossing over towards a multi-layered theoretical position constitutes what otherwise disintegrates and divides: a fragile but politically constructive space of un/belonging. This un/belonging, posited as a "nomadic position," allows us to see Irigaray's "disruptive excess," Butler's suspension of the category "gender," Kristeva's concept of "porousness," and Braidotti's embodied subject of becoming as converging in a common intention to elaborate a theory of cultural legality. After all, as Butler admits, against her earlier theoretical standing, it was Kristeva who said that Lacan made no room for the semiotic and insisted on offering that domain not only as a supplement to the symbolic, but as a way of undoing it. And it was Cixous who saw feminine writing as a way of making the sign travel in ways that Lévi-Strauss could not imagine at the end of *The Elementary Structure of Kinship*. And it was Irigaray who imagined the goods getting together, and even implicitly theorized a certain kind of homoerotic love between women. (Butler, *Undoing Gender* 208). In bringing this common intention together, the method of thinking I employed was that of a convergence of feminist thought, which, disabling fixed points of reference, shifts our attention towards interconnectedness, from the concept of difference towards a process of differentiation. Instead of polemical disagreements, visibly resulting in the fragmentation of feminist agendas, what is needed is an affirmative engagement in a feminist activism across Western and Westernized cultures. What is needed is a productive connection that will mobilize a common aspiration towards thinking through difference, and consolidate the very capacity to transform conditions. Considering the dangers and the potentials for global alliance as well as transformation, Braidotti's insistence on transforming possibilities might be difficult at times, but it certainly overcomes the feminist exploration of grief and negativity (and the passive mode of thinking that derives from it). As a mobile feminist consciousness, it moves beyond philosophical abstraction to find the way through and beyond it, without assuming the position of dominance or mastery. Mobility, multiplicity, and political flow are not the end of agency, but the very condition of its feminist premise.

In this concluding frame, I return to my central argument that the witch figure, deployed in the 1970s to convey the diasporic status of a female sexuality, has undergone significant theoretical transformations over the last three decades. These transformations reflect on central traits in the reformulation of second-wave continental and Anglo-American feminist thought into third-wave feminist postulates of transnational difference and the heterogeneity of women's agendas. The latter, dislocating the centrality of the dominant subject, inevitably comes to the conclusion that the subject is never strictly defined by gender. What is and what will be incessantly produced are waves of transnational immigration, wars, cultural and political displacement, rapidly developing technologies (of communication as well as of the body), and therefore waves of continually new inequalities and new forms of difference. The challenges for feminism are in this sense inexhaustible, and have as much to do with mainstream North American and European capitalist and post/communist histories as with the specificities of feminist cultures within these histories, to which the concept of "difference" is undeniably fundamental.

Conclusion

Based on tenets of the framework of comparative cultural studies, a framework that pays particular attention to all minorities, the marginal, and the Other and embraces a nonessentialist world view, the narratives analyzed in the first chapter of my book illustrate the second-wave feminist sense of urgency and the need to create a common identification with the historical invisibility of women as suggested in Luce Irigaray's notion of bringing together mothers and daughters. The figure of the "witch" represents here a dimension of radical (feminist) identity that inserts the history of her oppression into contemporary ideological and political spaces. Conveying the tension between past and present, the witch becomes a central signifier of women's cultural un/belonging, a metaphor for *herstory*, that is, a form of feminist mythology constituted in relation to and as an alternative to the established male-centered master narrative. Consequently, I read the narratives selected for my analysis as literary unveilings of the "witch" in her negotiations to reenter history as a speaking, autonomous, and self-reflective subject. Shifting the critique from the witch as a source of *herstorical* fantasies to the properties of the witch as archaic mother, in my second chapter I focus on primary maternal loss, depicting cultural constructs of mothers and daughters expelled outside the symbolic structure.

These narratives converge in the recognition of anoedipal debt to the mother trapped within constructions of phallocentric discourse. As phallic rather than *omphalic* depictions of mothers (*omphalos*, the navel, as the scar left by separation), I view these narratives as both participating in and failing Judith Butler's strategies of subversive repetition. These narrative representations embody the instability of culture and its symbolic structure, disturbing gendered forms of identity, and collapsing into Julia Kristeva's notion of the abject that designates bodily discharges, excrements rendered alien, and the expulsion from culture. The narratives analyzed in my final chapter engage with the feminine as contesting its own metaphorical representation as explicated theoretically in the work of Rosi Braidotti. In my own reading and analysis I suggest a new theoretical framework for explicating the transgressive locations within the feminist discussions of the social. Thus, in discussing these *transgressions* I propose to disconnect theoretically feminine subjectivity from repression, negative ambiguity, and ultimately depression as the only alternatives

Conclusion 173

to sublimation. Instead, I focus on a reading that accounts equally for the shifts in theoretical thinking about agency transgression. And, finally, I formulate these shifts as defying dualistic, oppositional, and melancholic reasoning in order to mobilize multipronged and constructive responses across trans-Atlantic and trans-European feminist divides.

Works Cited

Abel, Elisabeth, Barbara Christian, and Helen Moglen, eds. *Female Subjects in Black and White: Race, Psychoanalysis, Feminism*. Berkeley: U of California P, 1997.

Anderson, Pamela Sue. *A Feminist Philosophy of Religion: The Rationality and Myths of Religious Belief*. Oxford: Blackwell, 1998.

Anzaldúa, Gloria. *Borderlands: The New Mestiza: La Frontiera*. San Francisco: Aunt Lute Books, 1997.

Armstrong, Nancy. "Some Call It Fiction: On the Politics of Domesticity." 1990. *Feminisms: An Anthology of Literary Theory and Criticism*. Ed. R. Warhol and D. Price Herndl. New Brunswick: Rutgers UP, 1997. 913-30.

Atwood, Margaret. *Alias Grace*. Toronto: M&S, 1996.

Bal, Mieke. *Reading Rembrandt:Beyond the Word-Image Opposition*. Cambridge: Cambridge UP, 1991.

Balibar, Etienne. "Culture and Identity (Working Notes)." Trans. J. Swenson. *The Identity in Question*. Ed. J. Rajchman. London: Routledge, 1995. 173-96.

Baym, Nina. "The Madwoman and Her Languages: Why I Don't Do Feminist Literary Theory." 1984. *Feminisms: An Anthology of Literary Theory and Criticism*. Ed. R. Warhol and D. Price Herndl. New Brunswick: Rutgers UP, 1997. 279-92.

Beauvoir, Simone de. *The Second Sex*. 1949. Trans. Howard Madison Parshley. New York: Knopf, 1993.

Bhabha, Homi K. "Freedom's Basis in the Indeterminate." *The Identity in Question*. Ed. J. Rajchman. London: Routledge, 1995. 47-61.

Bhabha, Homi K. *The Location of Culture*. London: Routledge, 1994.

Boer, Esther de. *Mary Magdale: Beyond the Myth*. Harrisburg: Trinity P International, 1996.

Bovenschen, Silvia. "The Contemporary Witch, the Historical Witch, and the Witch Myth." 1978. Trans. Jeannine Blackwell, Johanna Moore, and Beth Weckmüller. *German Feminist Writings*. Ed. P.A. Herminghouse and M. Mueller. London: Continuum, 2001. 229-32.

Braidotti, Rosi. *Metamorphoses: Towards a Materialist Theory of Becoming*. Cambridge: Polity P, 2002.

Braidotti, Rosi. *Nomadic Subjects*. New York: Columbia UP, 1994.

Brilliant, Richard. "Kirke's Men: Swine and Sweethearts." *The Distaff Side: Representing the Female in Homer's Odyssey*. Ed. Beth Cohen. New York: Oxford UP, 1995. 165-73.

Brison, Susan J. *Aftermath: Violence and the Remaking of a Self*. Princeton: Princeton UP, 2002.

Bronfen, Elisabeth. *The Knotted Subject: Hysteria and its Discontents*. Princeton: Princeton UP, 1998.

Busheikin, Laura. "Is Sisterhood Really Global?" *Ana's Land: Sisterhood in Eastern Europe*. Ed. Tanya Renne. Boulder: Westview, 1997. 12-21.

Butler, Judith. "Discussion of Stanley Aronowitz's 'Reflections on Identity.'" *The Identity in Question*. Ed. J. Rajchman. London: Routledge, 1995. 129-44.

Butler, Judith. *Gender Trouble: Feminism and the Subversion of Identity*. London: Routledge, 1990.

Butler, Judith. *The Psychic Life of Power: Theories of Subjection*. Stanford: Stanford UP, 1997.

Butler, Judith. "Subjection, Resistance, Resignification: Between Freud and Foucault." *The Identity in Question*. Ed. J. Rajchman. London: Routledge, 1995. 229-49.

Butler, Judith. *Undoing Gender*. New York: Routledge, 2004.

Camp, Claudia. *Wisdom and the Feminine in the Book of Proverbs*. Sheffield: Almond, 1985.

Campbell, Kirsten. *Jacques Lacan and Feminist Epistemology*. London: Routledge, 2004.

Carter, Angela. "Black Venus." 1980. *Burning Your Boats: Collected Short Stories*. London: Vintage, 1996. 231-44.

Carter, Angela. *Expletives Deleted: Selected Writings*. London: Chatto & Windus, 1992.

Carter, Angela. "Impressions: The Wrightsman Magdalene." 1992. *Burning Your Boats: Collected Short Stories*. By Angela Carter. London: Vintage, 1996. 409-16.

Carter, Angela. "The Lady of the House of Love." 1975. *Burning Your Boats: Collected Short Stories*. London: Vintage, 1996. 195-209.

Carter, Angela. *The Sadeian Woman: An Exercise in Cultural History*. 1979. London: Virago, 2000.

Carter, Angela. "The Scarlet House." 1977. *Burning Your Boats: Collected Short Stories*. Vintage, 1996. 417-28.

Caruth, Cathy. "Introduction: Trauma and Experience." *Trauma: Explorations in Memory*. Ed. Caruth. Baltimore: Johns Hopkins UP, 1995. 3-12.

Chanter, Tina. "Introduction." *Feminist Interpretations of Emmanuel Levinas*. Ed. Tina Chanter. University Park: The Pennsylvania State UP, 2001. 1-27.

Christ, Carol P. *Rebirth of the Goddess: Finding Meaning in Feminist Spirituality*. New York: Addison-Wesley, 1997.

Cixous, Hélène. "The Book of Promethea." 1983. Trans. Ann Liddle and Susan Sellers. *The Hélène Cixous Reader*. Ed. Susan Sellers. New York: Routledge, 1994. 121-28.

Cixous, Hélène. "Extreme Fidelity." 1984. Trans. Ann Liddle and Susan Sellers. *The Hélène Cixous Reader*. Ed. Susan Sellers. New York: Routledge, 1994. 131-37.

Cixous, Hélène. "The Laugh of the Medusa." 1975. Trans. Keith and Paula Cohen. *Feminisms: An Anthology of Literary Theory and Criticism*. Ed. R. Warhol and D. Price Herndl. New Brunswick: Rutgers UP, 1997. 347-62.

Cixous, Hélène, and Catherine Clément. *The Newly Born Woman*. 1975. Trans. Betsy Wing. Minneapolis: U of Minnesota P, 1986.

Clément, Catherine, and Julia Kristeva. *The Feminine and the Sacred*. 1998. Trans. Jane Marie Todd. New York: Columbia UP, 2001.

Clifford, James. *Routes: Travel and Translation in the Late Twentieth Century*. Cambridge: Harvard UP, 1997.

Colette. "The Rainy Moon." 1940. *Wayward Girls & Wicked Women: An Anthology of Stories*. Ed. Angela Carter. London: Virago, 1986. 87-135.

Creed, Barbara. *The Monstrous-Feminine: Film, Feminism, Psychoanalysis*. London: Routledge, 1993.

Daly, Mary. *Gyn/Ecology*. Boston: Beacon, 1978.

Deleuze, Gilles. "Mysticism and Masochism." 1967. Trans. Michael Taormina. *Desert Islands and Other Texts, 1953-1974*. Ed. David Lapoujade. New York: Semiotext(e), 2004. 131-34.

Deleuze, Gilles, and Felix Guattari. *A Thousand Plateaus: Capitalism and Schizophrenia*. 1980. Trans. Brian Massumi. Minneapolis: U of Minnesota P, 1987.

Derrida, Jacques. "Différence." 1972. *A Derrida Reader: Between the Blinds*. Ed. Peggy Kamuf. New York: Columbia UP, 1991. 61-79.

Derrida, Jacques. "Dissemination" 1972. *A Derrida Reader: Between the Blinds*. Ed. Peggy Kamuf. New York: Columbia UP, 1991. 112-39.

Derrida, Jacques. *Of Grammatology*. 1976. Trans. Gayatri Chakravorty Spivak. Baltimore: Johns Hopkins UP, 1977.

Dietze, Gabriele. "Overcoming Speechlessness." 1980. Trans. Jörg Esleben. *German Feminist Writings*. Ed. P.A. Herminghouse and M. Mueller. London: Continuum, 2001. 290-92.

Douglas, Mary Tew. *Purity and Danger: An Analysis of Concepts of Pollution and Taboo*. 1966. London: Routledge, 1969.

Dworkin, Andrea. *Woman-Hating*. New York: Dutton, 1974.

Einhorn, Barbara. *Cinderella Goes to Market*. New York: Verso, 1993.

Felman, Shoshana. "Women and Madness: The Critical Phallacy." 1975. *Feminisms: An Anthology of Literary Theory and Criticism*. Ed. R. Warhol and D. Price Herndl. New Brunswick: Rutgers UP, 1997. 7-20.

Finckenstein, Iris von. "w.i.t.c.h." *Walpurgistänze. Vehexte Geschichten*. Ed. Julia Peters. München: Knaur, 2000. 27-58.

Foucault, Michel. *Discipline and Punish: The Birth of the Prison*. 1975. Trans. Alan Sheridan. New York: Vintage, 1995.

Foucault, Michel. *The History of Sexuality*. 1976. Trans. Robert Hurley. New York: Vintage, 1990. 3 vols.

Foucault, Michel. "Rituals of Exclusion." *Foucault Live: Interviews, 1961-1984*. Ed. S. Lotringer. New York: Semiotext(e), 1996. 68-73.

Foucault, Michel. "Space, Power and Knowledge." *The Cultural Studies Reader*. Ed. Simon During. London: Routledge, 1993. 161-69.

Fraser, Nancy. *Justice Interruptus: Critical Reflections on the "Postsocialist" Condition*. New York: Routledge, 1997.

Fraser, Nancy, and Sandra Bartky. *Revaluing French Feminism*. Bloomington: Indiana UP, 1991.

Freud, Sigmund. "Inhibitions, Symptoms, and Anxiety." 1926. *The Standard Edition of the Complete Psychological Works of Sigmund Freud*. Vol. 20. Trans. James Strachey. London: Hogarth, 1959.

Freud, Sigmund. *Introductory Lectures on Psycho-Analysis*. 1932. Trans. James Strachey. New York: Norton, 1989.

Frymer-Kensky, Tikva. *In the Wake of the Goddesses: Women, Culture and the Biblical Transformation of Pagan Myth*. New York: Fawcett Columbine, 1993.

Gallop, Jane. *The Daughter's Seduction: Feminism and Psychoanalysis*. Ithaca: Cornell UP, 1982.

Gallop, Jane. *Feminist Accused of Sexual Harassment*. Durham: Duke UP, 1997.

Gallop, Jane. *Reading Lacan*. Ithaca: Cornell UP, 1985.

Gearhart, Sally Miller. *Wanderground: Stories of the Hill Women*. 1978. Boston: Alyson Publications, 1984.

Gibson, Andrew. *Postmodernity, Ethics and the Novel: From Leavis to Levinas*. London: Routledge, 1999.

Griffin, Gabriele, and Rosi Braidotti. "Introduction: Configuring European Women's Studies." *Thinking Differently: A Reader in European Women's Studies*. Ed. Gabriele Griffin and Rosi Braidotti. London: Zed Books, 2002. 1-28.

Guiley, Rosemary Ellen, ed. *The Encyclopedia of Witches and Witchcraft*. New York: Facts on File, 1989.

Hall, Stuart. "Cultural Identity and Cinematic Representation." *Black British Cultural Studies: A Reader*. Ed. Houston A. Baker, Jr., Manthia Diawara, and Ruth H. Lindeborg. London: Routledge, 1996. 210-22.

Hall, Stuart. "Old and New Identities, Old and New Ethnicities." *Culture, Globalization and the World-System*. Ed. Anthony D. King. Basingstoke: Macmillan, 1991. 41-68.

Harris, Bertha. *Lover*. Plainfield: Daughters, 1976.

Haskins, Susan. *Mary Magdalen: Myth and Metaphor*. London: Harper & Collins, 1993.

Haug, Frigga. "The End of Socialism in Europe: A New Challenge for Socialist Feminism?" 1992. Trans. R. Livingstone. *German Feminist Writings*. Ed. P.A. Herminghouse and M. Mueller. London: Continuum, 2001. 167-74.

Humm, Maggie. *A Reader's Guide to Contemporary Feminist Literary Criticism*. London: Harvester Wheatsheaf, 1994.

Institoris, Heinrich, Montague Summers, and Jakob Sprenger. *Malleus Maleficarum*. 1486. Trans. Montague Summers. Mineola: Courier Dover Publications, 1971.

Irigaray, Luce. "The Bodily Encounter with the Mother." 1982. *The Irigaray Reader*. Trans. and ed. Margaret Whitford. Cambridge: Blackwell, 1991. 34-46.

Irigaray, Luce. *Entre Deux*. Paris: Grasset, 1997.

Irigaray, Luce. *This Sex Which is Not One*. 1977. Trans. Catherine Porter and Carolyn Burke. Ithaca: Cornell UP, 1985.

Irigaray, Luce. "The Limits of Transference." 1982. *The Irigaray Reader*. Trans. and ed. Margaret Whitford. Cambridge: Blackwell, 1991. 105-17.
Irigaray, Luce. "The Poverty of Psychoanalysis." 1977. *The Irigaray Reader*. Trans. and ed. Margaret Whitford. Cambridge: Blackwell, 1991. 79-104.
Irigaray, Luce. "The Power of Discourse and the Subordination of the Feminine." 1975. *The Irigaray Reader*. Trans. and ed. Margaret Whitford. Cambridge: Blackwell, 1991. 118-32.
Irigaray, Luce. "Questions to Emmanuel Levinas." 1990. *The Irigaray Reader*. Trans. and ed. Margaret Whitford. Cambridge: Blackwell, 1991. 178-89.
Irigaray, Luce. *Sexes and Genealogies*. 1987. Trans. Gillian C. Gill. Ithaca: Cornell UP, 1987.
Irigaray, Luce. *Speculum of the Other Woman* 1974. Trans. Gillan C. Gill. Ithaca: Cornell UP, 1985.
Irigaray, Luce. "Volume Without Contours." 1974. *The Irigaray Reader*. Trans. and ed. Margaret Whitford. Cambridge: Basic Blackwell, 1991. 53-67.
Irigaray, Luce. "Women-Mothers, the Silent Substratum of the Social Order." 1981. *The Irigaray Reader*. Trans. and ed. Margaret Whitford. Cambridge: Blackwell, 1991. 47-52.
Irigaray, Luce. "Women's Exile." Trans. Couze Venn. *Ideology and Consciousness* 1 (1977): 62-76.
Jordan, Elaine. "The Dangers of Angela Carter." *New Feminist Discourses: Critical Essays on Theories and Texts*. Ed. Isobel Armstrong. London: Routledge, 1992. 119-31.
Kaplan, Caren, and Inderpal Grewal. "Transnational Practice and Interdisciplinary Feminist Scholarship: Refiguring Women's and Gender Studies." *Women's Studies on Its Own: A Next Wave Reader in Institutional Change*. Ed. Robyn Wiegman. Durham: Duke UP, 2002. 66-81.
King, Ynestra. "Toward an Ecological Feminism and Feminist Ecology." *Machina ex Dea: Feminist Perspectives on Technology*. Ed. Joan Rothschild. New York: Pergamon, 1983. 118-27.
Kofta, Krystyna. *Złodziejka pamięci* (Thief of Memories). Warsaw: W.A.B., 1998.
Kolodny, Annette. "Dancing Through the Minefield: Some Observations on the Theory, Practice, and Politics of a Feminist Literary Criticism." 1980. *Feminisms: An Anthology of Literary Theory and Criticism*. Ed. R. Warhol and D. Price Herndl. New Brunswick: Rutgers UP, 1997. 171-90.
Koltuv Black, Barbara. *The Book of Lilith*. York Beach: Nicolas-Hays, 1986.
Kors, Alan C., and Edward Peters. *Witchcraft in Europe 1100-1700: A Documentary History*. Philadelphia: U of Pennsylvania P, 1972.
Korte, Sabine. "Hexenhochzeit." *Walpurgistänze. Vehexte Geschichten*. Ed. Julia Peters. München: Knaur, 2000. 257-72.
Kraskowska, Ewa. "O tak zwanej 'kobiecości' jako konwencji literackiej" ("About a So-called Literary Convention"). *Krytyka feministyczna. Siostra teorii i historii literatury* (Feminist Critique: Sister of Literary Theory and History). Ed. G. Borkowska and Liliana Sikorska. Warsaw: IBL, 2000. 200-12.
Kristeva, Julia. *Black Sun: Depression and Melancholia*. 1987. Trans. Léon S. Roudiez. New York: Columbia UP, 1989.

Kristeva, Julia. *Desire in Language. A Semiotic Approach to Literature and Art.* 1977. Trans. Thomas Gora, Alice Jardine, and Léon. S. Roudiez. New York: Columbia UP, 1980.

Kristeva, Julia. *New Maladies of the Soul.* 1993. Trans. Ross Guberman. New York: Columbia UP, 1995.

Kristeva, Julia. *Powers of Horror: An Essay on Abjection.* 1980. Trans. Léon S. Roudiez. New York: Columbia UP, 1982.

Kristeva, Julia. *Revolution in Poetic Language.* 1974. Trans. Margaret Waller. New York: Columbia UP, 1984.

Kristeva, Julia. "Stabat Mater." 1977. Trans. Léon S. Roudiez. *The Kristeva Reader.* Ed. Toril Moi. New York: Columbia UP, 1986. 161-85.

Kristeva, Julia. *Strangers to Ourselves.* 1988. Trans. Léon S. Roudiez. London: Harvester Wheatsheaf, 1991.

Kristeva, Julia. "Women's Time." 1981. Trans. Toril Moi. *Feminisms: An Anthology of Literary Theory and Criticism.* Ed. R. Warhol and D. Price Herndl. New Brunswick: Rutgers UP, 1997. 860-79.

Lacan, Jacques. *Ecrits: A Selection 1936-1958.* 1966. Trans. Alan Sheridan. New York: Norton, 1977.

Lacan, Jacques. *On Feminine Sexuality: the Limits of Love and Knowledge, 1972-1973. Encore: Seminar of Jacques Lacan*, Book 20. Trans. Bruce Fink. Ed. Jacques-Alain Miller. New York: Norton, 1998.

LaCapra, Dominic. *Representing the Holocaust: History, Theory, Trauma.* Ithaca: Cornell UP, 1994.

Le Guin, Ursula K. *Dancing at the Edge of the World.* New York: Grove P, 1989.

Levinas, Emmanuel. *Noms Propres.* Montpellier: Fata Morgana, 1996.

Levinas, Emmanuel. *Time and the Other.* 1979. Trans. Richard Cohen. Pittsburgh: Duquesne UP, 1987.

Levinas, Emmanuel. *Totality and Infinity.* 1961. Trans. Alphonso Lingis. Pittsburgh: Duquesne UP, 1969.

Lévi-Strauss, Claude. *Structural Anthropology.* 1958. Trans. Claire Jacobson and Brooke Grundfest Schoepf. New York: Basic Books, 1963.

Levy, Anita. *Reproductive Urges: Popular Novel-Reading, Sexuality and the English Nation.* Philadelphia: U of Pennsylvania P, 1999.

Lewis, Alison. *Subverting Patriarchy: Feminism and Fantasy in the Works of Irmtraud Morgner.* Oxford: Berg Publishers, 1995.

Lloyd, Genevieve. *The Man of Reason: "Male" and "Female" in Western Philosophy.* London: Routledge, 1993.

Lyotard, Jean-François. *The Postmodern Condition.* Trans. Brian Massumi. Manchester: Manchester UP, 1984.

Maitland, Sara. *Women Fly When Men Aren't Watching.* London: Virago, 1988.

Makinen, Merja. "Angela Carter's 'The Bloody Chamber' and the Decolonisation of Feminine Sexuality." *Angela Carter: Contemporary Critical Essays.* Ed. Alison Easton. London: McMillan, 1985. 20-36.

Marcuse, Herbert. *Eros and Civilization: A Philosophical Inquiry into Freud.* Boston: Beacon, 1955.

McDowell, Deborah E. "Recycling: Race, Gender, and the Practice of Theory." 1992. *Feminisms: An Anthology of Literary Theory and Criticism*. Ed. R. Warhol and D. Price Herndl. New Jersey: Rutgers UP, 1997. 234-47.

Merchant, Carolyn. "Mining the Earth's Womb." *Machina ex Dea: Feminist Perspectives on Technology*. Ed. Joan Rothschild. New York: Pergamon, 1983. 99-117.

Miles, Geoffrey. *Classical Mythology in English Literature: A Critical Anthology*. London: Routledge, 1999.

Milgrom, Jo. "Some Second Thoughts about Adam's First Wife." *Genesis 1-3 in the History of Exegesis*. Ed. G.A. Robbins. Lewiston: Edwin Mellen P, 1988. 225-53.

Miller, Nancy K. "The Arachnologies: the Woman, the Text and the Critic." *The Poetics of Gender*. Ed. Nancy K. Miller. New York: Columbia UP, 1986. 270-95.

Millett, Kate. *Sexual Politics*. New York: Avon, 1971.

Mitchell, Juliet. *Mad Men and Medusas: Reclaiming Hysteria and the Effects of Sibling Relations on the Human Conditions*. London: Penguin, 2000.

Moi, Toril. "Feminist, Female, Feminine." *The Feminist Reader: Essays in Gender and the Politics of Literary Criticism*. Ed. Catherine Belsey and Jane Moore. New York: Blackwell, 1989. 117-32.

Moi, Toril, ed. *The Kristeva Reader*. New York: Columbia UP, 1986.

Moi, Toril. *Sexual/Textual Politics: Feminist Literary Theory*. London: Methuen, 1985.

Moltmann-Wendel, Elisabeth. "Feminist Theology." 1985. Trans. J. Bowden. *German Feminist Writings*. Ed. P.A. Herminghouse and M. Mueller. London: Continuum, 2001. 240-42.

Morgner, Irmtraud. *Amanda. Ein Hexenroman*. Berlin: Luchterhand, 1983.

Morgner, Irmtraud. „Making Use of Sexuality as a Productive Force: Karin Huffzky in Conversation with the East German Writer Irmtraud Morgner" 1975. Trans. P.A. Herminghouse and J. Clausen. *German Feminist Writings*. Ed. P.A. Herminghouse and M. Mueller. London: Continuum, 2001. 272-77.

Morrison, Toni. *Paradise*. Toronto: Alfred A. Knopf, 1998.

Moskowitz, Andrew K. "Scared Stiff: Catatonia as an Evolutionary-Based Fear Response." *Psychological Review* 111.4 (2004): 984-1002.

Nachman, Elana. *Riverfinger Women*. Plainfield: Daughters, 1974.

Nash, Rebecca. "Exhaustion from Explanation. Reading Czech Gender Studies in the 1990s." *The European Journal of Women's Studies* 9.3 (2002): 291-309.

Oakley, Ann. *From Here to Maternity: Becoming a Mother*. Harmondsworth: Penguin, 1981.

Padel, Ruth. "Women: Model for Possession by Greek Daemons." *Images of Women in Antiquity*. Ed. Averil Cameron and Amelie Kuhrt. Detroit: Wayne State UP, 1983. 3-19.

Patai, Raphael. *The Hebrew Goddess*. Detroit: Wayne State UP, 1990.

Peters, Julia, ed. *Walpurgistänze. Vehexte Geschichten*. München: Knaur, 2000.

Pippin, Tina. *Apocalyptic Bodies: The Biblical End of the World in Text and Image*. London: Routledge, 1999.

Plato. "Timaeus." *Timaeus and Critias*. Trans. Desmond Lee. New York: Penguin, 1977. 1-96.

Pratt, Annis. *Archetypal Patterns in Women's Fiction.* Bloomington: Indiana UP, 1981.

Purkiss, Diane. *The Witch in History: Early Modern and Twentieth-Century Representations.* London: Routledge, 1996.

Pusch, Luise F. *Das Deutsche als Männersprache. Aufsätze und Glossen zur feministischen Linguistik.* Frankfurt: Suhrkamp, 1996.

Rajchman, John. "Introduction: The Question of Identity." *The Identity in Question.* Ed. J. Rajchman. London: Routledge, 1995. vii-xvii.

Reich, Wilhelm. "Dialectical Materialism and Psychoanalysis." 1929. *Sex-pol: Essays, 1929-1934.* Trans. Anna Bostok, Tom DuBose, and Lee Baxandall. Ed. Lee Baxandall. New York: Vintage, 1972. 1-74.

Rich, Adrienne. *Blood, Bread and Poetry.* New York: Norton, 1985.

Rich, Adrienne. *On Lies, Secrets and Silence.* New York: Norton, 1979.

Rose, Jacqueline. "Feminine Sexuality: Jacques Lacan and the École Freudienne." *Feminine Sexuality: Jacques Lacan and the École Freudienne.* Ed. and trans. Juliet Mitchell and Jacqueline Rose. London: Macmillan, 1982. 27-57.

Rowbotham, Sheila. *Hidden from History: 300 Years of Women's Oppression and the Fight against It.* London: Pluto, 1973.

Rubin, Gayle. "The Traffic in Women: Notes on the 'Political Economy' of Sex." *Toward an Anthropology of Women.* Ed. Rayna R. Reiter. New York: Monthly Review, 1975. 157-210.

Ruether, Rosemary Radford. *Gaia and God: An Ecofeminist Theology of Earth Healing.* San Francisco: Harper, 1992.

Sanders, Andrew. *A Dead Without a Name: The Witch in Society and History.* Oxford: Berg, 1995.

Saramonowicz, Małgorzata. *Siostra.* Warsaw: W.A.B., 1996.

Schwarzer, Alice. „How It All Began: I Have Had an Abortion." 1981. Trans. N. Stephan. *German Feminist Writings.* Ed. P.A. Herminghouse and M. Mueller. London: Continuum, 2001. 220-22.

Segal, Lynne. *Why Feminism? Gender, Psychology, Politics.* Cambridge: Polity, 1999.

Sempruch, Justyna."Intercultural Dialogue on Gender and Education." *Introduction to Multiple Marginalities: An Intercultural Perspective on Gender in Education across Europe and Africa.* Ed. J. Sempruch, K. Willems, and L. Shook. Königsberg: Helmer, 2006. 13-40.

Showalter, Elaine. "A Criticism on Our Own: Autonomy and Assimiliation in Afro-American and Feminist Literary Theory." 1989. *Feminisms: An Anthology of Literary Theory and Criticism.* Ed. R. Warhol and D. Price Herndl. New Brunswick: Rutgers UP, 1997. 213-33.

Sissa, Gulia. *Greek Virginity.* Trans. Arthur Goldhammer. Cambridge: Harvard UP, 1990.

Smith, Barbara. *Towards a Black Feminist Criticism.* New York: Out & Out, 1977.

Sprengnether, Madelon. *The Spectral Mother: Freud, Feminism, and Psychoanalysis.* Ithaca: Cornell UP, 1990.

Strathern, Marilyn. *Gender of the Gift.* Berkeley: U of California P, 1988.

Szczuka, Kazimiera. *Kopciuszek, Frankenstein i inne. Feminism wobec mitu* (Cinderella, Frankenstein, and Others: Feminism and Myth). Kraków: eFKa, 2001.

Szczuka, Kazimiera. "Prządki, tkaczki i pająki. Uwagi o twórczości kobiet" ("Spinners, Weavers, and Spiders: Remarks about Women's Creativity"). *Krytyka feministyczna. Siostra teorii i historii literatury* (Feminist Critique: Sister of Literary Theory and History). Ed. G. Borkowska and Liliana Sikorska. Warsaw: IBL, 2000. 69-79.

Thürmer-Rohr, Christina. "Cross-Thinking/Counter-Questioning/Protest." 1987. Trans. L. Weil. *German Feminist Writings*. Ed. P.A. Herminghouse and M. Mueller. London: Continuum, 2001. 163-66.

Tokarczuk, Olga. *Dom Dzienny, Dom Nocny*. Wałbrzych: Ruta, 1998.

Tokarczuk, Olga. *E.E.* Wałbrzych: Ruta, 1999.

Tötösy de Zepetnek, Steven. "Comparative Cultural Studies and the Study of Central European Culture." *Comparative Central European Culture*. Ed. Steven Tötösy de Zepetnek. West Lafayette: Purdue UP, 2002. 1-32.

Tötösy de Zepetnek, Steven. *Comparative Literature: Theory, Method, Application*. Amsterdam: Rodopi, 1998.

Tötösy de Zepetnek, Steven. "From Comparative Literature Today toward Comparative Cultural Studies." *Comparative Literature and Comparative Cultural Studies*. Ed. Steven Tötösy de Zepetnek. West Lafayette: Purdue UP, 2003. 235-67.

Treut, Monika. "The Ceremony of the Bleeding Rose: Preliminary Reflections on a Film Project." 1984. Trans. J. Esleben. *German Feminist Writings*. Ed. P.A. Herminghouse and M. Mueller. London: Continuum, 2001. 234-36.

Walker, Alice. *In Search of Our Mothers' Gardens*. San Diego: Harcourt, Brace, Jovanovich, 1983.

Walker, Alice. *The Temple of My Familiar*. 1989. London: Penguin, 1990.

Walker, Barbara. *The Crone: Woman of Age, Wisdom and Ritual*. San Francisco: Harper Collins, 1985.

Walter, Natasha. *The New Feminism*. London: Little, Brown, 1988.

Warhol, Robin R., and Diane Price Herndl, eds. *Feminisms: An Anthology of Literary Theory and Criticism*. New Brunswick: Rutgers UP, 1997.

Warner, Marina. *Alone of All Her Sex*. London: Pan Books, 1990.

Webb, Kate. "Seriously Funny: Wise Children." *Angela Carter: Contemporary Critical Essays*. Ed. Alison Easton. London: McMillan, 2000. 192-215.

Weil, Kari. *Androgyny and the Denial of Difference*. Charlottesville: UP of Virginia, 1992.

Westwood, Gina. *Margaret Atwood's Alias Grace: A Readers Guide*. London: Continuum, 2002.

Whitford, Margaret. "Introduction." *The Irigaray Reader*. Ed. Margaret Whitford. Cambridge: Blackwell, 1991. 1-16.

Wittig, Monique. *Guérillères*. 1969. Trans. David Le Vay. Boston: Beacon, 1971.

Wittig, Monique. *The Straight Mind and Other Essays*. Boston: Beacon, 1992.

Wyatt, Jean. "The Violence of Gendering: Castration Images in Angela Carter's 'The Magic Shop,' 'The Passion of New Eve,' and 'Peter and the Wolf.'" *Angela Carter: Contemporary Critical Essays*. Ed. Alison Easton. London: McMillan, 2000. 58-83.

Index

Abel, 146
abjection, 14, 71, 73, 84, 89, 113, 121, 126, 128, 166, 172
   and female body, 33, 66, 78, 100, 161
   and herstory, 22, 26, 57
   and the sacred, 154, 156
   and witch, 14, 25, 48, 54, 115, 126, 140
   concept of, 73
   in Kristeva, 113, 121, 130
   maternal, 36, 67, 88, 113, 116, 120
abyss
   ancient Greek, 42
   and vagina castrata, 70
   in Apocalypse, 70
   in Atwood, 103
   in Carter, 73, 78
   in Cixous, 16
   in Deleuze, 112
   maternal, 60, 68, 70, 88
agency
   definition of, 122
   in Bhabha, 127
   in Braidotti, 123, 166, 171
   in Butler, 16, 62, 79, 118, 122, 162
   in Carter, 70
   in Cixous and Clément, 63
alterity
   (of the) witch, 28
   feminine, 15, 18, 30, 32, 33, 34
   in Cixous, 15
   in Cixous and Clément, 26
   in Derrida, 60
   in herstory, 7
   in Irigaray, 27
   in Levinas, 3, 15, 115
   lesbian, 32
   narrative of, 109
Anderson, 15
Anzaldúa, 156
aporia, 162. *See* Kristeva
   chora, 59
archaic mother, 98
   and monstrosity, 5, 66, 69, 70, 73, 84
   and omphalos, 67, 112
   and the sacred, 96, 154
   and the semiotic, 8, 59, 66, 79, 87, 97
   and transgression, 117
   and virginity, 94
   as Lilith, 134
   as witch, 9, 116
   in Atwood, 103
   in Butler, 60
   in Cixous and Clément, 28
   in Freud, 60
   in herstory, 19, 30, 32
   in Irigaray, 64, 94
   in Kristeva, 68
   in Morgner, 41
   in Walker, 35
   narrative of, 42, 106, 110, 111, 150, 162
Armstrong, 140, 141
Atwood, 8, 97, 98, 99, 100, 101, 102, 103, 104, 106, 107, 111

Baba Jaga, 84
Bal, 113
Balibar, 119, 122, 125, 166
Baym, 53, 75, 92
becoming
   in Braidotti, 123, 125, 126, 128, 170
   in Deleuze, 72, 80, 107, 112
becoming (-a-subject), 10, 61, 80, 110, 118, 126, 133, 147, 155, 157, 166
becoming (of identity), 9, 61, 69, 83, 105, 107, 112, 123, 138, 139, 150, 151, 158, 166, 168
Bhabha, 127
Bovenschen, 17, 29, 45
Braidotti
   on difference, 59, 62, 117, 166
   on embodied subject, 3, 11, 63, 124, 128, 170
   on femininity, 6, 23
   on feminist subjectivity, 55, 61, 63, 121, 123, 125, 133, 149, 157, 167, 168, 170
   on metamorphosis, 115, 124, 135

on nomadism, 123, 125, 170
on sexuality, 3, 61, 62
on transatlantic divide, 27, 62, 169
on transgression, 120, 121, 123, 125, 126, 166
Brilliant, 42
Brison, 85
Bronfen, 67, 81, 90, 102, 112, 113, 116, 150, 162
Busheikin, 9
Butler
on body, 2, 16, 25, 56, 113, 169
on desire, 70, 78, 115
on difference, 62, 64, 124, 166
on fantasy, 169
on femininity, 6, 27
on gender, 3, 4, 13, 15, 20, 34, 110, 170
on melancholia, 121
on mimesis, 57, 71
on power, 120, 125, 161, 166
on subjectivity, 157, 162
on subversion, 16, 49, 63, 84, 97, 116, 122, 126, 129, 150, 160, 172

Camp, 137
Campbell, 59
Carter, 8, 9, 10, 24, 33, 45, 69, 70, 71, 73, 74, 75, 76, 77, 78, 80, 86, 93, 106, 128, 130, 131, 132, 133, 134, 135, 136, 137, 138, 148, 153, 156
Caruth, 85, 160
Cassandra, 16, 89, 90, 91, 92, 93, 96, 106
Chanter, 6, 15
chora
as exile, 111, 117
in Kristeva, 118
in Plato, 59
semiotic, 8, 33, 59, 63, 67, 70, 78, 85, 93, 94, 97, 101, 105, 116, 161
Christ, Carol, 32
Christ, figure of, 130, 151, 153, 154, 156
Christian, 146
Cixous
in herstory, 5, 14, 15, 16, 20, 25, 26, 28, 41, 42, 48, 54, 95
on desire, 13, 24, 28, 111, 113, 126, 163
on Eve, 98, 152
on jouissance, 167
on Medusa, 13, 15, 135
on the maternal, 60, 63, 64, 117
Clément
on agency, 117
on alterity, 18

on body, 61, 63, 95, 111, 113, 126
on desire, 15, 24, 26, 28, 42, 43
on ecstasy, 24, 133, 154
on eroticism, 167
on porousness, 16
on the sacred, 97, 114, 115, 127, 128, 131, 132, 134, 139, 140, 144, 145, 147, 151
Clifford, 158
Colette, 47, 50
comparative cultural studies, 5, 6, 172
Creed, 5, 65, 66, 69, 70, 72, 73, 77, 87, 100, 101, 107, 109, 126, 146
crime story. *See* fait divers
cultural studies, 7, 113

Daly, 5, 7, 13, 14, 16, 18, 19, 20, 22, 23, 26, 34, 35, 45, 51, 57
death
and jouissance, 71, 72, 78, 112
and Totstellreflex, 86
and trauma, 104
in Atwood, 101
in Butler, 142, 169
in Cixous and Clément, 143
in Clément and Kristeva, 154
in Douglas, 56
in Freud, 81, 85
in herstory, 14, 16, 19, 22, 24
in Morgner, 44
maternal, 99, 101, 102, 105
narrative of, 50, 69, 74, 80, 81, 83, 84, 85, 88, 89, 95, 100, 110, 148, 150, 151, 153, 155, 162, 163, 164
Deleuze, 61, 67, 69, 107, 112, 116, 123, 167
Demme, Jonathan. *See* Silence of the Lambs
depression
and Cassandra, 93
in Atwood, 99
in Butler, 121
in Kristeva, 121, 144, 161, 166
narrative of, 141, 142, 160, 161
Derrida, 4, 10, 60
desire
and the sacred, 130, 135, 149, 155
and the unconscious, 60, 66, 81, 85, 86, 97, 100, 109
in Butler, 15, 65, 115, 118, 121, 167
in Carter, 134, 136
in Cixous and Clément, 13, 26, 28
in Deleuze and Guattari, 107, 116
in Foucault, 70
in Gallop, 88

Index

in herstory, 12, 13, 14, 17, 22, 24, 29, 30, 38, 46, 54
in Irigaray, 31, 36, 61, 63, 64, 65, 94, 97, 109
in Kofta, 161, 163
in Kristeva, 88, 93, 119, 120, 129
in Lacan, 13
lesbian, 32, 90, 91, 95, 96
monstrous, 84, 116
narrative of, 48, 49, 53, 70, 72, 74, 76, 78, 90, 94, 101, 102, 106, 111, 132, 136, 137, 145, 146, 155, 158, 161
phallic, 42, 50, 90, 92
semiotic, 68, 116
de Beauvoir, 18, 23, 31, 36, 39, 58, 80, 82, 99, 135, 140
de Boer, 131, 134
diaspora
  (of the) witch, 122
  and female sexuality, 2, 171
  cultural, 13
  in narrative, 159
  of Virgin Mary, 114
Dietze, 118
difference, 2, 3, 9, 34, 36, 38, 42, 55, 70, 74, 127, 166
  and monstrous feminine, 101
  concept of, 3, 11, 125, 170
  in Atwood, 98, 100, 104
  in Braidotti, 27, 123, 125, 166, 167
  in Butler, 124
  in Carter, 129
  in Derrida, 16
  in herstory, 17, 28, 30, 34
  in Irigaray, 49, 55
  in Kristeva, 153
  national, 163
  negativity, 5, 125
  of mothers and daughters, 95
  racial, 146
  recognition of, 1, 2, 8
  sexual, 4, 6, 13, 27, 55, 57, 60, 62, 63, 65, 117, 119, 124, 133, 155, 169
  transnational, 171
  West and East, of, 40
Douglas, 16, 25, 56, 140
drag
  in Butler, 121
  narrative of, 129, 138
Dworkin, 5, 7, 13, 18, 20, 21, 22, 28, 34, 51, 57, 61

Einhorn, 9
eroticism
  and death, 71, 78
  and masculine desire, 5, 48, 90, 91
  and therapy, 103, 110
  and the sacred, 115, 130, 133, 135, 136, 155
  and transcendence, 167
  and violence, 76, 79
  in Braidotti, 61, 149
  in Butler, 156
  in herstory, 50
  in Irigaray, 61
  in Morgner, 6
  lesbian, 95
  maternal, 91, 114, 145, 161
  of phallus, 48, 87
Eve, 16, 98, 103, 114, 135, 137, 145, 152, 154
exile, 53, 54, 117
  as abyss, 70
  in Black feminism, 34
  in Butler, 122
  in Irigaray, 13, 23

fantasmatic
  chora, 68
  in Butler, 20
  in herstory, 24, 29, 30, 34, 35, 40, 46, 53, 54, 55, 57, 59
  in Irigaray, 13, 27, 60, 63
  in Morgner, 39, 44, 45
  in Walker, 37
  mother, 117
fantasy, 1, 14, 19, 22, 27, 28, 30, 51, 57, 165, 166, 170
  and incest, 84, 117
  and race, 138
  in Black feminism, 34
  in Carter, 69, 75
  in Irigaray, 13, 40
  in Morgner, 39, 42, 44
  narrative, 3, 94, 157
  phallocentric, 53, 71, 115
  political, 14
  semiotic, 68, 78, 89, 90, 160
  and the unconscious, 104
fantasy of
  archaic mother, 8, 66, 84, 98, 111, 140
  gender, 5, 10, 15, 29, 55, 65, 71, 72, 110, 123, 124, 127, 142, 151, 154, 156, 165, 169, 170
  phallic mother, 77, 78, 93, 95
  pleasure, 72, 106, 137
  sameness, 77
  sexuality, 6
  the lesbian, 32
  witch, 1, 9, 11, 56, 165

fear
>in Atwood, 102
>in Carter, 72, 73, 78, 138
>in herstory, 18, 19, 22, 24, 26, 31, 32, 51
>in Irigaray, 67, 106
>in Kofta, 159
>in Maitland, 92, 97
>in Morgner, 40, 43, 44
>in Morrison, 144
>in Saramonowicz, 82
>narrative of, 84, 87, 88, 93, 94, 95, 102, 105
>of (the) archaic mother, 66, 68, 130, 135, 137, 155

Felman, 17, 24, 58, 71, 73, 74, 98, 99, 149
fetish, 48, 50
>ancient Greek, 90
>colonized, 136
>maternal, 95, 115, 117
>monstrous, 65, 66, 71, 77

Finckenstein, 9, 46, 48, 51, 53
Foucault, 22, 51, 64, 70, 76, 78, 101, 120, 121, 140
Fraser, 6, 55, 75, 117, 119, 120, 121, 128
fraud
>in narrative, 3, 44, 52, 89, 94, 96, 97, 111
>maternal, 95

Freud
>in Cixous, 135
>in Irigaray, 27, 64
>in Kristeva, 68, 100
>narrative of, 106
>on archaic mother, 66
>on catharsis, 48
>on death, 85
>on Dora, 108
>on E., 108
>on father, 71
>on femininity, 109
>on libido, 75
>on Oedipal mother, 60, 85
>on sexuality, 27, 66, 88, 90
>on split, 100
>on the uncanny, 73
>on the unconscious, 8, 60, 74, 79, 106
>on trauma, 81, 82

Frymer-Kensky, 42

Gallop, 25, 55, 60, 61, 62, 65, 68, 78, 88, 116, 117
Gearhart, 5, 7, 18, 23, 30, 31, 34, 36, 37, 41, 57
Gibson, 124

Grewal, 29, 127
Griffin, 119, 127
Guattari, 67, 107, 112, 116, 123
Guiley, 21

Hall, 156, 158
Harris, 18
Haskins, 131, 134
Haug, 40
heresy, 39, 119, 127, 151, 153, 167, 168
Herndl, 10, 13
herstory, 18, 29, 46, 53, 172
>as fantasy, 20, 26, 33, 38
>as hysteria, 17, 24
>in Cixous, 14

household
>concept of, 140
>in Morrison, 142, 144, 146
>patriarchal, 98, 99, 109
>subversion of, 44, 106, 110, 126, 138, 140, 141, 148, 149

Humm, 34, 35
hysteria, 8, 17, 21, 53
>feminist, 55, 57

incest, 65, 84, 87, 117
instability, 111, 113, 120, 123, 159
Irigaray
>on archaic mother, 28, 114
>on becoming, 108, 125, 126, 128
>on chora, 59, 67
>on Clytemnestra, 55, 67
>on desire, 18, 31, 36, 53, 61, 65, 94, 97, 109, 155
>on difference, 11, 13, 15, 27, 49, 55, 107, 133, 166
>on hysterical fantasmatic, 27
>on jouissance, 60
>on libidinal economy, 23
>on mimesis, 37, 49, 53, 94, 168
>on the feminine, 5, 61, 63, 109, 165
>on the maternal, 144, 149
>on transcendental subject, 115, 122, 147, 167
>on women's exile, 13, 53, 56, 68, 76

Jezebel, 16, 130, 135, 137, 138
Jordan, 69
jouissance, 5, 49, 60, 71, 72, 82, 83, 88, 91, 92, 131, 132, 134, 139, 143, 167

Kaplan, 29, 127
King, 30, 33
Kofta, 147, 156, 160, 162, 164
Kolodny, 31, 38

Index

Koltuv Black, 42
Korte, 9, 46, 47, 48, 50, 51, 52, 53
Kramer, 21
Kraskowska, 80, 157
Kristeva
  on becoming, 110
  on carnivalesque, 29, 129
  on chora, 59, 67, 118
  on desire, 137
  on different legality, 4, 139
  on porousness, 16, 128, 170
  on primary narcissism, 83, 88
  on sexuality, 24
  on sublimation, 120, 161
  on the abject, 113
  on the maternal, 59, 60, 68, 73, 93, 96, 112, 114
  on the sacred, 114, 127, 129, 132, 133, 145, 153
  on the semiotic, 112, 121, 129, 168
  on the symbolic order, 30, 54, 56, 61, 106
  on transgression, 119, 139, 147, 160, 166, 167
  on virginity, 152, 155

Lacan
  on lack, 54, 86
  on mirror stage, 59, 75, 161
  on paternal metaphor, 160
  on phallus, 25
  on real, 60, 66, 117
  on split, 13
  on the feminine, 27, 48, 92, 109, 170
  on the unconscious, 64, 65, 75
LaCapra, 21
Lévi-Strauss, 170
Levinas, 4, 5, 15, 55
Levy, 71
Lewis, 38, 39, 40, 43, 44, 45
le Guin, 44, 139, 150
Lilith, 16, 41, 42
  in Morgner, 43
  in Carter, 133
Lloyd, 15
loss, 61, 165, 167
  in Atwood, 101
  in Braidotti, 121, 122, 125
  in Butler, 97, 121, 142
  in herstory, 24, 37, 41
  in Kristeva, 119, 121
  in narrative, 139, 142, 150, 158, 159
  maternal, 8, 59, 67, 75, 112, 117
  negation of, 68
  of identity, 160

Lyotard, 128

madness
  ancient Greek, 91, 92
  in Cixous, 63
  in herstory, 35
  in Irigaray, 55, 67, 109
  in the 19th century, 99
  maternal, 110
  of Cassandra, 90
  of daughter, 83, 97, 98, 101, 105, 109, 111
  of Mary Magdalene, 135
Maitland, 38, 89, 90, 91, 93, 94, 95, 96, 97, 106
Makinen, 69, 79
Marcuse, 12, 41
Mary Magdalene, 16, 128, 130, 131, 132, 133, 134, 139, 153, 156
masquerade, 52, 53, 109, 112
matriarchy, 18, 32, 37
McDowell, 54
Medusa
  and the lesbian subject, 95
  in Cixous, 13, 14, 15, 28, 135
melancholia
  in Braidotti, 121, 122, 123, 166
  in Butler, 15, 60, 71, 121, 167
  in Kristeva, 121
  in narrative, 44, 73, 99, 123, 140, 141, 143, 158
memory
  and fantasy, 3, 28, 29, 89, 94, 157
  in Butler, 68
  in herstory, 21
  in Irigaray, 65
  narrative of, 35, 36, 74, 75, 78, 79, 81, 95, 96, 100, 103, 104, 150, 157, 158, 159, 160, 161, 162, 164
  of mother, 88
  traumatic, 85, 86, 88
Merchant, 33
metamorphosis, 16, 51, 115
  and la mestiza, 139
  in Braidotti, 133
  in Cixous, 24, 26
  in Morrison, 144, 147
  in Tokarczuk, 153
  of Mary Magdalene, 135
Miles, 90
Milgrom, 41, 42
Miller, 54
Millett, 12
mimesis, 13, 37, 49, 52, 57, 72, 94, 123, 168

Mitchell, 60, 76, 80, 81, 82, 85, 87, 99, 102, 103, 105, 106, 108, 109, 116
Moglen, 146
Moi, 5, 6, 16, 18, 34, 37
Moltmann-Wendel, 39
monstrous feminine, 1, 5, 101, 122, 126
Morgner, 6, 8, 15, 38, 40, 41, 42, 43, 44, 45, 46, 57, 58, 77
Morrison, 10, 140, 141, 142, 143, 144, 145, 146, 147, 153, 156
Moskowitz, 81, 86
myth, 35, 148, 150
   ancient Greek, 39, 66
   in Black feminism, 9, 17, 34, 35
   in Braidotti, 123
   in herstory, 5, 12, 14, 17, 18, 20, 23, 30, 37, 53, 57, 172
   in Morgner, 42, 45
myth of
   archaic mother, 41
   lesbian culture, 30
   Medusa, 16
   Oedipus, 79, 81, 84
   Pandora, 40
   Penelope, 106
   vaginal orgasm, 93
   vagina dentata, 7, 74
   Mary Magdalene, 134

Nachman, 18
Nash, 9
nomadic, 7, 48
   fantasy, 123
   in Braidotti, 123, 170
   subjectivity, 125, 127, 131
non-place. *See* Augé

Oakley, 12
omphalos
   (scar), 67, 68, 90, 112, 113, 145, 172
otherness
   (of the) witch, 3, 18, 143
   concept of, 13
   fantasmatic, 24, 27
   feminine, 6
   in Atwood, 102
   in Braidotti, 11, 62, 133, 168
   in Carter, 75, 132
   in Cixous, 26
   in Gearhart, 32
   in Irigaray, 15, 49, 55
   in Kofta, 163
   in Kristeva, 112, 129, 130
   in Levinas, 15
   in Tokarczuk, 110

monstrous, 71
national, 162
of gender, 65
of Jezebel, 137
of Lilith, 42
of Mary Magdalene, 131, 132
racial, 34, 49
sexuality, 78
the sacred, 154

Padel, 91, 92
Pandora
   in Goethe, 40
   in Morgner, 40, 41
paranoia
   in Kristeva, 114
   narrative of, 164
Patai, 41
Pippin, 70, 71, 73, 137
Plato, 59
possession, 26, 29, 37, 40, 47, 49, 91, 92, 98, 99, 135
Pratt, 23, 35, 51, 55
Purkiss, 12, 14, 17, 20, 21, 23, 24, 28, 29, 51, 56, 57, 69, 96, 140, 143, 146
Pusch, 14, 19

Rajchman, 168
rape
   in Carter, 79
   in herstory, 20, 23, 24, 32
   in Irigaray, 50
   narrative of, 81, 86, 102
   phallic, 117
Reich, 12
resistance, 3, 5, 9, 10, 17, 20, 79, 117, 140
   concept of, 115, 123, 170
   gender, 56
   in Braidotti, 125
   in Clément, 140, 154
   in Kristeva, 165
   in Levinas, 55
   in narrative, 80, 82, 154, 160, 162
   politics of, 29
Rich, 23, 64
Rose, 75, 76
Rowbotham, 12
Rubin, 39, 84
Ruether, 30, 31, 41

sacred, the
   and the maternal, 10, 114
   in Carter, 128, 131, 132, 133, 134, 135, 136
   in Clément and Kristeva, 114, 115,

127, 128, 131, 133, 145, 153, 154
  in herstory, 16, 33
  narrative of, 139, 140, 151, 153, 154, 156
Sanders, 19, 127
Saramonowicz, 79, 81, 83, 84, 85, 86, 87, 89, 93
Schwarzer, 39, 42, 45, 46
secrecy, 44, 47, 48, 51, 80, 87, 111, 143, 145, 147, 160, 161, 163, 164
Segal, 9
semiotic
  and the archaic mother, 66, 79, 115
  and the phallic, 66, 92, 94
  and the sacred, 10, 155
  chora, 8, 33, 59, 67, 68, 78, 85, 93, 94, 101, 105, 116, 161
  fantasy, 68, 89
  in Braidotti, 123, 170
  in Butler, 64, 121
  in Cixous, 63
  in herstory, 37, 55
  in Irigaray, 60, 63
  in Kristeva, 112, 121, 130, 168
  language, 68, 76, 89, 97, 110, 116, 118, 125, 145, 149, 160, 161, 165, 169
  pleasure, 32, 36, 83, 87, 97, 130, 145, 147, 150
Sempruch, 9
sexuality, 2, 5, 6, 12, 24, 26, 50, 98, 102, 106, 114, 119, 120, 124, 155, 171
  and incest, 84
  and subjectivity, 8
  and the sacred, 130, 133, 137
  and the unconscious, 74
  anti-, 3, 23
  feminine, 1, 27, 34, 63, 129
  hysterical, 69, 100, 103, 143
  in Carter, 70, 73, 76, 78
  in herstory, 14, 18
  in Irigaray, 61
  lesbian, 23, 30, 31, 96
  monstrous, 1, 43, 66, 71, 88
  normative, 89, 91, 98, 108, 129
  in Braidotti, 61
Showalter, 18, 23, 34
Sissa, 92
sisterhood, 19
Smith, 34
spectacle
  in Cixous and Clément, 26, 28, 111, 126
  in Foucault, 101, 102
  in herstory, 22, 24

of archaic mother, 66, 149
of gender, 151
Sprenger, 21
Sprengnether, 66, 149
stigma, 9, 55, 58, 62, 105, 122, 138, 156, 157, 159, 166, 168
Strathern, 9
subversion, 2, 5, 44, 63, 97, 118, 126, 129, 130, 160
  archaic, 66
  concept of, 123
  fantasy of, 97, 151, 165
  gender, 4, 113, 128, 169
  in Morrison, 145, 147
Szczuka, 148, 149

television. *See* violence on television
therapy, 89, 104, 125
  and fantasy, 59
  the unconscious, 60, 64, 65
Thürmer-Rohr, 27
Tokarczuk, 106, 108, 109, 110, 111, 147, 149, 150, 153, 154, 156, 157, 164
Tötösy de Zepetnek, 7
trace, 15, 168. *See* Derrida
  archaic, 60, 66, 70, 74
  fantasmatic, 46
  feminine, 115, 131, 167
  semiotic, 121
trace of
  Mary Magdalene, 134
  omphalos (scar), 67, 162
  otherness, 3
  un/belonging, 2, 16
  Virgin Mary, 114, 133
  witch, 3, 56, 79
transgression
  and incest, 87
  and witch, 5, 25, 69, 117
  gender, 71, 77
  in Braidotti, 120, 122, 123, 125, 130
  in Butler, 121, 129
  in Douglas, 25
  in Kristeva, 120, 121, 127, 129
  in Morrison, 139, 142, 147
  in narrative, 50, 148, 151, 156, 160, 164
  of identity, 10, 119, 165, 166, 169
  of Mary Magdalene, 131
  sadomasochism, 78
trauma
  and memory, 21, 68, 85, 88, 96
  and omphalos, 67, 93, 113, 117
  and sexuality, 86, 103
  in Atwood, 104

in Freud, 81, 82
maternal, 84, 95, 160
narrative of, 116
sexuality, 91
Treut, 78

unconscious, the
and feminism, 46, 64, 68, 73, 74, 79, 93, 117, 126
in Atwood, 104, 105
in Freud, 8, 106, 115
in narrative, 35, 36, 75, 78, 80, 81, 83, 85, 88, 89, 101, 104, 110, 148, 161
and catatonia, 81
Unheimlich (Freud), 68, 71, 72, 73, 74, 100, 106, 109, 110, 112, 116

vagina castrata, 70
Venus, 10, 128, 132, 135, 136, 137, 138
virgin
ancient Greek, 133
and Cassandra, 92
and femininity, 16, 114, 152
and Mary Magdalene, 131, 133
and maternality, 94, 131, 132, 142, 152, 154, 155
and the lesbian subject, 89, 94, 95, 96
in Clément and Kristeva, 115
in herstory, 19, 25, 35, 56
in Irigaray, 67
in Kristeva, 114, 155
Judeo-Christian, 114, 130, 152
Virgin Mary, 16, 61, 83, 130, 132, 133, 134, 164

Walker, Alice, 5, 8, 30, 32, 34, 35, 36, 38, 49, 57, 58, 150
Walker, Barbara, 16
Walter, 9
Warhol, 10, 13
Warner, 114, 115, 130, 132, 133, 134, 142, 152
Webb, 138
Weil, 37
Westwood, 98
Whitford, 15, 27, 53, 55, 56, 83, 95, 97, 107, 155
witch
alterity of, 3, 15, 18
and ritual, 33
and the abject, 88, 112, 114, 116
and the colonial subject, 136, 137. See Jezebel and Black Venus
and the sacred, 130, 154
archaic, 65, 68, 79

as foreigner, 157, 159, 162
as healer, 30, 51, 146
as monstrous feminine, 71, 77, 80, 101, 110
as superwoman, 9
fantasmatic, 27, 53, 68
fantasmatic:in Cixous and Clément, 28
feminine, 115, 122
figure of, 1, 2, 16, 56, 116, 117, 124, 145, 172. See Lilith
household, 140, 141, 143
in Cixous, 25, 26
in herstory, 5, 12, 14, 16, 19, 20, 22, 23, 24, 45, 54, 58
in narrative, 7, 18, 49, 50, 51, 165
lesbian, 94
phallic, 68, 113, 117
pop-cultural, 1, 39, 46, 47, 48, 52, 84
transgression, 126, 127, 165, 167, 168, 169
un/belonging of, 11, 16, 55, 122, 124
Wyatt, 69

www.ingramcontent.com/pod-product-compliance
Lightning Source LLC
Chambersburg PA
CBHW061447300426
44114CB00014B/1874